Istanbul, City of the Fearless

Istanbul, City of the Fearless

*Urban Activism, Coup d'État,
and Memory in Turkey*

———

Christopher Houston

UNIVERSITY OF CALIFORNIA PRESS

University of California Press
Oakland, California

Cataloging-in-Publication Data is on file at the Library of Congress.

ISBN 978-0-520-34319-1 (cloth : alk. paper)
ISBN 978-0-520-34320-7 (pbk. : alk. paper)
ISBN 978-0-520-97467-8 (ebook)

Manufactured in the United States of America

28 27 26 25 24 23 22 21 20
10 9 8 7 6 5 4 3 2 1

This book is dedicated to Joel Kahn (1946–2017),
professor of anthropology, admired PhD supervisor,
beloved mentor, and deeply missed friend.

CONTENTS

CONTENTS

ACKNOWLEDGMENTS

It is a genuine pleasure to acknowledge the contribution of so many people to the researching, writing, and publishing of this book. Its genesis can be traced back to a walk in Istanbul one evening with a pal who remembered, as we passed his old high school, an assembly in the late 1970s when the entire student body had raised clenched fists in the air, in silent memory of a slain student activist. The story piqued my interest, and ever since, I have annoyed my friends and acquaintances, and their friends and acquaintances, to tell more about those years in Istanbul. Quite simply, the book could not have been written without them, since it is an account of their imaginative descriptions of activism, events, factions, places, and experiences in the city. Without being banal or simplistic, I wish to record my admiration for that generation's forbearance in suffering, for their graciousness toward their own and others' youthful and militant selves, and for the clarity decades later of their thoughts and emotions concerning those years of revolutionary fervor.

The book itself has been rather long in the making, and there are a large number of institutions and individuals that I must thank for supporting its composition. First, I am grateful to Macquarie University and its Department of Anthropology here in Sydney for providing an environment that values collegiality and teaching, while structuring time for its members to pursue both fieldwork research and writing. Colleagues are one's best teachers. Greg Downey and Lisa Wynn have been supportive departmental heads throughout the process of the book's writing, and the University facilitated research leave in Istanbul.

Staff at the German Oriental Institute in Istanbul, and Tomas Wilkoszewski in particular, tolerated my endless requests for tattered newspapers and faded copies

ix

of old leftist journals bundled up in the depths of the library. It has also been an educational pleasure to be involved in Tomas's own doctoral research program over the course of the project. The Anthropology Department at Princeton University provided a wonderful home for six months in 2018, which facilitated completion of the work, while also allowing my son and I to fall in love with New Jersey's native animals, including squirrels, gophers, deer, and raccoons! Special thanks there to Carol Zanca, Julia Elyachar, Onur Güney, Ryo Morimoto, Lawrence Ralph, and Nikos Michailidis for their friendship and hospitality, as well as to Carolyn Rouse, head of the department.

There is another group of individuals who I am very glad to mention, people who in a huge variety of ways, often without knowing the true import of their contribution, have added their defining touches to the shape and content of the book. These are Michael Jackson, Kenan Çayır, Joost Jongerden, Dilek Çilingir, Trevor Hogan, Robbie Peters, Faik Gür, Jean-Paul Baldacchino, and Kalpana Ram. As usual, my father, James Houston, edited the entire manuscript for grammatical and stylistic niceties, despite the bouts of illness that have laid him low over the last few years. A million thanks to filmmaker extraordinaire Max Harwood for his assistance on the manuscript's images, as well as for designing the cover of a music CD produced as a welcome break from writing anthropology.

Kate Marshall at University of California Press welcomed the book from the beginning, and I am deeply indebted to her work and support in fostering the manuscript through to publication. I also thank Enrique Ochoa-Kaup, and the entire editorial team for the further polishing of its prose. There are other publishers to thank as well. Versions of parts of chapters 1, 2, and 4 have been published in two articles as follows: portions of chapter 1 and 2 in "Politicizing Place Perception: A Phenomenology of Urban Activism in Istanbul," in *Journal of the Royal Anthropological Institute (JRAI)* 21, no. 4 (2015): 720–38; portions of chapters 1 and 4 in "How Globalization Really Happens: Remembering Activism in the Transformation of Istanbul," in *International Journal of Urban and Regional Research* 39, no. 1 (2015): 46–61.

It is a delight to name my family, to acknowledge their interest in the project, as well as their timely disinterest when my obsessions became too much. Love was also their mode of support. Thus in no particular order of significance I thank my mum and dad, my brothers and sister, and of course my two beloved sons, Raphael and Gebran, for whose edification in some small way I also wrote this book. My brother Nick Houston read the manuscript, and suggested a million good ideas, most of which I was too slow to adapt. Last, my gratitude, love, and respect to Banu Şenay, who in myriad ways supported this project from its inception. Without you, I'd still be on the introduction!

PROLOGUE

Those who thanked General Kenan Evren for stopping anarchy and for bringing calm after the 12 September coup d'état did not remember him on its anniversary.

Buried in the state cemetery, Kenan Evren's grave did not receive a single visitor, nor was it decorated with flowers or wreaths.

—"KENAN EVREN'IN 12 EYLÜL YALNIZLIĞI" (*The Loneliness of Kenan Evren on 12th September*), in Cumhuriyet *newspaper, 13 September 2018*

LIST OF POLITICAL PARTIES,
ORGANIZATIONS, AND GROUPS

Acilciler	Urgent Revolutionaries
Akıncılar	Raiders [Muslim youth wing of MSP]
AP	Adalet Partisi (Justice Party)
Aydınlık	Enlightenment
CHP	Cumhuriyet Halk Partisi (Republican People's Party)
Dev-Genç	Türkiye Devrimci Gençlik Federasyonu (Revolutionary Youth Federation of Turkey)
Dev-Lis	Devrimci Liseliler (Revolutionary High School Students)
Dev-Sol (DS)	Devrimci Sol (Revolutionary Left)
Dev-Yol (DY)	Devrimci Yol (Revolutionary Path)
DH	Direniş Hareketi (Resistance Movement)
DHKP-C	Devrimci Halk Kurtuluş Partisi-Cephesi (Revolutionary People's Liberation Party-Front)
DİSK	Devrimci İşçi Sendikalari Konfederasyonu (Confederation of Revolutionary Trade Unions)
HB	Halk Birliği (Peoples Brigade)
HK	Halk Kurtuluş (Peoples Liberation)
HS	*Halk Sesi* (journal) (*Peoples Voice*)
HY	Halk Yolu (People's Path)
İGD	Ileri Genclik Derneği (Progressive Youth Association)
İLD	İlerici Lise Derneği (Progressive High School Students Association)
Kurtuluş	Liberation
MHP	Milliyetçi Hareket Partisi (Nationalist Movement Party)

MSP	Milli Selamet Partisi (National Salvation Party)
Partizan Yolu	Partisan Path
PDA	Proleter Devrimci Aydınlık (Proletarian Revolutionary Enlightenment)
PKK	Partiya Karkerên Kurdistan (Workers' Party of Kurdistan)
SP	Sosyalist Partisi (Socialist Party)
Sürekli Devrim	Continuous Revolution
TEP	Türkiye Emek Partisi (Turkey Workers Party)
THKO	Türkiye Halk Kurtuluş Ordusu (People's Liberation Army of Turkey)
THKO-TDY	Türkiye Halk Kurtuluş Ordusu-Türkiye Devrimci Yol (Turkish Peoples Liberation Army—Turkish Revolutionary Path)
THKP-C	Türkiye Halk Kurtuluş Partisi-Cephesi (People's Liberation Party-Front of Turkey)
THKP-C/MLSPB	Türkiye Halk Kurtuluş Partisi-Cephesi / Marksist Leninist Silahlı Propaganda Birliği (People's Liberation Party-Front of Turkey/Marxist Leninist Armed Propaganda Brigade)
TİKP	Türkiye İhtilalci İşçi Köylü Partisi (Revolutionary Workers' & Peasants' Party of Turkey)
TİP	Türkiye İşçi Partisi (Workers Party of Turkey)
TSİP	Türkiye Sosyalist İşçi Partisi (Turkish Socialist Workers Party)
TKP	Türkiye Komünist Partisi (Turkish Communist Party)
TKP-ML–TİKKO	Türkiye Komünist Partisi (Marksist Leninist)—Türkiye İşçi Köylü Kurtuluş Ordusu (Communist Party of Turkey (Marxist Leninist)—Workers' Peasants' Liberation Army of Turkey)
TKP/ML	Türkiye Komünist Partisi/Marksist Leninist (Communist Party of Turkey/Marksist Leninist)
Türk-İş	Türkiye İşçi Sendikaları Konfederasyonu (Confederation of Turkish Trade Unions)
Vatan Partisi	Fatherland Party (founded by Dr Hikmet Kıvılcımlı)

1

Spatial Politics, Historiography, Method

Introduction

Bu şehirde ölmek yeni birşey değil elbet
Sanki yaşamak daha büyük bir marifet!

(Ha, to die in this city brings no new thrill,
Living is a much finer skill!)

—CAN YÜCEL (2005), *"Yesenin'den Intihar Pusulası Moskova'dan"*

1.1 URBAN ACTIVISM IN ISTANBUL

Imagine a city characterized by the radicalization en masse of students, workers, and professional associations. Imagine as a core aspect of struggle their inventive fabrication of a suite of urban spatial tactics, including militant confrontation over control and use of the city's public spaces, shantytowns, educational institutions, and sites of production. Sounds and fury, fierceness and fearlessness. Picture a battle for resources, as well as for less quantifiable social goods: rights, authority, and senses of place. Consider one spatial outcome of this mobilization—a city tenuously segregated on left/right and on left/left divisions in nearly all arenas of public social interaction, from universities and high schools to coffee houses, factories, streets, and suburbs. Even the police are fractured into political groups, with one or another of the factions dominant in neighborhood stations. Over time, escalating industrial action by trade unions, and increasing violence in the city's edge suburbs change activists' perceptions of urban place. Here is a city precariously balanced between rival political forces and poised between different possible futures, even as its inhabitants charge into urban confrontation and polarization.

Imagine a military insurrection. Total curfew. Flights in and out of the country suspended, a ban on theater and cultural activities, schools and universities shut down. Removing books from library shelves that the new regime might find suspicious. "Wanted" posters pasted at ferry terminals, civil police watching for suspicious

1

responses. Whole suburbs targeted for "special treatment." Mass arrests and torture, random identity checks in public places, the sudden cutting of roads by police and the searching of buses, assaults on the houses of activists, summary executions. Martial law turning the city into another country. "It was as if time stood still," said Ömer (Türkiye İşçi Partisi, or Workers Party of Turkey)[1] Imagine for hundreds of thousands of people fear of arrest seeping into consciousness, a fear of torture, and of telling under torture when they had a rendezvous or where they had last visited an organization house. Picture body habits changing overnight, in anticipation of future regulations of the junta. Shaving your head in order to stay at the university (Vassaf 2011: 5). "I didn't go out much in those years," said one activist.

The city is Istanbul in the years 1974–1983. For militants,[2] what is it like to *dwell* there? How do they transform its places and mood, and respond to others' remaking of its affective atmospheres and spaces? What of the urban environment itself, synesthetically known by the "whole body sensing and moving" (Casey 1996: 18): how does it sound, feel, smell, and appear? And what of the decades since then, forgetting and remembering it, your activism and its small part in the making of the city's chaos? Snatch of a song, rhythm of a chanted slogan, anniversary of the death of a comrade, son, or friend. Each live on in the museum of the mind, in the pains of the body, in the affect exuded by objects and photos, and in the intersubjective imagination of daughters and sons who listen to your stories.

Istanbul, City of the Fearless is a study of urban activism in those years, ruptured by the 1980 military coup d'état—12 Eylül (12 September) in the political vernacular—that brought a decade-long, fragmented social struggle to a bloody close and instituted nearly three years of martial law. Military dogma has it that the coup's precipitating cause was the "terrorist" actions of urban militants and the anarchical state of the city. In response the junta's new dispensation instituted in the authoritarian 1982 Constitution was designed to prevent their recrudescence in the politics of the present ever after. The third military intervention in Turkey's Republican history, 12 Eylül led to the replacement of the liberal 1961 Constitution by one demonstrably less democratic. Loyalty to the ideology of Atatürk was declared the sole guiding principle of the Turkish state and society, with no protection afforded "to thoughts or opinions contrary to ... the nationalism, principles, reforms and modernism of Atatürk" (Constitution of the Turkish Republic 1982). Civil society associations and political parties alike had to show allegiance to these defining characteristics or face prosecution by the Constitutional Court.

---

1. I have changed the names of activists, but not the political faction they belonged too, nor their gender. The first time I mention the name of a political group or faction I translate it into English. Thereafter I use the Turkish abbreviation. See the list of names of political organizations.

2. I use *activist*, *militant*, and *partisan* interchangeably in this book to refer to the active members of different political factions.

Today the institutions of military tutelage remain in place, from the National Security Council to the Higher Education Council, despite the pressure for constitutional change that has partially characterized Turkish politics over the last decade and a half. As much as in the bodies and memories of a generation, 12 Eylül endures in such political instruments, conditioning contemporary Turkish social life, reason enough to learn more about the period that gave it birth. Its ongoing influence in politics means that this book is simultaneously an anthropological study of the recent past *and* of the present, of how two significant urban events—the spatial activism of revolutionary movements in the 1970s, and the 1980 coup d'état—not only transformed Istanbul in those years but also exerted their force and influence into the future, becoming sources of novel spatial arrangements, new social divisions, and of inhabitants' altered perceptions and memories of the city.

In the years immediately before the 1980 military coup Istanbul was experienced as a city in crisis, described by activists as "electric," "chaotic," or "strained." For Ertuğrul, it was "tense, like a family used to violence and waiting for it to happen" (Devrimci Yol [hereafter Dev-Yol, Revolutionary Path/Way]). Others remembered its sounds as raucous and threatening. Activists' perception of the partisan, fragmented, and unstable qualities of the city reflects a period in which their own actions inflicted a radical contingency upon its spatial organization and order of places. Conventions of engagement, movement, and relationship, partially fostered by material arrangements, were replaced by an uncertainty about the "spatial economy" of places (Lefebvre 1991: 56). For Istanbul's strongly ideological activists, the stress of the city meant sense and sensibility became acutely attuned to the semiotics of different political fractions, to the behavior of groups of people and to political signs encoded in the urban environment. A rapidly accumulating (and changing) spatial knowledge about when to move around the city, where not to go, how to sit in the coffeehouse, and who to avoid became a potentially life-and-death practice of urban living.[3] Recognizing the political alignment of others as communicated through their bodies was critical. Paying attention to the acoustic cues resounding in public space—say to the singing of certain songs on the ferry by a group of people—might save one from a beating.

Activists' embodied sensory experience of the city, their changing urban knowledge and emerging sense of place were intimately related to political practices of organizing, mobilizing and agitating. Perceptions of Istanbul derived from activists' purposive attitude toward the city, oriented by the "task" of revolution. Walls were noticed for the possibilities they afforded posters and graffiti, reverberant streets for the cascading of sonic amplification. Squares were assessed for the concatenating choreography of gestures and slogans, the time between train stations

---

3. According to Zürcher (1995) in the year before the coup up to twenty people a day were slain in urban conflict.

for the shaping of a "shock" speech. Yet because activists were dispersed among rival groups, the affordances furnished by the urban environment were sometimes formally divided up between groups and sometimes fought over, adding affective registers of amity and enmity to their experiences of the city. Differences between leftist groups concerning Turkey's situation spilled over into conflict between fractions, contributing to militants' feelings of living in an intensely stressed and merciless city.

In brief, in the second half of the 1970s the activists of the socialist factions and the cadres of the ultranationalists together sought both to control and to remake the city, in the process changing radically the experiences and practices of place-making for their own members and for the rest of the city's inhabitants. Their combat in, with, and over the city, their taking possession of its public spaces and institutions through occupying force, and their attempted creation of politically autonomous zones of self-governance in the city's deprived shanty-towns were significant strategies in their appropriation, occupation, and transformation of space. The description and analysis of activists' experiences connect to other matters that I discuss in this book. These include the city's political geography and its key sites of conflict and mobilization; violence as both spatial practice and generator of urban space; militants' perceptions of political fractions and of political ideologies; the junta's post-coup strategies for urban pacification; contrasts in the socio-material structure and spatial organization of Istanbul before and after the coup; and the significance of activist practices and the coup for understanding the neoliberal "globalization" of Istanbul in the decades after.

Spatial Politics

Although this book's first concern is the perception of urban activists in Istanbul, the larger context of their experience of the city involves their participation in spatial politics, an under-theorized subject for these critical years. By *spatial politics* here I mean the generation and transformation of space–both symbolic and physical–by a range of social actors, including legal and illegal organizations, the State, the junta, businesses and property developers, private builders, urban designers, and ordinary residents. I use it to include political factions' appropriation and transformation of the city's expanding buildings, streets, and institutions, as well as their gaining control of an area and defending and changing it in conformity with, in disregard of, or in opposition to the intentions of its authorities, builders, or other factions. The junta, as "architects" of the coup, pursued spatial politics too, intentionally orchestrating the sound, appearance, and uses of the city.

On both a more concrete and macro level, the spatial politics of earlier eras in urban Turkey have been well studied, most thoroughly in Sibel Bozdoğan's (2001) work on the architectural culture, design, and buildings of the Republican state in the single-party period (1923–1950). Although the new monumental and modernist architecture that Bozdoğan analyzes in 1930s Ankara was only patchily present in Istanbul, it too was transformed in those very same years. In it the primary endeavor of Turkey's first Kemalists was not to construct or reassemble Istanbul's built environment but to *disassemble* its population, their nationalist program targeting Greeks, Armenians, and Jews for expulsion from the city while Turkifying its economy (Aktar 2000). The result was de-peopled places and displaced people (see chapter 3).

Urban planning, too, has continually remade Istanbul over the Republican period, first in the work of famed urbanist Henri Prost, author of the master plan for the city in 1937 and its chief planner between the years 1936–1951 (Pilsel and Pinon 2010), and then in the substantial transformation of Istanbul by the Democrat Party in the years 1950–1960, led by Prime Minister Adnan Menderes. Murat Gül's *The Making of Modern Istanbul* (2009) focuses on the urban development of the city in the 1950s, including the chiseling out of its major thoroughfares— for example Aksaray Caddesi, Beşiktaş Meydanı, Vatan, and Millet Caddeleri or Tarlabaşı Bulvarı—that still give the older parts of the city much of their skeletal form. Yet his book has the same bias as Bozdoğan's, concentrating on the emerging structure of the city—what Gül calls its morphology—and not on its inhabitants in relation to it.

Compelling as both these analyses are, they are circumscribed by their focus of study, concerned as they are for only half of what Bernard Tschumi (1994) has described as the "violence of architecture." By this Tschumi means not only the "violence" inflicted upon inhabitants by the material and symbolic arrangements of architecture and urban structure, but also a second dimension: users' "violence" against places themselves in their transformation—temporary or permanent, authorized or transgressive—of the built environment. For Tschumi, the violence of architecture is not just a metaphor, given the reality of certain sites that destroy emotional and bodily integrity—for example, in the spatialized brutality of prisons and of their soul-shredding sonic design (see chapter 7), or the construction of buildings over and out of the ruins of others.

Yet as metaphor, too, the violence of architecture captures the intensity of relations between buildings-spaces and their users: the ever-present reciprocal and *frictional* confrontation in which buildings qualify actions, just as actions qualify buildings (Tschumi 1994: 122). The metaphor can be expanded as well, illuminating how buildings redefine, diminish, and highlight other buildings, and how users' actions impinge upon—rub up against—the actions of other users. Once we include both the planned and unplanned sonic/heard, olfactory/smelt, and textured/felt dimensions of the built environment in our analysis, the tracing of users' violent engagement with Istanbul's assemblages of urban space and with each other becomes a task in which the multisensory nature of the city and of the human body need to be taken into account.

My focus on activists' social construction of space in Istanbul is not, then, in the main concerned with the political intentions embedded in planning interventions and architectural sites in the city, as many recent studies on the built environments of Istanbul, Ankara, and Izmir have been (Holod and Evin 1984, Yeşilkaya 1999, Kolluoğlu-Kırlı 2002, Çelik 2007, Bertram 2008). Nor does it concentrate on the city's spatial formation as generated by the social relations of the capitalist mode of production (e.g., Keyder 1999), although I do write about both of these processes in chapter 3. Rather, it foregrounds the second dimension of the violence of architecture, in an attempt to bring the vital social movements of the late 1970s, the activists of the leftist factions and the cadres of the ultranationalists, into relationship with the historically evolving spatial organization and built environments of the city. Together they changed radically the experience of inhabiting Istanbul, both for their own partisans and for any politically neutral public.

1.2 ISTANBUL 1974–1983

Why arrow in on the period 1974–1983? Is there not artificiality in bracketing off these years from the influence of earlier social processes and events that bequeathed to activists already-instituted imaginaries, heroes, political practices, and urban environments, even as they sought to create insurgent social-historical habits and arrangements? Despite this risk, 1974 seems to herald the emergence of a city qualitatively different from the Istanbul of the early 1970s. The coalition cobbled together by Süleyman Demirel to form Milliyetçi Cephe, the first "Nationalist Front" government in April 1975, included the "fascist" Milliyetçi Hareket Partisi (MHP [Nationalist Movement Party]), which was given two ministries despite having won only three seats in the five-hundred-member parliament.[4] (In the 1977 election the MHP polled 7 percent of the votes and increased their seats in parliament to seventeen.) Ministers enabled the "infiltration" and "pillaging" of state institutions by their own party members, as well as turning a blind eye to the organized "Turkist" violence that began to characterize urban places. Less than a year earlier, in July 1974, an amnesty extended to political activists by the short-lived Ecevit coalition government released thousands of leftist intellectuals, trade unionists, student leaders, and journalists imprisoned after the March 12, 1971, military intervention and declaration of martial law (including the poet Can Yücel).

4. There is an issue with the nomenclature used by protagonists to describe combatants in the political struggle in these years. *Fascist* is the word used by leftist groups to describe the commandos they were confronted by. The rightists called themselves "idealists," inspired by the ideals (*ülküler*) or principles of Turkism. Similarly, the Ülkücü labeled all leftist groups "communists," despite profound differences between them.

The Istanbul many returned to had changed. For example, according to Hüseyin (TKP, Turkish Communist Party) until the early 1970s "Istanbul ferries and train were divided into two sections, first and second class. But even if you had the money you couldn't enter first class unless you were known. Ecevit abolished this in 1973." The most liberal constitution in the Republic's history (in 1961) had legalized the establishment of class-based parties, and by 1965 the Workers Party of Turkey had emerged as an electoral force. Its internal fragmenting in the late 1960s, and then its being closed down after the 1971 intervention for (among other things) its recognition of Kurdish rights at its fourth congress in 1970, boosted the appeal of more revolutionary ideologies, and by the mid-1970s a host of radical socialist, communist and anti-imperialist groups were active in the city. These legal and illegal leftist parties and organizations sought to mobilize the inhabitants of the workers' suburbs on the edges of a rapidly expanding Istanbul, and all over the city their university and even high-school youth groups were active in educating students in their analyses of Turkey's retarded social development. At the same time, labor militancy was growing among workers in state industries and in large private factory plants, with membership in unions fractured between two major rival confederations, DİSK (Confederation of Revolutionary Trade Unions) and Türk-İş (Confederation of Turkish Trade Unions). That same 1961 constitution (and then more fully Ecevit government policy in 1974) had given unions the right to educate workers upon the signing of a collective agreement; paid leave was funded by the employer. These privileges encouraged union activities, and by 1979 more than one million workers were organized in unions, the majority of them in Istanbul (Mello 2010).

A broad and eclectic range of civil society associations, parties, and organizations had also organized to oppose the Demirel coalition. According to Faik (Aydınlık [Enlightenment]), "When I came out of prison in 1974, I was surprised by the strength of the leftist groups. They were everywhere and very lively." They had also become more factionalized: "The new TKP began to organize in 1973/4 as well, and had become influential. They gained control of DİSK. After the mid-70s the left groups divided into two fronts [cephe], Maoists and the Soviet aligned groups." Of course, an active and heavily factionalized radical leftist movement generated its own opposition, not only in employers' federations or in right-wing political parties vying for parliamentary domination, but also in the form of a para-military anti-communist organization, known as the "idealists" (ülkücüler), whose intention was to combat, violently or otherwise, the influence of the left (Çağlar 1990).

Another momentous event happened in late 1974: the first killing of a student since 1971. "I even remember his name," said Ömer (Birikim journal), "it was Şahin Aydın. He was stabbed to death by fascists outside a dispensary on Barbaros Boulevard." Around this time guns, too, became a feature of activist life: "All groups began to be armed after 1975–76, because of the violent anti-union attacks," said Erdoğan (Dev-Yol). Thus, activists encountered a new experience of urban life—the visceral phenomenon of violence. The bloodshed at the May Day rally of 1977 confirmed a new level of political polarization and provocation had been reached:

> I left Halk Kurtuluş [HK: Peoples Liberation] a few days before 1 May 1977, because I could see what they were planning to do, and I thought it was opening everything up to provocation. They were going to march into Taksim Square with guns, hoping for a fight [to avenge a death]. There was a story that someone from TKP had killed a member of HK, and that it was time to take revenge. The TKP and DİSK had already declared that they wouldn't let Maoist groups enter the square, as they were claiming the workers' day for themselves. The TKP did not object to Devrimci Yol cadres entering the square. The Dev-Yol militants stayed in front of the Hotel . . . and as they entered someone fired, and then automatic gunfire opened up from Etap Oteli and the waterworks building. (Salih, Kurtuluş [Liberation])

What makes 1983 the end of an era? Post 12 Eylül, the violent pacification of the city continued throughout the years of martial law (see chapter 7). Although the 1982 military constitution structured its working processes, the return to restricted parliamentary authority with the election of Turgut Özal as prime minister in November 1983 signified the cessation of the direct rule of the military junta. Indirect rule was assured through the operation of the new constitution. Kenan Evren remained president of the Republic. Despite this, civilian government facilitated the faint beginnings of a new experience of the city for its cowed and shocked inhabitants. For activists, too, politics began to take on different dimensions:

> It is clear that the feminist movement [and human rights] began in 1985 because it was almost the only legal way of doing politics. Thus, the first political march after 12 Eylül was a women's march from Kadıköy Yoğurtçu Park to Kadıköy Square. Before the march we went out at night to write about the protest and to put slogans on the wall. We went out late as a group, very made-up [çok süslenmiştik]. It was a cold, snowy night, and we caught a taxi from one place to another. The slogan was: "Women exist" ["Kadınlar vardır"]. Unlike the 70s, men could join in the march but only if they stayed silent and marched at the back (Berrin, HK).

Similarly, according to Filiz, the leftist organization Kurtuluş decided in 1985 that if two people with the same experience were to apply for the same position, the woman should be preferred.

In sum, the years 1974–1983 may be construed as constituting a distinct period for the city, characterized first by the fearlessness of mass urban mobilization and then by the fear of mass urban pacification, both of which marked indelibly, in their reckoning with Istanbul, a generation of activists. The years are punctured by the military coup in 1980 that initiated in the city an unprecedented phase of state terror.

Inhabiting Istanbul

How can we gain a preliminary sense of the finer contours of urban living in Istanbul in those years? Certainly the daily newspapers, although politically partisan, illuminate and extend political science and political economy perspectives, facilitating our imagining of the existential *affect* of the city, of how it was felt/perceived and spoken about, and thus known by its inhabitants. Even details of concrete if apparently random acts of Istanbul's inhabitants reveal something about the intersubjective relations in which they dwelt—for example, the stealing and cooking of a *süs köpeği* (small house dog) by two youths because they were hungry (*Tercüman*, 2 October 1977, p. 5); or the unintended death of a three-year-old girl in Gültepe, killed on her balcony in a fight between two groups by either an "accidental" bullet (*kaza kurşun* in *Cumhuriyet*, 11 October), or a "traitor" bullet (*hain kurşun* in *Tercüman*, published on the same day).

In 1977 the school term in Istanbul opened with a severe shortage of textbooks and teachers. At one school of fifteen hundred students, packed into a place designed for seven hundred, the students felt it more useful to play football than to sit in classrooms with no teachers (*Cumhuriyet*, 16 October 1977, p. 7). In the same year, electricity cuts became a feature of daily life; two hours each day rolling out in turn over every district of the city (although never between 12:00 and 1:00 p.m., or on Sundays) (*Cumhuriyet*, 21 October 1977). Price rises of basic goods in September 1977 brought severe hardship for Istanbul's poorer inhabitants, and rising school expenses meant that some families sent their children back to the village; many said that they could eat meat only during Bayram holidays. *Cumhuriyet* (16 October) published the "*yoklar listesi*" (list of missing goods) reporting which things were unavailable and where—salt in Malatya and Bursa; *tüpgaz* in Bingöl; *mazot* in Bitlis; cement in Mardin; wood in Adıyaman.

The list of price rises helps us understand a political campaign announced in *Devrimci Yol* newspaper on 24 October, bringing Dev-Yol's supposedly "anarchistic" and "extremist" actions into logical relations with the broader urban condition. "Faşist zülme ve pahalılığa karşı direniş kampanyası' açtığını bildirmiştir." (We declare the opening of a resistance campaign against fascist oppression and inflation.) As part of the campaign, a meeting at Sultanahmet Square involved ten democratic organizations protesting against the price hikes. Participants included Halkın Kurtuluşu (People's Liberation), YDGD (Patriotic Revolutionary Youth Association), İleri Müzik-İş Sendikası (Union of Progressive Music Workers), Perde ve Sahne Sanatçıları Sendikası (Union of Curtain and Theatre Artists), İleri Maden-İş (Progressive Mine Workers), Halk Ozanları (People's Poets/Minstrels), Kültür Derneği (Culture Association), Yurtsever Devrimci Giyim İşçileri (Patriotic Revolutionary Textile Workers), Fatih Halk Bilimleri Derneği (Fatih People's Science Association), Kartal İşçi Derneği (Kartal Worker's Association), and Gençlik Birliği (Youth Confederation). A group of women and children from Ümraniye's "1 Mayıs" suburb marched at the front of protesters, carrying posters saying: "There is no water, electricity or school in our *gecekondu*" (*Cumhuriyet*, 24 October 1977, p.5).

1.3 HISTORIOGRAPHY OF THE 1970s

There are further reasons, too, for excising and examining these years. For one, over the last three decades there has been little detailed study about urban social movements and the broader practices and perceptions of activists and politically oriented civil society in Istanbul in the second half of the 1970s. Similarly, the lived experiences of activists and the mood of the city during three years of martial law (1980–1983) have rarely been described, nor in that new context have the changed spatial and social relations of its inhabitants. Jenny White notes the existence of a "mass amnesia" about the period, so much so that after 1980 "the violence that had characterized the preceding decade was effaced from public consciousness. No one wished to discuss it, even once the danger of arrest had receded" (White 2002: 41). Indeed, for the period of military dictatorship most political science accounts have focused on the generals' managed return of government to restricted "civilian rule" as well as on the process of the drafting of a new Constitution, and have been unwilling or uninterested in writing about the perceptions and fate of activists.

This *absence* of research and lack of public knowledge is even more striking when we consider a subdued yet central understanding of Istanbul that has insinuated itself into the minds of its inhabitants and intellectuals alike: the 1980 military coup marks the great dividing line between the present "globalized" city and what is felt to be a foreign country of the past. For many analysts the 1980 coup d'état and its instituting of the Third Republic ushered in a new era in Turkish politics, a period characterized by the eclipse of previously dominant leftist movements and ideologies, and the emergence of an identity struggle between Islamists and secularists, as well as between pro-Kurdish movements and a bloody-minded State, all in the context of a newly liberalized, consumer-oriented and globalizing economy (e.g., see Houston 2001). Accordingly, most social science investigation of any particular contemporary urban phenomenon places its origin in the short *durée* of post-coup time.[5] More than ever, Istanbul is a polarized and crowded mega-city of inferior apartments, monuments, shopping malls, five-star hotels, and luxury housing developments. Studies of Istanbul's urban reconfiguration since 1980 have

---

5. Let me give two examples, each from the volume *Orienting Istanbul: Cultural Capital of Europe* (2010). Çağlar Keyder begins his narrative with a single paragraph on peasant modernization through urban migration to Istanbul in the 1960s and 70s, before proclaiming how "all this changed when Istanbul, in common with other globalizing cities of the Third World after the 1980s, experienced the shock of rapid integration into transnational markets and witnessed the emergence of a new axis of stratification" (2010: 26). Göktürk, Soysal and Türeli's introduction ignores the 1970s while claiming that "a new phase of urban restructuring begins with economic liberalization in the 1980s" (2010: 3).

focused on a vast range of subjects, from the rise of gated communities on its urban fringes (Geniş 2007) to studies of gentrification in the older suburbs (Ergun 2004); from exploration of the commodification of its public spaces (Öz and Eder 2012) to investigation of the influence on its secular politics of transnational organizations and of the supra-state project of the EU (Gökarıksel and Mitchell 2005); from tracking of the city's financial extension beyond Turkey itself (Sassen 2009) to analysis of new forms of social exclusion for the most recent generation of rural or Kurdish migrants to the city (Keyder 2005, Secor 2004). In each of them the coup indexes a formulaic baseline from which the trends of the present might be imagined, measured, and assessed.

Yet despite this widely held local knowledge concerning the defining significance of 12 Eylül as a threshold to a new global city, little research over the last three decades has focused directly on Istanbul and its activists in the critical years immediately before and after the coup. At worst, in some accounts 12 Eylül is barely mentioned, by-passed in the breathless rush to come to terms with neoliberal and global Istanbul. Sassen's article about Istanbul (2009) is a case in point. According to her paradigmatic sense of the term, Istanbul is now a "global city," identified by changing sets of numbers that measure its *flows* of money, people, and ideas. But in her analysis there are no national causes, actors, opponents, or makers of its "globalization," nor is there a discussion of the city's actual history apart from that alluded to in the title, its "history" as a place of "eternal intersection."

Why? Why this local (ac)knowledge(ment) that the military coup in 1980 is the crucial event in the long-term reengineering of the city, alongside an apparently effaced intellectual curiosity and public memory about what it was like to live, organize, agitate, mobilize, and suffer in Istanbul at that time?

One possibility is that the years constitute a collective trauma in the lives of many who lived through them, their excesses perceptually overwhelming and therefore difficult to comprehend. In his introduction to *The Making of Modern Turkey* Feroz Ahmad notes in a single terse paragraph on the 1970s that "political violence and terrorism, which have yet to be adequately explained, made the lives of most Turks unbearable" (1993: 13). Similarly, in her recent book *Muslim Nationalism and the New Turks*, Jenny White summarizes the decade in three brief paragraphs, relating how "violence and ideological extremism were inescapable." She finishes by recounting her relieved escape from the situation: "Having lived through three years of street violence in Ankara, where I was studying at Hacettepe University, I pocketed my master's degree and left the country in 1978" (2013: 34, 35).

Reflections upon my fieldwork and interviews with ex-activists add something critical to Ahmad and White's brief "outsider" comments on urban life. True, militants' accounts of activism in the years before 12 Eylül document their participation in acts of violent militancy, in what Samim described as their "'liquidation' of the felt validity of the revolutionary experience of others" (1981: 84). Yet unlike the characters in novels described by Irzık (2010) in her analysis of 1971 coup d'état fiction, who are invariably depicted as persecuted by the State despite their innocence, the activists interviewed for this research did not protest that their victimization as leftists was mutually incompatible with the experiential realities of engaging in democratic and sometimes revolutionary action, including their own acts of violence. Indeed, the interviews revealed something different—the capacity of ex-activists not just to remember their status as combatants in a civil war or as victims of horrifying human rights abuses post coup but also to acknowledge their own flawed *agency* as political actors.

Perhaps differences in accounts of those years disclose not only insider or outsider perspectives but also contrary *existential* perceptions? Ahmad and White's brief comments express a discomforting experience of passivity in the face of the actions and activities of others. By contrast, activists recollect their own sense of social efficacy extended against the friction of other actors. Activism by definition is a mode of embodied agency, and activists felt and hoped that they were remaking the world. Three years of martial law in Istanbul re-tuned the mood of residents in the city, enacting a perception of helplessness, and traumatizing activists and residents alike in the name of Atatürk.

Justifying the Coup d'État

There is more involved in this public and intellectual disengagement from the critical years before and after the coup, alongside any guilt, anger, or fear felt by militants or Istanbul's inhabitants about what they did or about what was done to them. The minimal comprehension of that period and the lack of public memory about it are demonstrated in the near complete absence of any officially sanctioned visual monuments to its most striking events. There is one moving, albeit unofficial, memorial to Metin Yüksel in the courtyard of Fatih mosque, leading member of the Muslim youth group Akıncılar, who in 1979 was murdered by MHP commandos after attending Friday prayers. His fallen body shape is etched into the paving stones of the mosque courtyard where he was slain. Prayers are still held there annually in his memory. The lack of sites of memory testifies to a *suppression* of militants' voices and perceptions and to an ongoing project by Turkish state institutions to obscure or depreciate the full gamut of acivists' political and social activities.

Most active in this project is the Turkish Armed Forces, which attributes responsibility for the military intervention to the collective anarchism, terrorism, and class separatism of the militants themselves. In his speech broadcast on State TV and Radio on the morning of the coup, General Kenan Evren drew attention to the "perverted ideologies" that made some people sing the "Internationale" in place of the Turkish national anthem. It is plausible to suggest that denigrating the activists of those years comprised a key policy through which the Turkish military legitimized its preeminent role in post-coup politics. This campaign also ensured the immunity from prosecution of the military personnel responsible for the gross human rights abuses carried out as a matter of regime policy after the coup. It was only thirty years after the intervention, with the junta leaders nearly all deceased, that the Turkish parliament abrogated the constitutional clause granting coup leaders amnesty from prosecution (see chapter 8). At the time of writing, tens of civil court cases have been launched against military personnel. The outcomes of these are uncertain.

In brief, a dominant discourse invokes the increasingly violent polity in the years before the coup as its very justification, binding for better or worse militants and coup-makers to each other. That narrative positions the activists of the late 1970s as the city's *fulcrum* generation, negatively but causally linked to the restructuring of Istanbul and of Turkey itself. Activists themselves live with that status, rejecting the implication that they deserved their arrest and torture while reflecting upon the failure of their struggle to transform urban society.[6] Indeed my interviews with ex-activists reveal how in retrospect they are intensely critical of the faults and shortcomings of their own groups and factions in the years before the coup (see chapters 2, 4, and 5), a critique, in short, of themselves, as well as an imagining of their own partial responsibility for the present flawed development and state of the city. This sober self-examination informs many ex-activists' identities and practices in the present.

Reference above to a "dominant" discourse suggests that it is insufficient to say that the 1970s have not been written about or analyzed. More precisely, it is the complex and varied modes of activism, including consideration of the diverse practices, motivations, experiences, intentions, and ethics of militants in the urban environment that have been simplified or ignored. By contrast, there is a large literature listing and explaining the context of events leading up to the coup. The best-disseminated account has been the discourse of the junta, broadcast (for years) after the coup in censored media space. Book chapters in general histories of "modern Turkey," often referencing the picture of the 1970s sketched out by the junta, comprise a second literature, while work oriented to dependency and world-systems theory is a third, analyzing the struggle over the political economy as a significant reason for social conflict.

The junta's narrative justifying the intervention was repetitive and clear, consistently made in speeches or interviews given by members of the National Security Council in the months after the coup and published in the strictly controlled

6. See the title *Bizim çocuklar yapamadı* (Our children couldn't do it) (Mavioğlu 2008), which in retelling the story of 12 Eylül and its aftermath echoes the reported words of the American consul in Ankara to the State Department on the night of the coup: "Our boys have done it."

press. It included the following claims: the armed forces are a disinterested institution sitting above the grubby affairs of politicians, political parties, and partisan
civil society, called upon to act for the benefit of the neutral citizens who are dis-
advantaged by the politicization of state services; indeed the intervention was an
obligation forced upon the military as a result of the conditions of its existence,
given the duty bestowed upon it by Atatürk to protect and guard the Turkish
Republic; it had warned the government and the opposition numerous times to get
their house in order, but they had refused to act to solve the biggest "regime crisis"
in the history of the Republic; the country was in peril on a number of fronts, particularly from the politicians' inability or refusal to protect the constitutional and
democratic institutions of the state and regime; further, a grave threat was posed
by the actions of *inside* and *outside* powers who armed, brainwashed, and released
militants into the environment, leading to anarchy, terror, and separatism, and to
the needless deaths of twenty or more young people each day.

Single chapters in general political histories of modern Turkey comprise a second literature describing the 1970s (see for example Zürcher 1995; Ahmad 1993,
2003; Pope and Pope 1997; Davison 1998; Howard 2001; Kalaycıoğlu 2005; Akşin
2007; Waldman and Çalışkan 2017; Ter-Matevosyan 2019). Although they usefully
chronologize an incredible array of events—elections, coalitions, prime ministers,
galloping inflation, price-hikes for food and oil, balance-of-payment deficits,
Cyprus tensions, strikes, acts of violence and assassination, notorious massacres—
in the main these chapters lack, paradoxically, both theoretical analysis *and*
description of actors' concrete experience and perspectives.

Further, the narrative of the junta influences much of their analysis. In more
than a few accounts, society is described as threatened by anarchy; activists are
reduced to "terrorists" and "extremists" fighting in the streets; and politicians are
criticized as incompetent, naive, or frivolous (Gunter 1989, Kalaycıoğlu 2005: 124),
and the military—far from being presented as turning a blind eye to or even spon-
soring certain perpetrators of urban violence—is portrayed as forced to disinter-
estedly intervene in society to resolve a social and political crisis for which (it is
implied) it had no responsibility in generating, in order to restore the tenets of the
Atatürk Cumhuriyeti (Atatürk Republic). To give just one example: in his introduction to Ersin Kalaycıoğlu's *Turkish Dynamics* (2005) Barry Rubin writes, "At
times, extremists of left and right fought in the streets. As a result, the military—
which saw itself as the guardian of Atatürk virtues—repeatedly had to intervene.
Yet if the system's problem was the sporadic coups, its strength was that each one
returned the country to a democratic system" (2005: xii). Clearly, the military constitution of 1982 did not return Turkey to a democratic system, at least in any normative sense of the word. Further, in some writings, activist violence is condemned
even as the violent imposition of non-violence for "civil" society is condoned (see
Gunter 1989 for an egregious justification of torture, while citing the military

regime's own publications after the coup as his chief source of information about "terrorist" events). In some of these accounts the coup is presented as enacting a necessary *depoliticization* of Turkish society rather than as simultaneously instituting a new political-economic model in its place. For example, in his chapter "The Troubled Years 1967–1987" in *Turkey: A Short History* (1998: 199), Roderic Davison repeats approvingly the military's argument that the 1982 constitution restricted the scope of democratic rights to prevent their abuse by those who sought to undermine democratic rights.

More interestingly, certain writers' assumptions about modernization, including a willingness to populate the binary categories of modernity and tradition with secularists and Islamists (e.g., Kalaycıoğlu 2012: 173), translate as a refusal to acknowledge one occluded but central dimension of the 1970s leftist-rightist ideological struggle: its character as an *intra*-Ataturkist dispute organized for many rightists and leftists around key Kemalist terms of nationalism/Turkism and anti-imperialism/independence respectively. Accordingly, the threat of "Islamic fundamentalism," and more specifically a rally held in Konya by the MSP (Milli Selamet Partisi [National Salvation Party) a week before the coup is often cited as another legitimate reason for 12 Eylül (see Zürcher 1995, Gunter 1989, Ahmed 2003).[7]

Last, in some chapters "Kurdish separatism"—not ethnic Turkish chauvinism—is mentioned as a threatening tendency in south-east Turkey, and presented as a lawful concern in inciting military intervention (see Davison 1998, Howard 2001, Gunter 1989). In his memoirs, Kenan Evren himself claimed that there were eight "separatist" (*bölücü*) organizations operating in the southeast of Turkey before the coup (in Pope and Pope 1997). In such explanations there is little acknowledgment of the oppressive long-term project of assimilation directed toward Kurds by the Kemalist state, immediately reinforced by the junta's banning of Kurdish after the coup. Nor is the notorious and extreme violence meted out to Kurdish inmates in Diyarbakır Prison after 12 Eylül much spoken about (see Odabaşı 1991), or the junta's reorganization in 1981 of Turkish nationalist outlets like the Turkish Historical Society and the Directorate-General of Intelligence and Research, aimed at producing propaganda about ethnic minorities (see chapter 7).

By contrast, for scholars versed in dependency theory and the world-systems school, the crisis of state-led import-substituting industrialization (ISI) in the 1970s determined conditions for conflict over the mode of capital accumulation and its distribution (see for example Gülalp 1997, Keyder 1993). An exemplary study in this vein is Çağlar Keyder's *State and Class in Turkey* (1987), which provides both a macroeconomic autopsy of the systemic failure of ISI in the 1970s and an account of its conditioning of political developments, including fragile and fragmented coalition

---

7. Kenan Evren specifically mentioned the Konya rally in his address to the press, September 16 1980, citing it as an example of the dangerous publicization of "reactionary" beliefs (2000: 23).

governments, failed populism, intra- and inter-class rivalry and antagonism, and radicalization of a segment of the population alienated from center left and center right parliamentary politics. Keyder sets the crisis in the larger context of the Turkish economy's incorporation into the world economy and division of labor, arguing that global capitalism provides a "set of constraints within which class struggle at the national level determines specific outcomes" (1987: 4).

In sum, presentation of the political or economic *background* to activists' actions and relationships has dominated accounts explaining the years before and after the military intervention, alongside much repetition of the utterances of the makers of the coup. An underlying concern of both the synoptic political science and political economy approaches has been the political implications of the rapid urbanization of Turkey from the 1950s onward, seen most strikingly in the spread of shanty towns in Istanbul outside the boundaries of the historic city (see chapter 3). In the process, either the political-economic interplay between global and local class-actors, dysfunctional urbanization, or the misadventures of a more narrowly defined political system have been *foregrounded* as the appropriate lens through which to inspect selected features of the decade, as well as to explain activists' activities. Indeed, economic developments are sometimes presented as the *cause* as well as the *context* of activists' actions, through the assumption that actors' calculation and pursuit of economic self-interest is the primary factor informing their motivations and decisions.

1.4 METHODOLOGICAL CONSIDERATIONS

I make these points not to overly criticize such analyses, but more importantly to note that none of these approaches asked activists *themselves* what they thought they were doing, nor placed much value upon describing and analyzing phenomena such as the built environment, militant bodies, movement around the city, places, moods, ethics, violence, ideologies, or factions as perceived and remembered by participants. Even the more thorough discussions (such as Erich Zürcher's 1995 *Turkey: A Modern History*) rarely encompass personal narratives, implying that individuals' lives and experiences are best comprehended by their being aggregated and subsumed within these public, more collective, events. Yet surely the opposite is equally true: an account of the death of a child and its traumatic effect on a family illuminates the significance of infant mortality rates as much as a statistical graph pegging out its comparative percentages (see Pamuk 2014 for a comparison with other countries of Turkey's declining rates between 1950 and 1980).

Equally curiously, the particularity of Istanbul and of its known, used, and efficacious places or built environments, in relation to which activists' political passions were stirred and stimulated, seems also to have disappeared in the accounts sketched out above. Yet the built environments and homes of the shantytowns were more than sites of generalized conflict and mobilization, and Istanbul itself more than the "spatial manifestation" (in factories, workshops, and offices) of capital accumulation or political crisis. *The city that people grow up in is an inhabited city*.[8] Writing about these years should also involve learning and revealing how activists heard, saw, felt, used and spoke about the city and its unstable parts, as well as their agonistic relationships with other emplaced inhabitants. Places were known through the senses of the body, and in situational and often-antagonistic relationship to other related places, not through their position on a map or, as in the case of the shantytowns, by their abstract apportioning in time, theorized as existing temporally somewhere between the city and the village.

"There was Kömürlük cafeteria in Aksaray, on the left of Tarlabaşı Bulvarı going toward the Marmara Sea, after the underpass; every group wanted to get control of it. Sometimes Dev-Yol occupied it, sometimes İGD [Progressive Youth Association]" (Ömer, İGD). Ümit remembered the same teahouse slightly differently: "On one side was the İGD Stalinists; on the other side farther down the row were the Maoists. No one ever passed between the groups or places." Leftists also patronized Turizm Tea Garden in Kadıköy, just as Barboros Café and Mühendisler Kıraathanesi in Beşiktaş were places where leftist students met. Kulluk Kahvesi in Beyazıt was notoriously MHP; and Diriliş Kıraathanesi in Süleymaniye was important for MSP and Akıncı (its youth wing) activists. Places and people were *singular*, and nomenclature expressed ownership, as well as actual or admired social practices. For example, according to Metiner (2008: 73), Muslim activists named Diriliş coffeehouse after the book *Diriliş neslinin amentüsü* (Creed of a reborn generation), by the writer and poet Sezai Karakoç.

Steve Feld stresses the affective dimensions of place names: "Because [they] are fundamental to the description and expression of experiential realities, these names are deeply linked to the embodied sensation of places" (1996: 113). After the coup the junta changed May 1st, the Ümraniye shantytown settled and named by its militant residents, to Mustafa Kemal. In the city of a thousand killings it is the *name* of each dead activist—Şahin Aydın or Metin Yüksel—that makes them particular persons, grieved for by those who knew or loved them.

We will see how else we may gain a *sense* of the city, and of how it was *sensed* by its politicized inhabitants, in chapters 2, 4, 5, 6, and 7, as well as in readings from newspapers and other archival material.[9] The primary source of this sense of their city is the activists' own accounts of their emplaced experiences and memories of Istanbul in the years before and after 12 Eylül. Analysis of them attests to activists'

---

8. Cf. Bachelard: "The house we were born in is an inhabited house" (1994: 14).

9. For example, see the often short lived (and now fading) archived journals of different political factions that analyzed social conditions in the years leading up to the coup and pronounced on both the current situation and the revolutionary strategy or tactics to overcome it.

own projects of spatial politics and production. Further, militants' generation of space occurred not only through their labor in the constructing of roads and houses in politically sympathetic shanty towns, but also in their theatrically embodied gestures, choreographed movements, and noisy exchanges in urban space, and in their symbolic, affective, and imaginative relations with it. This focus on activists' perceptions, urban knowledge, projects, and place-creation—for example through reverberating revolutionary songs—adds a complementary and much needed empirical dimension to the political economy and political science perspectives, while facilitating a necessary critique of the claims of the junta. It also enables us to learn from practitioners about the practicalities, potentialities, limitations, and pitfalls of urban activism.

Research Practices

Here let me briefly describe the central dimensions of the research process itself. Alongside written sources, the key material analyzed in this book derives from extensive interviews with ex-militants, which sought to facilitate autobiographical reflection upon their earlier selves and actions and upon the city (and its places) that co-constituted them. Over a dispersed period of nearly twelve months in 2009 and 2010, and then more briefly again in 2011, 2013, and 2014, I met with more than fifty people, men and women, from a variety of political organizations, including with militants from the violently anti-communist Nationalist Action Party (MHP). However, as will become clear in the book, there is a discrepancy in interview numbers between leftists and rightists that is reflected in the much greater depth of material on leftist practices, ideologies, activists, and (f)actions. Interviews often ran for two or three hours, and in many cases resulted in follow-up sessions. Interviewees ranged in age from forty-six to fifty-five, and were working in a number of areas, including journalism, television, unions, education, or in their own businesses. Many were still politically active in new associations. Interviewees were storytellers, presenting their versions of events. They were very interested in the perceptions of ex-revolutionaries (*devrimciler*) in organizations other than their own—a curiosity that was discouraged at the time, given antagonisms between groups. Indeed, one of their concerns was whether this study would do justice to militants' variety of experiences, given interviewees' realization of the particularity of the parts of the city they had been familiar with, as well as their intuition of political and socioeconomic differences between militants of different factions.

In the vast majority of cases, interviewees had been youthful members of a number of different organizations or factions from Turkish socialism's three major branches, the pro-Soviet factions (including the TKP); the Maoist sects (including HK); and more Latin American–inspired nonaligned groups, including Dev-Yol and Devrimci Sol (Revolutionary Left). In fact, over the decade of the 1970s as many as forty-five radical leftist groups were active. Interviewees recalled an intense factionalism and rivalry between leftist organizations for influence and initiative in urban militancy, detailing how certain groups refused joint cause with others, or even fought each other over a killing or an assault (see chapter 6). Violent conflict between leftist factions and between leftists and rightist groups was also connected to struggles over control of place. Official positions in the center of communism (USSR/China) had an effect on Turkish leftists too, with militants describing how political and ideological differences between factions were reinforced by minor nuances in clothing and style.

Despite this, militants' descriptions of their experiences revealed a common stock of performative spatial tactics shared across nearly all groups, including protests, strikes, sit-ins, revolutionary culture (theater, music), pirate speechmaking (on trains or in the cinema), marking and occupation of places, slum mobilization, organizational separatism, and ready recourse to violence (see chapters 2, 4, 5, and 6). None of these groups, with the exception of the MHP and the PKK (Partiya Kakeren Kurdistane [Kurdistan Workers Party]), exist in the present; although there are renamed organizations that trace their lineage back to the movements of the late 1960s and '70s.

Istanbul, City of the Fearless is also a study of memories. Even as activists recounted "raw" experience (things as they were or as they happened), in our conversations, both my leading questions and interviewees' present interests and intentions led them to foreground certain memories of spatial practices and the city and to relegate others to the "fringes" of consciousness. In this reassembling and new contextualizing of past memories, concern over the absolute veracity of activists' descriptions misses the way that in interviews telling is also a performance, as the literature on the constructive nature of remembering explores (Saunders and Aghaie 2005, Casey 1987). "I'm warmed up now," said Ulvi (MHP) as we spoke, "everything is fresh in my mind."

Indeed, in asking activists to attentively describe the sounds, appearances, and textures of the social environment in Istanbul, the interview process facilitated their reimagining of perception, as well as providing an opportunity to reorder memories in the present. "When the image is new, the world is new," says Bachelard (1994: 47). Careful description of a thing, an emotion or a relationship possesses a generative dimension. As Bachelard muses in *The Poetics of Space*, "Often when we think we are describing we merely imagine" (120). Equally significantly, ex-partisans' memories of Istanbul have been dynamically and ceaselessly reconstituted in the relational context of their ongoing engagements with the city's social and political worlds. As Lambek notes in describing people's ethical memories, specific incidents are located "within the stream of particular lives and the narratives that are constituted from them, changing its valence in relation to the further unfolding of those lives and narratives and never fully determined or predictable" (2010: 4). In the event of the interview, then, activists were able to engage in an act of "phenomenological modification" (Husserl 1962), taking up new perspectives, attitudes, and feelings toward people and events forgotten or perceived as having little significance at the time. Their new insights into the social relationships of the day have informed my own tentative, more synthetic, analysis.

I count this synthesis as classic ethnography, in that genre's most literal and basic sense: a crafted description (*grapho*) about people (*ethnos*), and more specifically about a class of people distinguished by their practices—activism—and their memories and understandings of Istanbul in the years immediately before and after the coup. Following Basso, we might also aptly call it a study of "lived topography" (Basso 1996: 58). It is ethnography in another sense also. It does not aim, through the empirical material and situation presented, to illuminate or progress any theoretical "problem" confounding or animating current debates within the academy. By contrast I prefer to engage with social theory in a more "micro" fashion—drawing out theoretical implications from activist practice and context, and using theory to illuminate aspects of those practices, while seeking to compose the richness, confusion, and reflexive dimensions of people's lives. Through these micro-excursions and comments and alongside the ethnography, I intend a "case-study" of phenomenological anthropology to emerge, an example of what a more phenomenology-inclined anthropology might sound and look like.

In short, *Istanbul, City of the Fearless* is my describing of activists' own ethnography of the city. Description—by both the activist and the anthropologist—is a complex activity. In his poem "Description without Place," Wallace Stevens (1990) draws attention to the *constituting* or *compositional* nature of description or of accounts of accounts. As he puts it, description is "a little different from reality: / The difference that we make in what we see." And not just in what we see. As writer of ethnography, description is the difference we make in what we write. Similarly, as phenomenology, the intellectual tradition that most values its enterprise, has long pointed out, the describing, interpreting, or imagining of anything is intimately connected to the consciousness and perceptions—to the intentions—of the describer, even as the describer's perception is an act mediated by a range of other processes. These include the describer's own history and prejudgments, including education in a discipline, and the intersubjective encounter of the interview.

Chapter Outline

To compose my descriptions I have divided the book into eight chapters. Chapter 2 identifies certain central themes of phenomenological philosophy that provide *City of the Fearless* with a suggestive language for apprehending activists' engagement with and experience of Istanbul. These include phenomenology's emphasis on human intentionality and its constituting awareness of events, places, and people, and its insights into how the event and pedagogy of activism involved militants in specific perceptual (phenomenological) modifications.

What is the relevant pre-history to 1970s activism? Chapter 3 recounts the history of the "violence of architecture" in Istanbul from the founding of the Turkish Republic in 1923 until the mid-1970s, to give readers some idea of the origins of the city's key features, which a multitude of political activists in the 1970s sought to control or revolutionize. One core historical process included the Turkish Republic's unrelenting de-Ottomanization of Istanbul, involving both the regularization of Istanbul through modernist planning, and its Turkification policies targeting its non-Muslim residents for expulsion. Another was the tremendous expansion of the city after the 1950s through rural-urban migration, and the burgeoning of the city's shantytowns (*gecekondu*), which became key theaters and crucibles of political conflict. According to Setha Low, "An ethnographic approach to the study of urban space includ[es] four areas of spatial/cultural analysis—historical emergence, sociopolitical and economic structuring, patterns of social use, and [its] experiential meanings" (1996: 400). I distribute discussion of these to various parts of the study, and areas one and two to chapter 3 in particular. In short, what was Istanbul like in 1974, and how did it get to be like that?

Chapters 4 and 5 explore activists' own production of space in Istanbul. To do so I *disaggregate* from partisans' narratives four major modes of politico-spatial practice, including their visual politics, their sonic politics, their occupation of space, and their performance of violence. Chapter 4 concludes by analyzing the content and meaning of factions' obituaries, and of statements from bereaved families for killed activists published in their newspapers or journals. Chapter 5 continues this exploration of activists' constitution of the city but arrows in on the political and ethical engagements of militant groups in three particular arenas in Istanbul's urban geography: in squatter settlements; in factories and workplaces; and in municipalities. *Ideological* activism in shantytowns, *labor* activism in factories and unions, and *urban* activism in Councils were core aspects of one single but bitterly factionalized revolutionary movement. This "interconnectedness" of the sprawling revolutionary enterprise is particularly important given junta claims that their intervention was necessitated by the "terrorism" of activists. Most groups did not pursue armed struggle.

Conflicts between militants, factions, ideologies, and ideologists revolved around two inseparable concerns: in order to make a revolution, what is our situation, and how is this to be done? Chapter 6 attends to a single broad theme with at least two dimensions—activists' perceptions of their factions, and of their factions' ideologies. The chapter moves back and forth between two foci: description of how partisans (personally and collectively) constituted or applied ideologies, and exploration of how the political/spatial actions, experiences, and decisions of militants were guided by the varied historical narratives, political claims, and economic models of leftist and rightist ideologies.

Coup d'état! Chapter 7 concentrates on three temporally experienced and inter-related themes. The first describes the junta's immediate spatial and activist politics after the military insurrection, embarked upon to punish militants and to intimi-date and pacify the city. The second involves investigation of activists' responses to this assault on Istanbul's urban bodies and places. The third section presents the junta's legal and institutional reconstruction of Turkish society, intended to drasti-cally and permanently reorganize its political practices. Taken together the themes chronicle Istanbul's shock entry into a reign of fascism and its preparation for a new authoritarian political and neoliberal economic order. Chapter 8 concludes *Istan-bul, City of the Fearless* by describing some of the ways that ex-activists and others in the present continue to reckon with the meaning of those events. In particular, it shows how acts of urban commemoration by leftist political parties, unions, and civil society groups communicate to younger generations both the aims of their struggle and the losses accruing to its participants.

The following chapter more directly addresses the phenomenological approach that orients the book's spatial analysis of the city. It affirms that at the crux of a phenomenological account of social life lies the matter of individual perception in any or all of its dimensions—corporeal, interactional, cultivated, political, and col-lective (Bachelard 1994, Casey 1996, Duranti 2009, Ram and Houston 2015). As people's orientations to the world change—say, by their living through a significant historical event such as the spatial convulsions wrought by urban militancy, or by a diminution of their bodily capacities by torture—so also do different properties of places, situations, emotions and people, once at the margins of noticing, come into focus. A phenomenological perspective illuminates a number of key social processes germane to understanding Istanbul in those years: activism and its mod-ification of place perception; militants' frictional fashioning of the affordances of the urban environment; the power of inhabited places through their spatial fur-nishment by others; songs', bodies', places' and things' holding of militants' memo-ries; and the contemporary politics impinging upon the forgetting and remember-ing of 1970s activism. In doing so *Istanbul, City of the Fearless* presents not only a social history but also a phenomenological study of political memory and com-memoration in the present.

2

Activism, Perception, Memory

12 Eylül Museum of Shame

The source of much of the key material analyzed in this book lies in the poetic descriptions of Istanbul's terrors and transformations communicated by ex-militants in extensive interviews. Given that 1970s activism and the coup occurred decades ago, I played particular attention in interviews to questions about activists' present-day remembering. Although heavily reliant upon those accounts, in this chapter I move back and forth between more and less subjective analytic discussion, seeking to distil from the experiences of individual partisans key social practices germane to understanding the city in those years.

The theoretical and methodological perspective known as phenomenology illuminates all of these processes. For phenomenology, human perception of the meaningful world is always *intentional*, experienced according to our interests, concerns, and attitudes, and thus also *temporal* and *spatial*. It is always also intersubjective, too, given the centrality of our knowing and perceiving *in relation* to others—*with* or *against* them—through which our varying intentions emerge. For phenomenology, subjects do not passively relate to given entities, people, events, and so on; rather, they *constitute* them—in Moran's words, make them acquire "objectivity-for-subjectivity" (2000: 15)—through making them the subject of attention according to their shifting intentions, moods, interests, and positions. Luft gives the example of a real estate agent who sees the house as an object of sale and business, and not primarily as a place for living (1998: 156). The dynamics of constitution can be described in other ways. For example, modifying the perceptual capacities or skills of people (i.e., through pedagogy in activism, say in the musical education that factions give to members through protest songs and marches) transforms the phenomenal world for them. It is through these modifications of perceptual attention, in which particular aspects of situations or environments are brought to the foreground while others fade to the background, that both the temporality of subjects' experience of the world, and the creation *in history* of perceiving subjects themselves, is made manifest.

As I show in this chapter, this quality of perception as a temporal process is vital for understanding the experience of militants during the years immediately before and after the coup. It also characterizes the emergent character of ex-activists' remembering (and forgetting) in the years thereafter, mediated as that is both by the state's project to discredit or even erase public knowledge of their activities, and by certain efficacious political developments in the 1990s and 2000s posited by activists themselves as significant in reforming the meaning of their past acts and experiences.

There are many benefits in bringing a phenomenological perspective to bear on activism and activists in Istanbul in the 1970s and '80s and on their transformation of urban environments. The minor intentional modifications effected in the interview process (as described in chapter 1) are best understood in relation to processes of perception more generally, described by phenomenology in its identification and exploration of an *elementary stance* through which humans live their lives. The prime dimensions of that stance most germane to the study of urban activism include the intersubjective condition of being-in-the-world; the emergent properties of both persons and environments that dwelling entails; the life-world as a field of practical engagement in everyday existence; and the significance of the moving ground of our bodies in perceiving, experiencing, and acting in the world (see Ingold 2000; Merleau-Ponty [1945] 2002; Luft 1998). In discovering this elementary stance— following Husserl, Bourdieu (1977) calls it the *natural attitude*—phenomenology also posits the necessity of its modification as prelude for individuals' more reflective self-awareness about it.

According to Luft, for Husserl the *natural attitude* "undergirds the everyday life that we live, as it were naturally, i.e. dealing in a 'straightforward' way with other human beings, animals, plants, things, making plans, performing actions, pursuing interests. . . . To call this 'situation' natural would be absurd for someone living in the natural attitude, yet making this mode of daily life explicit and thematic requires that we are no longer in it" (1998: 155). Levinas explains it somewhat similarly: "In the 'natural attitude,' man is directed toward the world and posits it as existing. . . . The existence of the world is 'the general thesis of the natural attitude.' This attitude is, according to Husserl, *essentially* naïve. . . . This naïveté consists in accepting objects as given and existing, without questioning the meaning of this existence and of the 'fact of its being given'" (1995: 121).

In Ingold's words, the availability of the world "is evident in our everyday use of the most familiar things around us, which, absorbed into the current of our activity (as indeed, we are ourselves), *become in a sense transparent*, wholly subordinated to the 'in-order-to' of the task at hand" (2000: 168) (my emphasis). To make a familiar thing nontransparent, or noticeable, requires an intentional modification, so that our sense of it changes as a consequence of our way of engaging with it (Duranti 2009: 209). For Husserl, this involves the bracketing, modification, or reduction of the natural attitude, particularly of its sensible assumption that the existence of entities, objects, values, and so on is independent of the work of consciousness in perceiving or constituting them. More specifically, Husserl's critique of the natural attitude involves "what is taken for granted in a culture that has been influenced by modern science" (Casey 1996: 13). As Levinas notes above, for Husserl, the naivety of early twentieth-century science consisted in its assumption that the natural world existed independently of the subject's—in this case the natural scientist's— apprehension or objectifying of it. To give just one example, an artist might notice a rock for its possibilities in an installation. A child might treasure a crystal given to her from a favorite aunt. A mining geologist may appreciate it for its mineral and chemical composition, its permeability or porosity, and for the size of its particles. By contrast, Myers (1991) tells us that for many Pintupi aboriginals in central Australia, a rock may be valued through its connection to Dreaming events, one small feature in a region of known and sacred places. In all cases, different educated, imaginative and affective perceptions govern actors' ways of reckoning with (the same) rock. Nothing, of course, stops an aboriginal geologist or artist from shifting between such perspectives. More generally, we might note that scientific disciplines (including anthropology *and* activism) teach novices and students a particular way of constituting the world.

Yet how does the "neutralization" (Levinas's term) of the natural attitude occur? Phenomenologists have posited different ways through which a more lucid ability to sense, identify, and describe one's subjective constituting of the world, including of the "interests that govern my manner of dealing with things" (Luft 1998: 156), may be activated. For example, the poet Wallace Stevens recommends cultivation of a hyper-attentiveness to the minutia, apparent ordinariness, multiple appearances (to consciousness), and constant (yet routinely unnoticed) changes of place in everyday existence as a method to modify ingrained perceptions arising from individuals' engagements in their everyday worlds (see Houston 2015a). Merleau-Ponty echoes such a method when he notes how a reflective break with the presupposed basis of any thought results not in the "return to a transcendental consciousness" ([1945] 2002: xii) but the opportunity to "wonder in the face of the world. . . . [The reduction] slackens the intentional threads which attach us to the world and thus brings them to our notice" (xv). Heidegger posits another well-known route out of the mundane, practical world: the *breakdown* of instruments or technologies—including our own bodies—habitually encountered only in their taken-for-granted "availableness." As Ingold explains, "things have to be rendered *un*intelligible by stripping away the significance they derive from contexts of ordinary use" (2000: 169) (emphasis in original). For Merleau-Ponty ([1945] 2002), analysis of people's experiences with impairments or with malfunctioning systems highlights the crucial importance for perception of the capacity for motility and action rooted in having a body. When we no longer can do things, due to assault, illness, injury, or age, our perspectives toward those things change. In *Outline* (1977), Bourdieu identifies how the event of social crisis may fracture the natural attitude and its conditioning by the *habitus*, whereas in *Masculine Domination* (2001) he argues that the ethnological investigation of another society facilitates reflexivity about one's own.

These analyses of existential situations—and deliberate methods—whereby people are made aware of their bodily enmeshments in place or of certain aspects of their mode of perceiving are particularly relevant in thinking about how Istanbul's politicized inhabitants sensed the city. Skilled and unskilled practices of urban militancy broke apart its existing and familiar spatial orchestration and intelligible rhythm. For example, we have already noted how militants' use of and attitudes toward places (such as the Kömürlük coffeehouse) involved careful monitoring and assessment of their relationship with its current occupiers. The self-security of partisans depended upon instantaneous acts of judgment, vital in a city of shifting intersubjective alliances and authority. Attunement to micro changes in the environment—a single word erased from a slogan daubed on a wall—constituted an active tracking of emergent properties of urban space. Activists cultivated a hyper-attentiveness to the city, becoming, as Wallace Steven recommended, poets of place-change. In brief, training or pedagogy in activism also neutralizes certain taken for granted, "natural" attitudes toward urban places and environments.

Sustained frictional interactions in city places were significant in generating an affective mood of activists, accustoming them to urban breakdown or crisis. "We went to Düzce for something in 1978, and I remember the immense, sudden relief of being out of Istanbul where no one knew you, with no danger of being killed or attacked. In the city everyone looked at each other with suspicion" (Ertuğrul, HK). Temporary removal from the situation made Ertuğrul aware of his natural attitude, of previously non-attended-to feelings intimately related to specific qualities of the city, majorly contributing to his experience of it. This backgrounded but embodied sense of danger meant "crisis" became an expectation, an event to be reckoned with, as Reşat's story about something that *didn't* happen reveals: "Once we heard the ülkücüler were marching from Sarıyer to Beşiktaş. We didn't want them to enter the lower gate [of the university], so we got a gun. We went into a dormitory to have gun training. The person teaching us accidently fired the gun, and someone fell over, screaming 'Mother, I'm ruined!' We panicked, sure that we had killed him. . . . When he recovered with no injuries he said, 'I was told it didn't hurt, so I assumed I was shot.'"

In the main, phenomenological perspectives have had little influence over orthodox Turkish political science, as can be seen in the accounts and analyses of the 1970s summarized in the previous chapter. For good reasons, perhaps, scholars have been more concerned with the political efficacy and genealogy of Kemalism, including with debate over its historical emergence and its key ideological components (nationalism, civilizationalism, modernism, etc.); with questions concerning its attempted remodeling of social life; with an interest in identifying its core producers/consumers, and by analysis of both the benefits that have accrued to its advocates and the repression (and social opprobrium) incurred by its opponents; and finally by its historical fate in relation to contemporary political changes. All of these have of necessity been considered both in the broader context of the dissolution of the Ottoman Empire and developments in the global economy. Further, until recently, many university academics themselves have been committed Kemalists, resulting in a synthesis between their perception and ethical approval of its political project and the scientific categories used to analyze its effects. Kandiyoti (2002) describes conventional social scientific analysis in Turkey in a somewhat similar way, claiming that it has generally privileged the juridico-political and institutional realms as its field of inquiry, while being less preoccupied with theorizing the connections or disconnection between everyday practices and state-driven modernization.[1]

By contrast, I hope to show in *Istanbul, City of the Fearless* how phenomenology's emphasis on human intentionality and its constituting awareness of entities, events, places, people, and so on may both inform and relativize more mainstream accounts of political and social relations in Istanbul in the 1970s and early '80s. Phenomenological anthropology contends that people's purposive actions, their affective states, their embodied experience, as well as the essential interactive quality of their lives should not be reduced to epiphenomena of objectified political-economic structures, simplified by cause-and-effect explanations, subjected too quickly to abstract theoretical or cultural models, or attributed to their following of rules. Similarly, social theories, philosophies, and historiographies should be assessed as much for their contribution to the transforming of their proponents' perceptions of, and scope for action in, the world as for their objective truth. Thus, one virtue of a phenomenological approach is its utility in exploring the conflicted intersubjective character of everyday, lived experience in Turkey in the years between 1974 and 1983, through its concentration on "human consciousness in all of its lived realities . . . and its priority given to embodied, inter-subjective, temporally informed engagements in the world" (Desjarlais and Throop 2011: 4).

1. In a 2005 overview of the literature on cities and globalization beyond Turkey, Davis notes that one consequence of the focus on the capitalist world system, transnational networks, and global trade is the relative paucity of anthropological studies on "urban experience" (2005: 97). This is still true of studies of 1970s Istanbul.

Although in anthropology explicitly phenomenological approaches have often privileged individuals (in their interrelationships) as the mediators of broader cultural processes (e.g., Desjarlais 2003), one major advantage of extensive interviewing of militants about their experiences is that it enables analysis of a more diverse account of their feelings and perceptions than would have been experienced by any one particular actor, given the variation of political practices across the city. From them the analyst may hazard wider conclusions. Indeed, Zigon notes that this is one key tool within the phenomenological kit: the ability to make analytic distinctions between (in this case) the lived sociability of activists' everyday spatial politics, and a more totalistic account of spatial politics in Istanbul made "after the fact of articulation in speech and thought" (Zigon 2009: 287). However, in analyzing interviews, I do not wish to create too hastily in ethnography or in analysis a more comprehensible assemblage of urban practices and places than was experienced by militant subjects themselves, given the way that their own collective actions often caused unbearable uncertainty regarding changing conventions of spatial relations, movements, and engagements. As Hüseyin (from Aydınlık) said, "It was a civil war, and death was very close."

2.1 ACTIVISM AND PERCEPTION

Alongside their practical and affective encounters with a "revolutionary" city, the event and experience of activism itself involved militants in specific perceptual (phenomenological) modifications. Activism involves a pedagogic method. Activist groups sought to educate militants, neutralizing in novices previously deposited attitudes toward the city and its parts and instigating in their place a "socialist (or fascist) way" of reckoning with it.[2] In redefining and politicizing selected intersubjective relationships of activists, factions and groups tried to reorient their perceptions of certain properties of those situations and things. Thus, workers were taught by leftist groups to re-recognize their employers as members of the bourgeoisie class or of the "oligarchy"; and rightists were encouraged by ultranationalist organizations to perceive that the nation demanded certain duties from their Turkishness. Skills mastered in engaging and inhabiting the city in a new way produced urban events, the collision of militants from different factions struggling to realize realities and assert interests. Some events were powerful enough to radically modify the consciousness of individual actors, rupturing previous political visions and practices, and recomposing them as transformed, singular subjects in the process (Humphrey 2008, Houston and Şenay 2017).

2. Duranti (2009) traces out how instructors in jazz classes try to develop in students a "jazz way" of listening to music.

In brief, activist training aimed to *politicize* what Husserl called the "phenomenological *epoche*"—that is, the "method[s] by which an individual is able to modify his or her orientation to the everyday world of experience so as to dislodge ingrained commitments to seeing only particular aspects of it" (Throop 2015: 75). Organizations, parties and factions used the term *consciousness-raising* to describe the strategies whereby impersonal backgrounds or horizons of experience that mediated activists' ordinary perceptions were brought to the foreground of attention. Like any acquired, new embodied knowledge, these intentional modifications were only partial, directing critical attention toward some identified social or ideological determinants of the natural attitude or of consciousness about something while leaving others unavailable to reflection. Up to a point, political groups "confirmed" Bachelard's claim that "it is better to live in a state of impermanence than in one of finality" (1994: 61).

Second, the sponsored modification of activists' perceptions and experience toward the city and its places of work, study, and public engagement involved more than their learning of new theoretical knowledge about society and history so as to discern its exploitative "determinate structures" and project how to transform them. More concretely, consciousness-raising involved activists in a range of new practices and relationships, including work in the shantytown (*gecekondu*) suburbs, where student-militants regularly went to sell journals, teach literacy classes, provide services (clinics, roads, legal and medical advice) and to protect the gecekondu from attacks on its places of meeting (see chapter 4). For male and female student-activists from Istanbul's more middle-class areas, successful service to and mobilization of gecekondu inhabitants required their conscious acquisition of a modified and gendered corporeal style. Awareness of techniques of the body (movement, comportment, mannerisms, and clothing) and communicable dimensions of affective existence (expressions of mood, sensibility, and humor) were crucial in forging intersubjective relations with residents. Thus, according to Şahin (from Partizan Yolu [Partisan Path]),

> You had to learn how to talk and act to older people. When we went to a house, they would prepare the *sofra*. You had to know where to put your legs. We had to know how to sit on the floor together. You wouldn't look eye to eye with the women nor shake their hands. I still don't shake the hand of covered women even when extended to me. The women in the house were covered; these suburbs didn't have "modern girls." They wore long dresses, with baggy trousers underneath and headscarves. To drink water we used a bowl, not a glass. You had to act as if this was natural to you, wait to talk; you shouldn't talk during the meal but only after the tea came.

Third, like any learning activity, activism involved apprentice militants in an attuning or sensitization of their perceptions to others' ways of sensing "by joining with them in the same currents of practical activity" (Ingold 2011a: 314). Factions and organizations were places of collective pedagogy and instilment of skills. Ideologies, too, are well understood in this way, disciplines that educate novices to direct attention toward things in their own particular terms as much as cosmology about the world. They are lived out before they are written out. Further, learning to perceive the city as crucible for revolution through practical activity crucially involved an ethical/sentimental education, the cultivation (in militants) of ethical dispositions that would notice (or infer) particular aspects of the environment—poverty, injustice, and inequality—or be moved by certain dimensions of people's lives. More generally, the moral sensitization of the perceptions of apprentice militants through socialization in activist practice reveals how *perceiving* the world involves or possesses intrinsically ethical and affective dimensions. In turn, this indicates that the anthropological study of ethics should be supplemented by an attention to "ordinary" perception.[3]

Fourth, the perceptual modifications incurred in becoming an activist involved ceaseless talk: the city became a differently inhabited place for militants in being spoken for as much as through being acted in.[4] A flourishing speech economy invested in oral interaction, dialogue, exchange, and debate at countless meetings, seminars, study groups, clubs, and commemorations produced more than transmission of, or knowledge about, Marxist theory, the Turkish nation, or the political economy. In being spoken for, selected aspects of place were disclosed to novices' perception. Equally important was "companionship in conversation."[5] This was a crucial element in stirring and suffusing affective states (emotions, sentiments, and moods) in both militants and in the city itself, and in generating intimacy and affection between members of a group or a faction.

In sum, and as each point above affirms, activism itself—like any skilled practice—is a mode of embodied phenomenological modification, transforming activists' attunement to the city and their interpretation of the "affordances" (Gibson 1979) that its parts provide. Revolutionary activity and intent provoked both new constitution

---

3. The reference here is to the title of Lambek's book, *Ordinary Ethics: Anthropology, Language and Action* (2010).

4. Cf. Ingold: "It is apparent that the world becomes a meaningful place for people through being *lived in*" (2000: 168) (emphasis in original).

5. The phrase comes from Silverstein's (2008) fieldwork with Sufi Islamic brotherhoods in Istanbul in the late 1990s. I use it to draw attention to an over-correction in recent anthropological work on perceptual enskilment and apprenticeship that emphasizes the imitative, body modelling, demonstrative, and repetitive dimensions of teaching and learning (see, for example, Marchand 2010: S8 and his phrase "knowledge beyond language") while downplaying oral articulation, verbal explanation and instruction. By contrast, in activism, talk is a pedagogical and emotional force, generative of the affective bonds experienced between leaders/teachers and militants, and between comrades themselves in activist groups. See Şenay (2015) for a similar discussion of the importance of conversation in the learning of the *ney* (reed flute) in Istanbul.

of and new receptivity to the urban environment's opportunities for action.[6] In discovering and pursuing new spatial practices, both revolutionaries and state authorities activated an affinity between the city and mass political action that does not exist in either the house or in the village: walls for inscribing dissonance; boulevards for marching in or barricading; public buildings for occupation; places for the amplification and feedback of attack and reverb; private associations for secrecy and dialogue; audiences to broadcast one's message to; strangers to address; passers-by to solicit; statues to drape with flags or slogans, to climb on or demolish; state cemeteries in which to commemorate or desecrate the famous dead; squares for mass meetings or punitive massacres; streets for mob lynching, or for dumping mutilated corpses. The city accommodates assassinations in crowded streets, and beatings in deserted lots or unlit alleys; it enables public hangings, and suicides, off bridges and tall buildings or in front of trains. It facilitates begging, and the showing of poverty. As Merleau-Ponty famously put it, "consciousness [of place] is in the first place not a matter of 'I think that,' but of 'I can.' In the action of a hand which is raised towards its object [say a wall on which the activist wishes to paint a slogan] is contained a reference to the object, not as an object represented, but as that highly specific thing towards which we project ourselves" ([1945] 2002: 137–38).

Significantly, however, activists' sensing and utilization of architectural affordances raise vital questions about the role and qualities of *places* in both soliciting and foreclosing on particular perceptions or embodied experiences of them. Thus, the processes by which activism charges or "electrifies" the affordances of the urban and built environment needs careful discussion (see Houston 2015b). Tim Ingold notes that in James Gibson's original formulation the world in which the perceiver moves around is already there, "with all its affordances ready and waiting to be taken up by whatever creatures arrive to inhabit it" (2000: 168). Further, for Gibson, this appropriation of environmental affordances occurs non-conflictually. Yet the affordances held in places gather residents who may seek to circumscribe the access of others to their offerings, or even to occlude their presence. Ingold's turn to phenomenology and what he calls a "dwelling perspective" presents a more dynamic, relational model of human interaction with the environment, with its focus on the work of consciousness in constituting environmental objects of experience. As Ingold writes, "Environment is a relative term—relative, that is, to the being whose environment it is" (20). Here aspects of the world *emerge* for the

6. Indeed, even a "passive" apprehension of place has to be *actively* absorptive, in the first instance by decisively stilling the body's movement in and between places. More than this, listening is an action, as the poet Orhan Veli attests: "İstanbul'u dinliyorum, gözlerim kapalı" (I am listening to Istanbul, with my eyes closed). Similarly, consider the key lines in Walt Whitman's ([1855] 1986) poem "Song of Myself": "Now I will do nothing but listen, / to accrue what I hear into this song, to let sounds contribute towards it."

perceiver in acts of educated and embodied engagement with it, including of course with other beings, both human and nonhuman. In examining perception, phenomenological investigation is analytically acute in identifying the (always temporally unfolding and educated) qualities and capacities—Ingold calls these "skills of perception"—of the *actor-subject* that enable *this* engagement or *that* experience of the world (of objects, environments, and others) to occur. By contrast, sometimes it is less sensitive in identifying the role of architects and their sponsors in intending (through design) the qualities and capacity of the *actor-object* (the thing that is perceived), which permits *this* experience or *that* evocation of it to occur.

Nevertheless, Ingold's work itself is not particularly helpful in sketching out the violence of architecture, or of the political and conflictual dimensions involved in people's interactional generation of their environment and its affordances. The claim is as much Ingold's as it is my own. As he himself notes, "the criticism that the political is conspicuous by its absence from my own attempts to formulate a dwelling perspective is entirely just, and troubling" (2005: 503). The very material affordances of the environment that were malleable to militants' projects and activities also had embedded in them the political intentions of their makers, configured in pathways and roads, artifacts and machines, buildings and interior design, architecture, zoning and urban planning. Here the fabricated efficacies of places and things themselves exerted perceptual power over their users, seeking to condition particular experiences and uses of them while actively contriving at activists' bodily motions. Shull's recent research (2012) on the engineering of experience in poker machine gambling is an awful case in point, where video graphics, ergonomic consoles, surround-sound acoustics, plastic-press buttons, marketing schemes, and player-tracking systems all conspire to trigger addiction through minute and synesthetic scripting of people's behavior. Such manipulative control of the environment, and the carefully calculated algorithms that seduce players to feed in more money by periodically cascading back a proportion of their losses, are designed by corporations, with their intentions in play.

Moreover, in their own adversarial appropriation of places and in their energetic modification of them, activists contended with other efficacious users of space, entering into conflict with them over access to and adaptation of urban affordances. Neither activism nor dwelling is harmonious. In chapter 1 we saw how for Tschumi the prime violence of architecture involves confrontation between buildings or planned spaces and their users. Yet friction *between* inhabitants themselves in their bitter performative conflicts over the city and its configured assets is equally important in qualifying users' spatial experiences and actions. In other words, the urban environment of militants was an intersubjective one, an emerging field of frictional relations and moods that gathered together and encompassed multiple actors. For individuals, regions of places—factories, schoolyards, student lodgments, shantytowns, town squares, houses—and peregrinations between them arose that were rich with the "wildness," bodily presence, threat, and power of other beings. In response, two key spatial strategies of militants involved the *occupation* and the *breaking* of another group's occupation (in Turkish *işgal* and *işgal kırmak*). To occupy meant to take control of a building or place (lodgment, school, factory, university department), to appropriate its resources and to expel members of rival groups so as to prevent their organizing there. Here we see an inversion of Ingold's insight that lives are led "not inside places but through, around, to and from them" (2011b: 148): the factional apartheid governing Istanbul's places sought to put a stop to the active perambulations of *wayfaring*, Ingold's preferred term for the experience of inhabiting the environment. Post-occupation, users' relationships with rivals were mediated through their possessive transforming of places' visual, acoustic, and performative elements.

Equally significant, the perceptual attunements constituted by enacting activism were not only instigated in confrontation with contemporaries. In the urban assemblage itself, the acts, agency, and efficacy of *predecessors* were also encountered. The intentions of the dead lived on in places, in their socio-material distributions, in their trails for movement, and in their scenes for action, thought, or expression; indeed, given their constant immersion in them places constituted activists' bodies as much as their bodies marked places. Ingold describes this process in somewhat neutral terms: "Human children," he writes, "grow up in environments furnished by the work of previous generations, and as they do they come literally to carry the forms of their dwelling in their bodies—in specific skills, sensibilities and dispositions" (2000: 186) "The house is a book read by the body," says Bourdieu (1977: 90). The words *previous generations* here are vague, as well as politically naive—in many urban places these past acts of spatial "furnishing" are more precisely described as initiated by militant groups, who may seek to effect a targeted *rupture* within the environment and its dwellers as much as to ensure continuity or evolution.[7] Indeed, in deliberate projects of *urbicide*, places and environments are as vulnerable to forced rearrangement and destruction as the people they house.

As we will see in chapter 3, in the course of the twentieth century Istanbul has witnessed a number of *ruptures* in its history of dwelling. Most significant is the forced migration or expulsion from the city of its indigenous Armenian, Greek, and Jewish inhabitants in the first four decades of the Turkish Republic (1920–1960), enabling others to benefit from their fashioning of its environment. In the novel *Huzur*, Ahmet Hamdi Tanpınar (1949–2011) describes another rupture, reflected in the perturbation and melancholy experienced by Istanbul's inhabitants at the Kemalists' selected transformation (in the same years) of the "sensuous presentations"

---

7. One such group (in Istanbul) has been modernist urban planners, named by Rabinow (1996) as "visualizers of a socio-technocracy." See chapter 3.

(Casey 1996: 22) of late-Ottoman Istanbul, including most palpably of the familiar sonorities of the city by the muting of Ottoman music. These two events were aspects of a nationalistic transformation of Istanbul, antagonistically aimed at its cosmopolitanism and at the life-worlds of its inhabitants.

The 1980 military coup and the junta's subsequent counterrevolutionary reassembling of the city caused a third rupture between inhabitants and environments in Istanbul. Activists in particular were systematically stripped of their ability to place-make, first in the dissolution through torture of the fragile concordances established between their bodies and Istanbul's places; second, in the prohibition forbidding collective interaction in public with other inhabitants of the city; and third, by denying them involvement in new post-coup political processes that generated revised affordances in the city. In brief, Edward Casey is wrong to say that places are "generative and regenerative on [their] own schedule" (1996: 26). Even as places are sui generis—nothing can ever not be in place—they also allow themselves to be recruited by the political imagination, their ongoing fabrication shrinking or expanding in-built affordances for action, in the process entitling some groups and disenfranchising others.

For a number of reasons, the work of Henri Lefebvre in *The Production of Space* might here be usefully contrasted with Gibson's naive presentation of environmental affordances, as well as with Ingold's (absent) political analysis. For one, the book was first published in 1974, making its analysis contemporary enough with the practices described above to have a descriptive, analytic, *and* politically invested relationship to militant leftist movements in that period.[8] A shared Marxist vocabulary informs both the broader socialist movement's effort in Turkey to situate individual experiences in the historical development of the political economy, and Lefebvre's text, as demonstrated for example in its stress on the centrality of the mode of production in the generation of spatial order. More specifically, the ambitions and tactics of these political movements account for what Lefebvre describes as the "special practical and theoretical status" that he gives to the category of *appropriation* in the book (1991: 368).

To identify the importance of appropriation, Lefebvre identifies three aspects of social space: first there is a society's "spatial practice," "which embraces production and reproduction" (1991: 33) and "secretes that society's space" (1991: 38). Secondly, there exists "representations of space" or conceptualized space, the space of planners, urbanists and, most paradigmatically, of architects. This is a "visual space, a space reduced to blueprints, to mere images"—the architect has a "representation of space, one which is bound to graphic elements—to sheets of paper, plans, eleva-

---

8. *The Production of Space* was translated into English only in 1991, which has meant its orientation to the urban social movements of the 1970s is often overlooked. (Lefebvre had already in 1970 published a book on the 1968 Paris events, titled *L' Explosion*.)

tions, sections, perspective views of facades, modules, and so on" (1991: 361). Last (and confusingly named) there are "representational spaces," the spaces of users and inhabitants, *spaces as lived* (not conceptualized). "When compared with the abstract space of the experts, the space of the everyday activities of users is a concrete one, which is to say, *subjective*" (1991: 362). It is also the "dominated—and hence passively experienced—space that the imagination seeks to change and *appropriate*" (1991: 39) (my italics).

Lefebvre's notion of appropriation involves more than inhabitants' negating of urban space, their using of the city as the setting for political struggle, or even of their *diverting* of existing space for new purposes (1991: 168). Ideally, it also entails the creation of *counter-spaces*, of a new urban morphology. Hence Lefebvre gives cardinal importance to class struggle: because the "secretion" of space in capitalist society is dominated by the bourgeois class, only class struggle has the capacity to transcend the passivity of users of space, creating in the process new environments, places, and interrelationships.[9]

Despite the rather schematic nature of his model, Lefebvre's theory illuminates certain dimensions of activists' experiences and practices in Istanbul. However, their accounts encourage us to revise certain of its emphases. For example, *The Production of Space* displays an orthodox Marxist preference for tracing out how the programming of everyday life by the capitalist mode of production renders the users of space passive. Thus, actors enter capitalism's "secretion of space" after the fact of its production, which simultaneously preconditions their relationships, actions and consciousness in it: "Every space is already in place before the appearance in it of actors; those actors are collective as well as individual subjects inasmuch as the individuals are always members of groups or classes seeking to appropriate the space in question. This pre-existence of space conditions the subject's presence, action and discourse, his competence and performance; yet the subject's presence, action and discourse, at the same time as they presuppose this space, also negate it" (Lefebvre 1991: 57).

As we will see in chapters 4 through 7, the situation in Istanbul was much messier. By paying particular attention to the phenomenological dimensions of social life—in this case to how activists perceived phenomena (bodies, factions, violence, places, ideologies, suffering)—we grasp better how urban things were constituted by militants' intentions and simultaneously reckoned with. It is not a criticism of Lefebvre's *The Production of Space* to note that its positing of three dimensions

---

9. For Gibson, affordances of the natural environment are offered to dwellers for their adaptation and use. By contrast Lefebvre assumes the fabrication of space by human labor through the political economy, in which oppositional socialist groups are forced to seize the (non-neutral) affordances of the city created by capitalism, affordances that advantage the dominant class and incite other inhabitants to attempt to transform them in social movements.

of social space is in its own terms a "representation of space." Yet Lefebvre clearly values a phenomenological "bias" in urban research when he argues in the same work that some artists, and even a few writers and philosophers "who *describe* and aspire to do no more than describe" (1991: 39) may *engage* in their work with space as "directly *lived* through its associated images and symbols" (1991: 39) (my emphasis).

2.2 REMEMBERING ACTIVISM

Long a world city, Istanbul's more recent "globalization" is by now old news. Hyped by travel agents, lauded by cultural brokers, marketed as a bridge spanning East and West by the tourism and culture industries, the image makers and money makers agree: Istanbul is fashionably global, its markets and food places, its Sufi lodges and gay bars, its museums, mosques, mosaics, and *manzara* (landscapes) exhibited and consumed on- and off-line, by a flood of tourists and by the city's own residents, twenty million people or more.

See Istanbul and die, says the poet Can Yücel.

Istanbul is all this, and much more. Do the extraordinary changes in its built environment and its sense of place post-coup mean that *Istanbul, City of the Fearless* is a study of a city and of a time that exists only in memory? This side of 12 Eylül, are activists' spatial politics, experiences, and memories of the years before and after the coup—their private and arcane knowledge—of historical interest only? Are those years sealed off from the decades that succeeded them? Are 12 Eylül and the military government a door that opened to Istanbul's neoliberal or "global city" future by slamming it shut upon the past?

In these next two sections I show that this is indeed partly true. Revolutionary Istanbul lives on in the memories of its ex-activists. But it lives on, too, in their learned capacities and accumulated reflective wisdom that even now give depth to and partially orient the lives of hundreds of thousands of citizens living in the city. Casey describes this process in his book *Remembering*, noting how "orientation in place . . . cannot be continually effected *de novo* but arises within the ever lengthening shadow of our bodily past" (1987: 194). In this process, militants' embodied and emplaced historical memories and perceptions of the city prevent any easy articulation with the shallow self "free of any particularist spatial ties" (Gökarıksel and Mitchell 2005: 150) imagined and mobilized by neoliberalism, and sometimes assumed by analysts to be a plausible account of social agents' modified dispositions and ethical consciousness (Hilgers 2013). The selves that ex-activists are in the process of becoming—just like the city that they are continually in the process of inhabiting—depends in part upon their memories of and reflections upon their earlier actions, convictions, and experiences. Elsewhere, Casey writes of the "incoming" of places into the body. Places, he notes, "constitute us as subjects. . . .

To be (a) subject to/of place is to *be what we are as an expression of the way a place is*" (2001: 688, emphasis in the original). Accordingly, a history of the sedimentation and hierarchy of places in people's bodies exists according to the intensity of experience encountered in them, even as places themselves are altered by people's actions. Although this constituting of self through its marking by places is cumulatively produced over a lifetime, the city before and after 12 Eylül powerfully impressed its presence upon militants, interacting with and reorienting their earlier socialized bodies and personae.

Certainly the material infrastructure of much of the 1970s city has disappeared, in particular in the transformation of Istanbul's housing. The gecekondu suburbs of the 1960s and '70s with their small, separate houses have been transformed into *apartkondu* (four- to ten-story buildings). They are no longer on the periphery of the city. On the other hand, gentrification has conserved and spruced up the buildings of older, more central areas but contributed to the massive emigration of their earlier residents. Even the perduring monuments of the physical environment (mosques, museums, palaces, villas, administrative buildings, etc.) have been upgraded or restored, their lines of sight and their sightlines exposed through simplification of their surroundings, their sounds made more audible (or muted), their occupants changed, their functions transformed.

Of course, not every bit of Istanbul has changed. The three- or four-story apartment blocks put up in the 1960s in lower-middle-class suburbs like Aksaray are still there. Yet when Fırat, an ex-MHP sympathizer, took me on a tour in 2013 of Şehremini in Istanbul's historic peninsula, where he had lived through the years before and after the coup, we did not encounter a single sign of the spatial politics of the 1970s. Like blood spilled in a stabbing on the stairs of an apartment block at night and washed away by the early morning cleaner, it was as if the era and its acts had never occurred. Fırat recognized few people in his old neighborhood, and Şehremini's present occupants did not share his or his generation's intimate memories of emplaced events experienced there. In brief, if memory requires anchoring or harboring in peopled places, activists' option "to go back to a place [they] know, finding it full of memories and expectations, old things and new, the familiar and the strange" (Casey 1996: 24), is severely compromised in Istanbul.

Nevertheless, sometimes it is the very change of place that compels memory. Differences in places' inhabitants, activities, appearances, smells, and sounds evoke absences.[10] A peaceful street reminds one of a violent march; polite police

10. In her autobiography about growing up in Istanbul, Ayfer Tunç writes movingly about the relationship between memory and absence:

Painted on one wall were robust and merry young girls and boys wearing white swimming costumes playing with a ball in the sea, and on the other wall was drawn a row of young girls, whose arms were stretched out towards each other's shoulders. ... They made Süreyya Beach

stir up fears of a baton: the body remembers in its quickening of breath, sweating, or feelings of nausea. Similarly, the forced transformations of sonic place after the coup made activists remember the mood of a time. Filiz (TKP) recalled how, before the military intervention, singing the party's song together with a thousand people "made us feel we all shared the same views on life." The events of 12 Eylül fractured this acoustic solidarity: in our interview (thirty years later) Filiz still remembers weeping a year after the coup at hearing in passing a snatch of a familiar (but prohibited) march hummed in the street under someone's breath. Aural awareness is a powerful if sometimes backgrounded force bearing memories and carrying political subjectivity. In Nesrin Kazankaya's play Quintet, bir dönüşün beşlemesi (Quintet: A transformation in five parts), a leftist activist returns to Istanbul for the first time in twenty years after fleeing the coup for Europe: meeting up with her old friends and comrades, the ex-revolutionaries best reconnect with the singing of a march ("May 1st"). The now-businessman husband joins in despite earlier bitter arguments over politics. Like places, then, songs hold memories, as do objects: "There was an urban myth of the 'gri-mavi van' [gray-blue Ford van]. We knew among ourselves that it was the van of the undercover police. Whenever we saw one, we would run or duck for cover. In Montreal after the coup, whenever I saw one, I still ran for cover. Of course, in Istanbul most vans of that color were not carrying police. But once it came true: we were stopped and frisked by four police who came out of a gri-mavi van! Luckily, we were going to the cinema, and we convinced them of that" (Kenan, HK).

Further, alongside places, songs, and objects "where memory crystallizes and secretes itself" (Nora 1989: 7), the city is "physically inscribed" in a generation of activists.[11] As described by Kenan above, he fled at the very sight of a gray-blue van in Montreal years after his regular exposure to police practice in Istanbul, an embodied reenactment that referenced a personal and collective history. Similarly, Şahin (as we have already seen) still finds himself reluctant to shake the hand of a covered woman, even when extended to him. Casey calls this "body memory" (1987: 146ff), the way that something kinesthetically learned in conscious (or semiconscious) imitation of others' mannerisms, movements, and comportment may

---

and the railway cheerful. . . . One day the wall was knocked down, and a wide road built between the beach and the railway line. The absent wall made me ruefully realize for the first time that the small things that add colour to our lives will disappear, are able to be lost. (Tunç 2001: 13)

11. Cf.: "the house we were born in is physically inscribed in us. . . . The feel of the tiniest latch has remained in our hands" (1995: 14, 15). Wallace Stevens's poem "To an Old Philosopher in Rome" reveals how the images of intimacy attracted by the "house" (and collected in Bachelard's The Poetics of Space) can also be extended to the city: "The sounds drift in. / The buildings are remembered. / The life of the city never lets go, nor do you / Ever want it to. It is part of the life of your room. / Its domes are the architecture of your bed' (Stevens 1990: 510).

become habitual action over time, an embodied modification thereafter ingrained in militant habit. In body memory, the past is revived by its active entry into present actions. In just this way both urban violence and torture, too, are remembered by the body, in an ache, an itch, impairment, or trauma—an invasion of the body by its past that transacts memory, whether wanted or not.

Yet activists remembered reflexively as well: habitual body memory is not the same thing as retrospective "memory of the *perception* of the body" (Casey 1987: 162, original emphasis), as Levent's recollection of Fatih shows: "By 1978 the sound of gunfire in the night was common in Fatih, as people attacked the university lodgments. But despite all this, the sounds I remember most about Fatih are the sound of people talking, of women neighbors chatting, of children calling from the street to their mothers or neighbors. People had their own whistles, everyone with their own melody, just as with nicknames."

For Levent, Fatih is a "geometry of echoes."[12] They are the echoes that similarly give depth to and partially underpin the lives of hundreds of thousands of other ex-activists living in the city, a class of people often highly active in politics still. The emplaced and powerfully affective multisensory memories initiated by the spatial militancy of those years, including from post-coup torture, mingle with (and even limit) ex-activists' perceptions in the present. Some are unable to participate in political life altogether, as intended by the junta. Interviewees were aware of friends and ex-comrades who had never come to terms with the things that happened to them in the years of martial law. If being unable to come to terms with past experience is another form of remembering, it testifies to how the past "follows us at every instant ... pressing against the portals of consciousness that would fain leave it outside" (Bergson cited in Ingold and Hallam 2007: 11). None the less, this pressure was also politically generated: after the coup, the State punished many people involved in activist movements through the banning of their employment in government ministries; discrimination against them via expulsion from study and work; and the withholding of passports or, for political refugees overseas, stripping them of citizenship. Nine thousand members from Maden İş (Mineworkers Union) were blacklisted and unable to gain employment in that field again.

Revolutionary Istanbul and its events live on in ongoing legal trials too, petitioning or extracting memories from activists and overturning both the junta's efforts to mandate closure and different governments' wishes to enforce statutes of limitations. To give just one example, in July 1980 Kemal Türkler, founder of DİSK and chairman of the union Maden İş, was murdered in the street outside his house

---

12. Cf. Bachelard: "The old house, for those who know how to listen, is a sort of geometry of echoes. The voices of the past do not sound the same in the big room as in the little bed chamber, and calls on the stairs have yet another sound" (1994: 60).

in Istanbul. The public prosecutor indicted four Ülkücü militants for the killing, who were acquitted by one court, only to have that verdict quashed by another. Three decades later, in 2010, the first court ruled that the case had to be dropped because of lapse of time.[13] Outside the court, the then DİSK chairman vowed to continue the legal process, and in 2013 the accused murderer was once again on trial. In court Kemal Türkler's daughter remembered the event she witnessed: "I was 18 years old when my father was killed in front of me. I saw with my own eyes three people kill my father in interlocking fire. I saw the murderers, and I recognize them. Indeed, I even saw which gun jammed. For a full 31 years I have lived out this scene many times, I am still living it."[14]

In sum, rather than being "lost forever" with the radical transformation of Istanbul, the city of the fearless continues to live on and with its ex-activists. A city that has been experienced "is not an inert box. Inhabited space transcends geometric space" (Bachelard 1994: 47). Indeed, far from sparsity of recall, the power of places, songs, objects, legal techniques, and bodies to evoke memories and affect through their registering of inhabitation and trauma reveals a lingering *surfeit* of particulars concerning those years. The reason is clear: individuals' memories of the past and their perceptions of the present are intimately related. This relationship explains how the interview process itself facilitated awareness of things once unnoticed or unutterable: because the past is not set off from the present as completed event (fading with the passing of time), its prompted remembering (in interviews) allowed new impressions to come into being, according to activists' present perspectives.

2.3 POLITICIZING ACTIVISM

Alongside the dynamic constitution of ex-militants' memories of revolutionary Istanbul in the ongoing context of their engagements with the urban world, activists retrospectively identified at least two other efficacious *political* developments as significant in informing and transforming impressions and assessments of their past experiences and actions. One significant event concerns the decades-long legitimation crisis of Kemalism, the foundational ideology of the Turkish Republic. Activists' first disappointment with Kemalism can be traced back to the 1971 military intervention, which dashed the (in retrospect) naive 1960s hope of many leftists that a progressive faction of the military might join in a "national democratic revolution," in a replay of the 1920s. An equally important factor in activists' own critical realization of Kemalism's repressive character can be traced back to

13. "Kemal Türkler davası düştü," *Hürriyet*, 12 January 2010, accessed 20 December 2018. http://www.hurriyet.com.tr/gundem/kemal-turkler-davasi-dustu-16423709,

14. "Kemal Türkler cinayet davası yeniden başladı," *Posta*, 27 February 2013, accessed 12 January 2018, http://www.posta.com.tr/yazarlar/nedim-sener/kemal-turkler-cinayet-davasi-yeniden-basladi-164407, ().

the torture dealt out as a matter of course to hundreds of thousands of people arrested after 12 Eylül. The consequence has been a pressing need felt by activists in the 1990s and 2000s to critically reexamine Kemalism's pristine years in search of clues to the abuses of the junta. In the process, they have been forced to uproot commitments to previous ways of configuring ethico-political perceptions and urban militancy. As previously mentioned, in the 1970s, both leftists and rightists found powerful support for their respective programs of revolution and nationalism in founding tenets and practices of the state Kemalist project. Indeed, according to Serdar (Kurtuluş),

> In the 1970s no one knew that we were all Kemalist. I'll explain with an anecdote. In 1968 the US fleet came to Istanbul. The left declared that it would never come ashore; they got some boats and prevented some of the sailors from landing. It was said, "we threw them into the sea" [*denize döktük*]. The phrase was connected to the official history of the "Liberation War," which anyway is a hoax. The Greek army invaded Anatolia (encouraged by the British), and it was the British who threw some Greeks overboard when they were fleeing from the Turkish army in Smyrna. Now that it's time for the left to differentiate itself from Kemalism, it is hard for it to do.

Here Serdar identifies how leftists' response to an ostensibly novel event—the visiting of the US Sixth Fleet as part of NATO arrangements in 1968—was interpreted by protestors through an analogy generated from the official history of the founding of the Republic, a temporally backgrounded aspect of activists' education deployed to orientate action in a changed situation. Similarly, Ertuğrul (Biliş Trade Union) critically analyses how in the 1970s certain tenets of Kemalism—we might call them horizons of the past that entered into activists' perceptions both as history of one's body and as recollections, habits and moods—were taken up by many activists to constitute a political program:

> At the 1920 Baku congress, in an act of political desperation, the Comintern declared eastern people were oppressed peoples of the world—oppressed by imperialism. It was a declaration of the right of nations to self-determination. We [the left] began to confuse nationalism with anti-imperialism, which is an aspect of capitalism. Kemalism was nationalist, statist, and populist, never Marxist or working class. It was a national independence movement. If you are not essentially an anti-capitalist movement, then you gravitate to the nation-state, especially when it has the rhetoric of anti-imperialism. You support local elements [bourgeoisie, state, progressive peasants] against foreign imperialism. And there you have the lineage from *YÖN* [leftist Kemalist journal 1961–67] through *Devrim Dergisi* [*Revolution*, a journal in late 1960s] to the fascism of today's *Türk Solu* [Turkish Left, journal and name of an ultra-nationalist, socialist group active in the present]. This is a leftist sickness in Turkey.

Both Serdar's and Ertuğrul's comments express a fundamental modification in their present perception of their own faction's political practice in the 1970s. Many of the ex-activists I interviewed were now acutely critical of Kemalism, its ambiguous history, and its ongoing political influence. Similarly, nearly all had disengaged from contemporary attempts of leftist Kemalists (such as *Türk Solu*) to mobilize support around a laic-Islamist polarization in their attempt to reinvigorate a Kemalist program, including a continuation of its historic Turkification project directed at Kurds.

A third account of transformed awareness is given by leftist journalist and writer Hasan Cemal, who in 1969 started writing in the left-Kemalist journal *Devrim* (*Revolution*), mentioned by Ertuğrul above. In a foreword written in 2008 for ex-Akıncı militant Mehmet Metiner's book *Yemyeşil şeriat, bembeyaz demokrasi* (Green shariah, white democracy), Cemal reflects upon his own recently published book: "It is never easy to come to terms with the past nor to confront yourself. I, too, could no longer escape my past. Indeed, this is what I tried to explain in my book *Let no one be angry, I wrote myself*. In it I endeavored to explain how my political identity developed, where my political ideas derived from and which mistakes I made" (in Metiner 2008: 16). Cemal also references his journey away from the certainties of what he calls "Jacobin" Kemalism. In his book, Metiner, too, describes a parallel political evolution, from his militant years in the late 1970s as a member of an Islamist youth organization, to his rejection in the mid-1990s of the foundational tenets or paradigm of "Jacobin" Islam, including abandonment of his 1970s fantasy of forcing sharia law on the population through establishment of an Islamic state.

A second and equally powerful event identified by activists as crucial in radically modifying the meaning of their 1970s activism, in particular for revolutionaries and parties identified with the communism of the Soviet Union, was the collapse of that regime in 1989. For many activists (especially those affiliated to, or members of the TKP), the demise of Soviet communism as an alternative modernity caused a painful reorientation of perceptions of their acts and ideals pursued in that intense and formative period. T. S. Eliot's lines from the play *Murder in the Cathedral* capture something of TKP activists' discomfited position in the shift to a post–Cold War world: "The last temptation is the greatest treason: To do the right deed for the wrong reason." Akın's more prosaic words express the same sentiment: "We learned that for all those years we had pursued not an empty [*boş*] politics, but worse, a *wrong* one. This was a bigger trauma for us than 12 Eylül." Testifying to the intrinsically temporal and affective character of consciousness, and to how memory both retains and reinterprets past experience in each new moment of meaning, Filiz (TKP) describes a similarly shattering perceptual modification in 1988 and its reconstituting of other entities and relationships:

> My father was a Democrat Party parliamentarian. He was arrested in the coup [1960] and stayed in prison for two years; I remember visiting him in Kayseri when I was

six. I was always interested in politics, and realized later that I got my feelings of justice [*adalet duygusu*] from him. I never knew that my father paid for roads, etcetera from his own pocket. We owned land, were very rich, but I was uncomfortable with our wealth. I first began getting interested in politics through reading novels, and felt uncomfortable at injustice. Sometime in the 1970s my father gave me a Solzhenitsyn novel, but I refused to read "bourgeois" lies/literature. When I went to Moscow for three months in 1988, I was criticizing the *perestroika* politics, and a party historian gave me the same novel. "This is true," he said, and I began to cry. I was changed.

Softly, almost in passing, she added, "What a pity I was never able to talk about this with my father before he died."

Both accounts reveal the weighty loss of an esteemed political ethic, so that activists' past cause of revolution is felt to have lost its footing in any legitimate continuing struggle. Militants' feelings of shock and sadness were connected to the great sacrifices they had made—in some cases involving a rift with family—for principles that they no longer perceived to be true.

Importantly, it was not just TKP members and sympathizers who in interviews reflected on acts and practices performed for reasons now perceived as wrong. Activists from virtually all factions expressed an intense ambivalence about those years of sound and fury. Thus Nuriye (THKP-C) (Turkish People's Liberation Party-Front) noted that, "We [the left] also did wrong things that we haven't come to terms with. How could we have entered into the killing of a seventeen-year-old ülkücü so easily?" Ömer (MHP) felt that "there was no time to think, we were drowning in events/action. There was no balance. Our movement started in love and ended in a lake of blood." Mehmet Metiner (see above) remembered slapping someone for eating during Ramazan, and confessed that then "everyone sought to gain control before someone else, with the aim of restricting the world of those others. Perhaps the government would change but the logic of authority and nature of it would have been exactly the same. The hand that held the stick would have been different but the stick would still have worked" (2008: 83). Ümit (Dev-Sol) said something similar, that in those years "normal things were abnormal; abnormal things became normal. We saw ourselves as heroes [*kahramanlar*]. The junta killed hundreds of people, but if we came to power, we would have killed thousands." And Erdoğan (Kurtuluş) noted pensively that "if we hadn't been so ambitious or impatient, and just tried to provide services to the poor, we would have been more successful. And if we weren't so fragmented among ourselves. . . ." Finally, Özlem (THKP-C) diagnosed the reason for the unhappy and asymmetrical relationship between political factions and local people in the shantytowns (see chapter 4): "We wanted to replace the existing order. But gecekondu people wanted to create an order. They didn't care that someone lived in a *köşk* (mansion), like we cared; they wanted food, work, and a house. We were valuable to them because we gave: importantly, we looked like we were strong and capable. But they were also scared of us: I raised a finger to a man who hit his wife, and we put them in danger as the fighting spread."

2.4 COMMEMORATING ACTIVISM

Most significantly, ex-militants' chastened perspective on the spatial politics of the period before the military coup reveals a profound ambiguity over whether, or how, to *commemorate* their project of revolution, whose rationale or romance has been modified in the light of disillusionment with Kemalism, socialism, and anti-communism.[15] For many activists there has been no easy acceptance of vindication or vice, victimhood or virtue that might *modulate* or *temper* the profusion of affective memories immanent in bodies, places, objects, and sounds; no shared collective memory that might authorize an agreed-upon narrative of the past. Even the military do not celebrate 12 Eylül. Casey argues that commemoration inheres in the action of "carrying the past forward through the present so as to perdure in the future" (1987: 256). He goes on to say that the past can only be honored and preserved in this way "if it has attained a certain consistent self-sameness in the wake of the *perishing* of the particulars by which it had once presented itself" (256, my emphasis). Which particulars must perish so as to generate the "selfsameness" of the past? Whose past is to be memorialized in its reenactment? If many ex-activists in the forty or more years since those years have elected not to commemorate their acts despite an abundance of particular memories of the city, could not this, too, constitute an honoring of the past? Rather than signifying something negative—say the absence of an ethically efficacious common narrative regarding their past deeds—non-commemoration may express humility on the part of ex-militants, generated by an awareness of the moral ambiguity of their actions. With memorialization is born the first lie.

One consequence, however, as we have noted already, is the difficulty activists have had in translating the dramatic sense and context of their memories of urban politics in Istanbul to non-activist others, even to their own children. Further, alongside this reluctance of many ex-revolutionaries to mythologize or lionize the spatial activism of their generation, we must revisit military actors' strategies to manufacture a public condemnation of it, so as to better comprehend how up until recently each has combined to make commemoration of those years so problematic. Noting

15. One exception to ex-activists' general unwillingness to commemorate their past is the celebration of 1 Mayıs (Labor Day) in Taksim Square, which in 2010, 2011, and 2012 attracted huge crowds. Since 2010 a wreath-laying ceremony mourning the 1977 massacre has become an integral part of Labor Day demonstrations. Despite this common front there has been no definitive agreement concerning the identity of the perpetrators of the 1977 killings, and differences between leftist factions concerning events on that day still linger amongst ex-militants.

that forgetting is not a "unitary phenomenon," Paul Connerton (2008) identifies a number of its forms. As we have already seen in their expunging of place names, the junta has pursued his first type, "repressive erasure." It was exercised most systematically in their *prohibition* of the publishing of activists' written or spoken defense or of their petitions in the huge number of court cases opened up by army prosecutors in military courts in the immediate years after the coup. In reporting the list of charges against activists—typically armed robbery, murder, bombing of property, arson, escaping from prison, membership in an illegal organization, communist propaganda, separatist activities and so on—newspapers were forbidden to print that confessions were extracted under torture, or that defendants were not allowed to read to the courts prepared statements.[16] The result was that throughout those years there was no legitimate or sanctioned way for militants to publicly testify to or justify their intentions and experiences. Thus, Filiz felt that "Turkey lived through fascism in the '80s, though even now it is not said very openly. It was hard to know what was happening after the coup: You heard that so and so was arrested, that *x* was killed, or *y* tortured, that this house had been searched. In this way people lived through a massive trauma."

Connerton's second and third types, "prescriptive forgetting" and "forgetting that is constitutive of a new identity," do not apply, as they involve a decision to consciously forget—perhaps in an amnesty (literally, to not remember)—that which once was known, not to assign to oblivion past actions that have never been remembered. His fourth, fifth, and sixth types are not relevant here. However, his last form, which he calls "forgetting as humiliated silence," is more suggestive. This is a forgetting that is not solely "a matter of overt activity on the part of a state apparatus" (2008: 67) but also expresses civil society's exhaustion and disillusion with a project, as well as its experiences of shame and fear. In particular, the trauma of mass torture of activists in prison, their returning home injured and broken with no prospect of redress or rehabilitation, and "legal" press censorship in the 1980s and '90s (engineered through the 1982 constitution) all combined to produce decades of censorship and self-censorship, of buried grief and strictly controlled memories. Jenny White found that still in the late 1990s there was a "lingering pain among a lost generation of men and women who had fought as students in the 1970s for something they had believed in, had lost friends to killings and torture, and had themselves suffered in jail or gone into hiding" (2002: 41). As the

16. One typical example, from *Tercüman* newspaper (19 November 1980), reported on one of the mass trials of the "illegal" (*yasadışı*) organization Dev-Yol. The headline read, "Death penalty requested for 30 Dev-Yol members." The military prosecutor charged them with being members of an illegal organization "whose aim is to change constitutional law and institutions, and the constitutional order by armed force and to bring in a society founded on the dictatorship of a single class."

poet Abbas Beydoun notes for Lebanon after the civil war, "the right to forget [became] obligatory forgetting" (in De Cauter 2011: 424).

During those decades, activists' adoption of a fugitive silence as a means of "un-remembering" both their own worst actions and the worst actions done to them must have been an essential act of survival. But the slow demilitarization of Turkey amid the struggle to create a post-coup Constitution in the first decade of the new century—and as chapter 8 explores, this counts as a third political development allowing occluded aspects of activism and Istanbul to be perceived—has released a massive reservoir of activists' memories of their experiences, especially concerning 12 Eylül and the years of martial law.[17] Published memoirs of political activities and experiences in the years before the coup have been less common but in *Havariler* (Disciples), Zileli (2002) recounts his years as a founding member of the Aydınlık movement.

Along with this revived facility in recalling perceptions of the city, leftist ex-activists have initiated a new memory-work project, titled *12 Eylül Utanç Müzesi* (*12 Eylül Museum of Shame*). The traveling museum gives visitors permission to remember events and acts that had been long muted in daily interaction. Its website explains that it is "the first serious attempt to create a memorialization site to reveal the brutality of the 1980 military coup while struggling to foster the democratization process in Turkey. Those who initiated the project are victims of the indiscriminate violence of the Turkish Armed Forces, mainly in the 1980s. Therefore, struggling against unjust state practices allowed the organizers to experience a degree of healing."[18]

Here we encounter two further reasons for activists' publicizing of their memories of the city: the museum enables a counter-recollection for post-coup generations whose memories have already been induced by the junta's discourse, while also enacting a therapeutic remembering of those years for its creators (and by extension for other ex-militants as well). In collecting and exhibiting various material objects—Deniz Gezmiş's coat, Mazlum Doğan's shirt, the mimeograph machine owned by İbrahim Kaypakkaya, Mahir Çayan's vest—the traveling museum intuits the potent influence these possess empowered by the lived bodies that used them. All four were militants of leftist groups in Turkey killed or executed by the state in the early 1970s.[19] Their names are important, as heard in their

17. For example, see Alişanoğlu's (2005) *Netekim 12 Eylül 'de geldiler: Bir idamlığın trajiko-mik anıları*; Mavioğlu's (2008) *Bizim çocuklar yapamadı: Bir 12 Eylül hesaplaşması*; Öztunç's (2008) *Ülkücüler 12 Eylül'ü anlatıyor*; Küçükkaya's (2011) *Darbe şakacıları sevmez: Bir ailenin 12 Eylül günlüğü*; Görsev's (2011) *3 yılda 6 tutukevinde: 12 Eylül anıları*; Asan's (2010) *12 Eylül sabahı*; and Saymaz's (2012) *Oğlumu öldürdünüz arz ederim: 12 Eylül'ün beş öyküsü*).

18. See the website, http://www.memorializeturkey.com/en/memorial/309/.

19. Interestingly, in its focusing on the gross human-rights abuses of the Turkish government and military against the leftist movement of the 1970s, '80s and '90s, the museum of shame "forgets" the intense factionalism in those years that perturbed so many activists in the interviews.

recital in the battle slogans of THKP-C, Dev-Yol and Dev-Sol up until the coup: "Mahir, Hüseyin, Ulaş: *Kurtuluş'a kadar savaş*" (Mahir, Hüseyin, Ulaş: War until liberation). Similarly, for revolutionaries who experienced the military courts, the exhibited trial proceedings are not just a piece of paper: the museum's collecting of legal documents and files of prisoners killed or executed under the junta preserves intensely expressive memories, securing the past in the present. The power of these artifacts to incite a visceral affective state in visitors—vivifying body memories—is revealed in Cafer Solgun's account of his painful visit to the museum:

> A few days ago I went to the 12 *September Museum of Shame* exhibition. It was my friends, the Revolutionary '78ers, who had curated it. I should confess I had manufactured many excuses, not to go to the museum, but to not go. It took time for me to admit it to myself, but if I went, I would grieve, I would remember, I would weep.... But if I didn't go, it would have been as if I had committed an offence against my friends whose photos, clothes, personal belongings, and last letters were exhibited there. I knew myself: I went. I knew that I would cry, but I went. I wouldn't be able to say anything to those who asked about my feelings and thoughts, but I went. I wouldn't be able to write a single word in the visitor's book because my hands would be trembling, but I went. I went and as soon as I entered the door I found myself in a time tunnel.
>
> Our friends "who had been lost" ... Our friends who had been killed by torture ... Our friends who had been killed by execution ... Our friends who had lost their lives in hunger strikes, in death fasts ... Our friends who had been killed in "clashes" ... For us that was 12 Eylül; torture, murder, fascism.[20]

One final example, that of the opening, almost in the same year, of another, very different museum, demonstrates the alteration that urban activism makes in perceiving, remembering, and commemorating Istanbul. As we have seen, the *Museum of Shame* assembles things that possess intense affect for leftist activists, bestirring dormant moods and reawakening ex-militants' sense of places' presence. Violence is remembered by its configuring of places. Much more famous is Nobel Prize–winning author Orhan Pamuk's *The Museum of Innocence* (*Masumiyet müzesi*), displaying a contrasting set of objects from the very same years (1974–85), artifacts and ephemera commemorating the relationship of two lovers with a now no-longer-existing Istanbul from his novel of the same name. It is a museum of a fictional story. Both museums reflect a labor of love in attending to and conserving things and places that held and afflicted the beloved. Yet it is the peculiarity of each set of objects—the gallows that executed Deniz Gezmiş; the lipstick-stained butts of cigarettes smoked by Füsun (the narrator's love)—that radiate different memories and emotions, constituting and mourning, in the ensemble assembled in the *Museum of Shame*, a socialist perspective of the city and its past.

20. C. Solgun, "12 Eylül utanç müzesi," *Taraf*, 23 September 2013.

CONCLUSION

In sum, if both the interviews with ex-militants' and the *12 Eylül Museum of Shame* reveal that revolutionary Istanbul lives on only in memory, this does not mean that its existence is any less real. As we have shown, memories exist not just in the mind but also—more so—in the world, in objects and things, in sounds and songs, in the city and in its (absent) places, in legal events, and in the temporal habituation to them of activists' lived bodies. All of these store and stir militants' memories of the past even as the value and meaning of remembered practices and experiences wax and wane with new acts of political participation and judgment. Memories can be stabilized but are never completed.

These particular acquired stances of political action, place perception, sentiment, and ethics are urban and activist. In the pedagogic process, the inevitable social friction that activism incites reveals the conflicted interaction that characterizes the sensing and appropriating of affordances of place, both between living beings (including animals and humans) and between the living and the dead in the fraught passage of furnished environments from one generation, or from one group, to another. Activism as a pedagogy and process of skilled practice trains not only practitioners' awareness of the urban environment but also their *ethical* capacities, displacing and redirecting existing modes of socialized engagement with the surrounding world and implicating them in particular tasks concerning ways of acting toward and talking about the city and its inhabitants. Here, at the close, is a more adequate description of how political-economic and phenomenological perspectives inform each other: for the rest of their lives, activists' memory of this key "horizon of the past" (Husserl in Moran 2000: 162) ensures its reawakening or revivification to consciousness in any new auspicious event or appalling episode in Turkish politics, of which, since 1980, there have been many. For ex-militant Ümit, to give just one example, participation in the unexpected explosion of urban activism in Istanbul in 2013, over the government's proposed privatization and redevelopment of Taksim's Gezi Park, immediately recalled—and problematized—one certain taken-for-granted aspect of the 1970s. For him, most striking about the Gezi protest were the peaceful relations between the groups, individuals, and civil society organizations that participated in and supported the protest—the rainbow symbol of Istanbul's emerging LBTG groups, waved alongside the flags of Turkey and those of socialist factions, of football teams, and Kurds. "We weren't like that," he commented ruefully. In his remembering, encompassing less resemblances and more contrasts between urban movements and their repertoires of spatial tactics thirty years distant from each other, memories of the past flash up against the unfolding present, instigating a new fragile knowledge of a different history of Istanbul's inhabitants' reckoning with the city.[21]

---

21. The verb *flash up* references Walter Benjamin's Thesis VI: "To articulate the past historically does not mean to recognize it 'the way it really was.' It means to seize hold of a memory as it flashes in a moment of danger" (1940).

In the next chapter we turn to the past again, but on a different scale. In it I compose a selective and specific history of the development of Istanbul from the founding of the Turkish Republic in 1923 up until the mid-1970s, to give readers some idea of the origins and development of the key features of the city in 1975 that multitudes of political activists in the years before and after the coup sought to control or revolutionize. What were the primary sociopolitical and economic processes that reassembled the city up until 1974? In brief, in unintended preparation for the emergence of the activists of the 1970s and for the city of the fearless, who set the stage, how did they do it, and what was it like?

3

De-Ottomanization, Modernism, Migration

A Selective History of Istanbul, 1923–1974

As one of the great cities of the planet, Istanbul has properly been the subject of a vast body of writing. A proportion of it sits on shelves in the Greater Istanbul Municipality bookshop beside the funicular railway exit in Galata, groaning under the weight of local histories of each of the city's older neighborhoods, supplemented by exegeses of their representations in a thousand and one novels, songs, films, and poems. More recently established suburbs are less well celebrated. Almost every issue of any Middle East journal reviews new material on Istanbul's social history, provisioning, political institutions, labor relations, socio-spatial differentiation, sexual practices, religious governance, architecture, consumption habits, sartorial dress, and aesthetic traditions, from any of its many ages. Then there are the centuries of writings from its own inhabitants and of travelers from eastern and western origins, captivated or overwhelmed by its size and complexity.

Sedimented with the detritus of two empires and dense with Muslim and non-Muslim places, four hundred fifty years of Ottoman rule resulted in a peninsula dotted with buildings, fountains, mosques, libraries, and so on, inscribing in place the benevolence and power of the dynasty.

To spite this endless archive, in this third chapter I want to compose from a range of sources a selective history of the "violence of architecture" in Istanbul from the founding of the Turkish Republic in 1923 up until the mid-1970s.[1] In so doing, I

---

1. If 1923 is a key date, the 1913 military coup by the Committee of Union and Progress (CUP, or the Young Turks), of whom Mustafa Kemal had been a prominent but not overly influential member, signaled the practical end of the Ottoman Empire and its ruling dynasty, and the beginning of a new historical era. Üngör (2011), for example, traces out the continuity in CUP—Kemalist resettlement and population policies in Eastern Anatolia, from 1913 to 1950.

hope to give the reader some idea of the origins and frictional development of the city's key morphology and environments that a multitude of political activists in the late 1970s sought to control or revolutionize. What was Istanbul, theater and crucible of political conflict, like in 1974, and how did it get to be like that? Radically remade through neoliberal economic policies in the decades after the 1980 coup, Istanbul is a city whose built environment in the nineteenth century alone had already been reassembled by world-scale processes, both by reforms in institutional practices of government and by escalating flows of European capital that greatly extended the city's urban footprint in the late-Ottoman years. After the establishment of the Republic, four processes transformed Istanbul again: first, a nationalist project aimed at the expulsion of its non-Muslim population (Aktar 2000); second, modernist urban planning initiatives, new architecture, and Marshall-plan money; third, on-again, off-again state policies of national developmentalism that characterized not just the first fifty years of the Republic (1929–1979) but a global system of partially self-regulating and only "banally" different nation-states (Keyder 1987); and fourth, mass migration that swelled its population, size, workforce, and wealth.

For simplicity's sake, I have divided this history into six sections. First, 3.1 sketches out a brief prehistory of urban developments in Istanbul in the late-Ottoman period, to give readers some idea of the emergence of its south-north segmentation. Then, sections 3.2, 3.3, and 3.4 on Kemalism, Turkism, and Modernism respectively describe and analyze the Turkish Republic's unrelenting de-Ottomanization of the city, which extends from the single-party period into the mid-1960s. By *de-Otto-manization* I mean not only the reconstruction and regularization of Istanbul through modernist planning initiatives in the 1930s and 1950s, but also the equally important Turkification policies that targeted its non-Muslim residents for insignificance and impoverishment. The last two sections, 3.5 and 3.6, examine the tremendous expansion of the city since the 1950s through rural-urban migration. In its discussion of the spread of the *gecekondu*, 3.6 briefly explores two theoretical approaches, modernization and dependency perspectives, which were influential in the mid-1970s in explaining Turkey's situation. For activists from different factions, variations of these accounts partly illuminated the explosive growth and uneven development of Istanbul, mediating how they perceived the emerging urban landscape, while simultaneously informing their spatial politics in it. As we have already noted, theoretical perspectives contributed to the generation of activists' experiences of dwelling in and political uses of the city. For that reason, it was no coincidence that most factions sought to produce their own journal or newspaper, as well as to restrict their cadres' reading of the publications of rival groups (see chapter 6).

3.1 LATE-OTTOMAN ISTANBUL

In 1923 Istanbul was a city bequeathed a history and symbolism that did not easily harmonize with the new political reality emerging in Ankara. An imperial and cosmopolitan port city and a center of commerce, consumption, and production, Istanbul's built environment reflected both nineteenth-century Ottoman modernization and European economic influence. Unlike Rabat in Morocco or Algiers in Algeria, Istanbul was not a colonial city structured by a racial segregation between indigenous and European "quarters," or characterized by severe overcrowding and underdevelopment in the "native" zone (see Rabinow 1989, Abu-Lughod 1981). Istanbul's Jewish and Christian neighborhoods were not segregated nor even exclusively non-Muslim, and its large Christian and Jewish communities were neither settler colonialists nor a comprador bourgeoisie acting for foreign powers.

According to Şevket Pamuk, two significant features distinguished the late-Ottoman empire from other comparable "'underdeveloped" countries. First, the empire was never, officially or unofficially, colonized by any European power, meaning the Ottoman state did not lose its political sovereignty. Secondly, adapting to its advantage certain technologies of governance trialed in Europe or in European colonies, the Ottoman central state in the nineteenth century was able to strengthen its position against rival social groups and local elements in its own domain (i.e., vis-à-vis movements of regional autonomy, "feudal" landowners, local leaders, tribal confederations, and rich merchants). In the wake of territorial losses in the Balkans (and the proclamation of an Independent Greece in 1830), Ottoman reformers placed a new importance on consolidating control over the eastern peripheries of the empire, including extending direct rule over the Kurdish and Arab provinces (see Houston 2008). Indeed, for Deringil, the late-Ottoman state "came to perceive its periphery as a colonial setting" (Deringil 2003: 311, 312). Pamuk concludes that in the century before the First World War the globalization of the Ottoman economy progressed "not through a working coalition between commercial capital, large landowners and foreign capital but in the struggle, bargaining and agreements between European states and capitalists, and the central Ottoman state" (2014: 159).

In short, in the "long" nineteenth century, modernization of the state, and the growing participation of the Ottoman Empire in a newly emerging global economy transformed its capital Istanbul. Deringil notes how the paradigmatic institutions of the modern state—mass schooling, a postal service, railways, lighthouses, clock towers, lifeboats, museums, censuses and birth certificates, passports and parliaments—were all aspects of, or followed after, the Tanzimat reforms of 1839 (Deringil 1998: 9). With the establishment of other changes—the standardization of weights and measures; the establishment of population registers and cadastral surveys carried out in the form of the first modern Ottoman census in 1831 and in the establishment of a Cadastral Department in 1858; new laws facilitating the private ownership of land and property; the standardization of language, first attempted in the 1880s with the designation of Turkish as the sole language of

Ottoman administration; and the standardization of legal codes, begun with the rationalization of *sharia* law in 1869 throughout the Ottoman domains—by the beginning of the twentieth century, Istanbul had become a new city. Indeed, Çelik (1986: xv) notes that the nineteenth century changes in Istanbul's physical form "planted seeds for an evolution that continues to the present day." For both Çelik and Tekeli (2009), Ottoman authorities' transformation of Istanbul's urban fabric, including the establishing of the city's first municipal council in 1855, involved the appropriation and application of three disciplines, themselves newly constituted in Europe. These were legislation regarding city planning issues; new urban design principles; and new architectural building types embedded in the urban environment.

Together these developments made Istanbul a "boomtown."[2] It was a city that in the second half of the nineteenth century expanded rapidly in both area and population, particularly through the construction of new suburbs on the ridges and slopes north of the Golden Horn beyond the bounds of Pera, as well as along the Bosporus shoreline. Spreading from Tünel to Şişli and out to Maçka, they became home to both the bureaucrats of a growing modernizing Ottoman state and a wealthy trading-commercial-merchant class whose businesses articulated with an expanding world economy, together at times making up one-quarter of the city.[3] In the same decades, less prestigious suburbs such as Tarlabaşı, Dolapdere, and Kasımpaşı were developed on the non-seafront side of the ridge. By the mid-nineteenth century, the migration of the sultanate out of the peninsula and to the north had taken place as well, in the building of the seafront palaces along the Bosporus shoreline by Armenian court architects Garabet and Sarkis Balyan, including both Beylerbeyi and Dolmabahçe, with its iconic public clock tower.[4] In the same years, three major connecting roads were built that still funnel traffic through the city: the expansion of the Divanyolu in the historic peninsula, the Karaköy-Ortaköy road that goes alongside the Bosporus, and the Taksim-Şişli thoroughfare that heads north along the Bosporus ridge (Çelik 1986: 159).

For Esen, the unique "spatial filter" that facilitated the break from what became the "southern" city was the *apartment*:

> The thing we call the suffocating customs of the neighborhood which we often define in the religious/cultural field, is nothing but a series of rites and mores forcing the redistribution of social resources: therefore, the neighborhood can also be read as a

2. See Orhan Esen, "Becoming Istanbul," accessed 6 February 2016, https://www.academia.edu/6746986/Kuzey_Istanbulluluk-eng_Becoming_Istanbul.

3. Esen, "Becoming Istanbul."

4. Esen notes that until then, most clocks were in mosques, to guide worshippers in the five daily prayers.

physical/spatial obstacle in front of the emergence of capital accumulation and a modern bourgeois class. Keeping at arm's length from the neighborhood is thus a compulsory step for social strata who want to take part in the capital accumulation cycle in the modern sense. A high-density settlement beyond the Golden Horn and at the top of the ridge, separate from the others also witnesses the birth of a class that has increasingly minimized its social relationships with the old city.[5]

Unlike Tekeli, however, who asserts that this spatial and class differentiation should also be described as a distinction between modern and traditional "culture-camps," Esen notes how the poorer southern neighborhoods were modernized in the same years, most notably by urban planning regulations enforced after regular fires that burned through local districts (see also Çelik 1986: 53–55, on the 1856 Aksaray fire and the redesign of the suburb). Nevertheless, by 1923 a "dual" city was fixed in place, its socioeconomic differentiations territorialized on a spatial basis. Istanbul's northern suburbs became the abode of the new Republican elites, who construed the areas within the old city walls as the habitat of unenlightened conservatives.

3.2 KEMALISM AND THE DE-OTTOMANIZATION OF ISTANBUL

Almost immediately after the instituting of the Turkish Republic in 1923, the Republicans expelled the last Ottoman *padişah* [Sultan] from the city of Istanbul, sending him and his family into exile. Ownership of family palaces was transferred to the Turkish Republic. The new national assembly gathered in Ankara, dominated by the will of Mustafa Kemal and his followers. The creation of new inhabitants for a new society, to be achieved through the establishment of a number of new social institutions, as well as through the assembling or rearranging of urban environments, engaged the political imagination of the Kemalists. A huge literature has zeroed in on these formative years in an attempt to describe and diagnose the young Republic's political program. Orthodox political science accounts have often described its social trajectory as "secularization," "modernization," or "Westernization" (Berkes 1964), anodyne words that do scant justice to its radical social engineering and systematically violent actions within its new boundaries.[6] Historical reassessment has coined different terms to characterize its activities and ideology: Touraj and Zürcher (2004) describe the social project of the Turkish regime as "authoritarian modernization"; Çağlar Keyder (1987) draws attention to similarities between Turkish Kemalism and Italian fascism; Ayhan Aktar (2000) (and others) identify its Turkification politics; while Sayyid

---

5. Esen, "Becoming Istanbul."
6. See Houston (2015c) for further discussion.

(1997) argues that the work of Mustafa Kemal in Turkey and the discourse of Kemalism should be understood as generative of a new political paradigm for the wider Muslim world.[7]

What did the policies of the single-party period encompass? Parla and Davison (2004) have identified how the Kemalist project of laicism involved neither a pact of mutual noninterference between Islamic organizations and the state, nor the elimination of Islam from a reconstructed public sphere. Rather, it comprised the incorporation within, and subservience of, a nationalized Islam to the state institution, informed by a political theology known as the Turkish-Islamic synthesis (in Turkish, *dini-Türkçülük*).[8] Facilitated by the institution of the Directorate of Religious Affairs in 1924, the Kemalist construction of a vernacular or idiomatic national religion, grounded upon support for selective Sunni teachings, created a Sunni-Turkish Islam that supported state policy and sought to nationalize religious sentiments. In the process the state disregarded the inner-plurality of Islam, marginalizing the religious practices of Alevism adhered to by a substantial proportion of the Turkish and Kurdish population. Yet at the same time Alevism, too, was "nationalized": Dressler (2013) identifies how early Republican intellectuals such as Fuat Köprülü incorporated it into the imagined Turkish nation by tracing its genealogy back to an indigenous Turkish shamanism, thus representing Alevism as carrier of an original pre-Islamic (and pre-Arab) Turkish culture. As we will see in chapter 4, that particular reading was made to have dire consequences for some Alevi in the late 1970s.

In the introduction to the volume on *Kemalism* in the *Political Thought in Modern Turkey* series, Ahmet İnsel begins his essay by stating, "Milliyetçilik ve medeniyetçilik, Kemalizmin iki aslı oğesidir" (Nationalism and civilizationalism are the two foundational elements of Kemalism) (2001: 17). What might be meant by

---

7. Further complicating claims regarding Turkey's "Westernization" was the Kemalist state's active economic and cultural relations with the Soviet Communist Party in the Republic's first fifteen years. This relationship was not surprising given the proximity of the Soviet Union and the power of its discourse regarding the revolutionary modernity at work there, rhetoric similarly heard in the future-oriented speech of the Kemalists in Turkey, and expressed most lucidly in the CHP's "arrow" of "*transformationism.*" Cultural exchange reached a high point in the 1930s, when Soviet filmmakers made *Ankara—The Heart of Turkey*, and Russian composer Dmitri Shostakovich performed in Ankara, Izmir, and Istanbul (Clark 2013).

8. The "Turk-Islam" synthesis is often argued to characterize the policies of the junta in the period after 12 Eylül, represented by the military's introduction of compulsory religious lessons in schools, and its mosque-building program, even in Alevi villages. But the 1924 institution of the Ministry of Religious Affairs (Diyanet), whose brief included the production and management of Islam, properly contextualizes these initiatives. Copeaux (1996) analyzes the longevity of the key word *hizmet* (service) in the Turk-Islam synthesis that references the Turkish nation's "outstanding" and "impartial" service to Islam, noting its continuous presence in school textbooks on Islam from the early 1930s until the present.

"civilizationalism," given that it is not one of Kemalism's six arrows? Civilizational-ism should be understood as a principle and process that binds them all together. It entails presumption of the universal status of contemporary European civilization combined with a desire to selectively adopt certain of its forms—republicanism, laicism, technology, and aesthetic modernism (most particularly in music, archi-tecture, literature, and the plastic arts). Equally important, the carrying out of a civilizational transformation simultaneously entailed the abolition of Ottoman institutions and the suppression of Islamic aesthetic traditions such as *tekke* (or "sufi") music.

Civilizationalism is not a synonym of Westernization. In it instead the "West," the "republic," the "nation," "revolution," and even "Islam" are better understood in Castoriadis's terms as *imaginary significations*—that is, new forms, ideas, and images through which Kemalist society instituted itself. "Every society defines and develops an image of the natural world, of the universe in which it lives ... in which a place has to be made not only for the natural objects and beings important for the life of the collectivity, but also for the collectivity itself, establishing finally, a certain world-order" (Castoriadis 1987: 149). Kemalist society's institution of a certain world-order through its creation of core imaginary significations was made neither in isolation from other societies nor in sole reference to any single one of them. Rather as we have already seen above, it was made in *knowing relation* to a number of them, via appropriation, mimicry, antagonism, improvisation, transformation and development, including its inheriting of a long history of Ottoman reflection on the adequacy of its existing social institutions. In the pro-cess, Kemalism created its own social-historical forms, investing selective signifi-cations and figures derived from both Ottoman society and European historical experience (including that of the Bolsheviks) with new meanings. This was not simple emulation, as is implied in the term *Westernization*, but self-institution through representation, interpretation, translation and evaluation (of a context, history or tradition). In Castoriadis's words, "the old [foreign] enters the new with the signification given to it by the new and could not enter it otherwise" (1997: 14).

Yet the Kemalist self-institution, as İnsel notes above, was founded on more than its constructed synonymy between civilization and European modernity, accompanied by a related orientalist discourse on Islam. Privileging its transform-ative "civilizing" of Ottoman Muslim society overlooks its equally significant nationalizing project, characterized not only by corporatist-style economic devel-opment policies (or nationalist developmentalism) from the early 1930s on but also by its positing and favoring of a master ethnic identity in the midst of a mul-ticultural population. In other words, Kemalism in the single-party period was characterized by a dual politics. First, it involved an *excluding modernism* partly operating as a form of status distinction distinguishing an enlightened class from suddenly backward Muslims. And second, it encompassed a *radical Turkism* directed against both non-Muslims (in particular against Greeks, Armenians, and Jews) and non-Turks (in particular against Kurds). Initiated by its cultural revolution, Kemalism's language purification campaign conjoined both these political stances, combating the claim to sovereignty exerted by Arabic and Persian "loan-words," heard as threatening the integrity of the nation's own worldview, and substituting them with newly minted Turkish replacements (Lewis 1999). The language mobilization campaign prohibited the speaking and writing of Kurdish, suddenly creating new linguistic minorities in Turkey and excluding them from monolingual state institutions within the national territory. Cultural revolution also involved the creation of a new national arts repertoire, constructed sometimes through the disaggregation and nationalizing of what were previously *trans-regional* cultural-artistic traditions and skills that overlapped ethnic and religious communities (Hough 2010).

Thus, one more concrete description of the Kemalist revolution is Sibel Bozdoğan's (1994) definition of it as a project of de-Ottomanization.[9] Bozdoğan discerns its focus on the transforming of the visual appearance of the urban landscape and its inhabitants as a key mode of social change. Typically, the same conviction that form could transform content was applied in the Soviet Union. For Kolluoğlu-Kırlı (2002), de-Ottomanization involved the eradication of Ottoman spaces, as pursued, for example, in the rebuilding of the fire zones in Izmir and Salonika by the Turkish and Greek nation-states respectively, which obliterated all traces of their respective non-Turkish and non-Hellenistic habitational history.

In Istanbul, where did de-Ottomanization and *Turkist civilizationalism* converge? One point was in the practice of urban planning and the construction of a number of new buildings and public parks/places in modernist style in which Islamic comportment was censured. Another was in the closing down of significant high-culture Islamic religious institutions and sites, for example, the city's four Mevlevi lodges in Galata, Üsküdar, Yenikapı, and Bahariye. Yet much more significant than both of these was the targeting for forced migration of the non-Muslim Ottoman populations living in Istanbul, who were already marked as alien in newly emergent nationalist space by the mutual deportation of orthodox Greeks from Turkey and Muslim citizens from Greece in 1923. Its result was both displaced people and de-peopled places. Although both of these practices of de-Ottomanization—Turkism and modernism—were mutually reinforcing in their transformation of Istanbul up until the 1960s, it is instructive to look at each in turn.

9. Somewhat paradoxically, the growing literature on "Ottoman" cities also notes their heterogeneity (see Eldem et al. 1999). This is in keeping with a more general trend among urban historians to move away from typological models of the "Ottoman" or "Islamic" city to focus on more nuanced considerations of relevant *regional* histories.

3.3 TURKISM

The emergence of nationalism in Ottoman lands in the nineteenth and early twentieth centuries constituted a rival theory of political and state sovereignty, attacking symbols of dynastic authority yet adapting their justifications and rituals of legitimacy for nationalist rule. New states and their leading cadres constituted their authority through a discourse organized around the key terms of ethnicity, race, and nation on the one hand, and independence and development on the other. Their populations, however, were not ethnically homogenous, and their urban centers were richly cosmopolitan. To give just one example, Mignon (2014) traces out the role of non-Muslims in the development of Turkish-language literature in the late nineteenth century, noting that the first *Turkish* novel was written in Istanbul in the Armenian alphabet in the 1870s.

Despite that reality, each post-Ottoman ethnic-state *constituted* as a problem the fact that in its newly inscribed territories there dwelt people who practiced a variety of religious creeds and who spoke different languages from the national majority, necessitating a political decision regarding their "management." Grounding their political power in the fabrication of a new ethnic subject, the Committee of Union and Progress Government (1912–1918), in the context of war and European encroachment, was less concerned with democracy than with improving the efficacy of state administration. Dündar (2001) describes how the Unionists commissioned anthropological and demographic research into Kurds, Armenians, Alevi (Kurdish and Turkish), Greek, and Turkmen communities in both the western (Aegean) and eastern (Kurdistan) extremities of Ottoman territory, designed to facilitate their planned resettlement as part of each region's Turkification. These were provinces that the Young Turks' own census research had shown to be ethnically and religiously highly heterogeneous (Dündar 2014). Similarly, analysis of Kemalist anthropology written in the 1930s and 1940s reveals its commitment to demonstrating the Turkish origins of Muslim minorities in Anatolia, most ardently of the Kurds. This search explains why in those years physical anthropology became its dominant theoretical mode, involving among other things extensive craniometrical surveys that "proved" a common (Turkish) ancestor of Turks and Kurds in Anatolia (Toprak 2012).

For those unable (or unwilling) to become Turkish, in particular for non-Muslims and Kurds, the consequences of Turkism were catastrophic. "In 1913, one out of five persons in the geographical area that is now Turkey was a Christian; by the end of 1923, the proportion had declined to one in forty" (Keyder 2003: 43). Calculating from the Ottoman census of 1906, in real numbers this equates to the loss of approximately 2,600,025 people in a decade, or a decrease in the Christian population from 3,000,000 to 375,000. Strikingly, a similarly radical demographic change occurred in reverse in the Balkans in the last years of the nineteenth century and again with the Balkan war of 1912, with the ethnic cleansing and flight of hundreds of thousands of Muslims into Anatolia and Istanbul, shaping new political conflicts there in turn (McCarthy 1995).

In the case of the Christians, the two biggest causes for this massive population loss was the Young Turks' deportation and mass killings of Armenians during the First World War (Weiss-Wendt and Üngör 2011), and the compulsory (and irrevocable) population exchange between Greece and Turkey in 1923, which together with the war in Anatolia between the Greek army of occupation and the Turkish nationalists led to the fleeing or expulsion of some 1.4 million Anatolian "Rum" (Christians). Most recent historical research has agreed that the Republican state inherited and built on the initiatives of the Committee of Union and Progress (see Zürcher 1984, Keyder 1987, Deringil 1998, Dündar 2001, Der Matossian 2014), with the Republicans continuing their policies of *Turkification*. Keyder makes the point that whereas for Greece this huge influx of Anatolian Christians in the early 1920s presented in the first instance as a massive economic burden for an already distinct polity, in the Turkish case the expulsion of the generally well-educated and commercially inclined Greeks was a constituting act of the new Turkish nation-state (Keyder 2003: 44).

Not all Christians and Muslims were "unmixed" in this population exchange. Greeks in Istanbul and Muslims in Thrace were exempted from this mutual expulsion of indigenous inhabitants. According to Oran (2003), some one hundred thirty thousand Greeks in Istanbul were denoted as un-exchangeable, with a similar number of Muslims excused from deportation in western Thrace. Their rights as minorities were sketched out in Article 2 of the Convention Concerning the Exchange of Greek and Turkish Populations signed at the Lausanne Peace Conference in 1923. In both Turkey and Greece, however, these rights were regularly denied, leaving Oran to conclude that "the experience of those who were allowed to stay proved to be more difficult than those who had to leave" (101).[10] Indeed, in the long term this population, too, was forced to leave. In 1974 the number of non-Muslims (Greeks and Armenians) dwelling in Istanbul was a tiny fraction of the population that had lived in the city in the first years of the Republic.

What was the fate of those in Istanbul who in 1923 "were allowed to stay"? More precisely, what were the reasons for them, too, leaving the city, delayed as it was? Oran (2003) notes how the treatment of Christian and Muslim minorities in Istanbul and Thrace respectively waxed and waned according to relations between the Turkish and Greek states. Yet over and beyond this, a more significant cause of their leaving, affecting Armenians and Jews as well as Greeks, was the remorseless and unrelenting ethnic nationalism of the new citizenship and economic regime

10. See Oran (2003) for a discussion of the comparable discriminatory policies pursued by Greece against its Muslim population after 1923.

pursued in Turkey in both the singly-party and multi-party period, expressed through a number of discriminatory laws directed at both non-Turks and non-Muslims. One of the first signs of the problematic cultural status of Istanbul's non-Muslims was the government's seizure of the building and library (*Syllogos*) of the Greek Literary Society in 1923. Its rich archives were partly taken to Ankara, partly distributed to other libraries in Istanbul. In an act of symbolic violence, the impressive building became the headquarters of the CHP until its disappearance from the city's urbanscape with its demolition in 1955 (Alexandris 1983: 132). In his autobiography Niyazi Berkes tells a revealingly nationalist story about this library, which comprised thousands of volumes in many different languages. Working in the Ankara People's House in 1932, he was asked to catalog a collection, "whose contents (still in boxes) were taken from the library of a secret Greek organization in Istanbul in the years of occupation and brought to Ankara under the orders of Gazi [Atatürk]" (Berkes in Aktar 2006: 252). Aktar notes that this explains how Berkes became familiar with the travel diaries and literature of Europeans writing about the Ottomans that he later discusses in his influential work *Türkiye'de çağdaşlaşma* (*The Development of Secularism in Turkey*).

A second act constituting non-Muslim residents as problems was the 1927 and 1933 "Citizen Talk Turkish" campaigns, directed at the *sound* of other languages in urban space. In Bursa the municipal government "passed a decree banning the uses of languages other than Turkish in public" (Cağaptay 2006: 26). But even before this (in 1925), the Turkish state terminated certain rights guaranteed to Christians by the Lausanne Treaty, leading to the abolition of minority family and personal law and the imposition of a new curriculum on the fifty Greek schools in Istanbul, along with the appointment of Turkish teachers to them. The most important Greek high school for girls was closed down for eighteen months in 1925–26 because a statue of the founder of the school in its courtyard was clothed in Hellenic dress (see Alexandris 1983: 131–43).

Around the same time a huge number of other laws were announced designed to *Turkify* the economy. For example, some forty thousand Istanbul Greeks who fled the city in 1922 were barred from returning (despite their non-exchangeable status), and their property confiscated. According to Alexandris, by 1924 the "most valuable properties of the absent and Hellene Greeks [including the Pera Palas Hotel] had been largely distributed amongst ministers and notables of whom İsmet Pasha is one" (1983: 118). In 1925 Greeks were barred from travel outside of Istanbul without state permission, and in 1928 they were forbidden to own property outside the Greater Istanbul City area (Alexandris 1983: 140). In the same year, all non-Muslim employees were fired from the Istanbul Water Utility at the request of the Ministry of Reconstruction and Resettlement (Cağaptay 2006: 28). Further, in 1926 the Parliament passed a law that declared that only Turks could be government employees. Military commissions were reserved for Turks, and in their compulsory

military service non-Muslims were forbidden from bearing arms. Minorities were
also banned from establishing Boy Scout units. In 1928 Ankara legislated that doctors, dentists, midwives, and nurses, too, had to be Turks. A 1932 law allocated a
number of professions to Turkish citizens, banning "non-citizens, especially some
Istanbul Greeks, who were Hellenic citizens, from a variety of jobs. . . . More than
15,000 Greek Christians left the country as a result" (Cağaptay 2006: 70).

In 1931 the Parliament severely restricted press freedom, while also ruling that
only Turkish citizens could own magazines or journals. Even before this, fear of
prosecution under the law against "insulting Turkishness" meant that the Greek
press in Istanbul was severely curtailed in their ability to criticize State policy: in
1929 the newspaper *XpoviKa* was closed down after being charged with precisely
this crime (Alexandris 1983: 140). Indeed, according to Keyder, the only people
prosecuted by the "insulting Turkishness" laws in the 1920s and '30s were non-
Muslims. He notes the fate of an Armenian woman who was imprisoned under the
act for complaining about the closure of a ticket booth that caused her to miss
the train.[11]

The result of all these measures was a steady decrease in the non-Muslim population of Istanbul. According to Alexandris the population of Istanbul in 1924 was
1,065,866, of which 279,788 were Greeks, 73,407 were Armenians and 56,390 were
Jews. The census of 1927 shows a large decrease in the city's population, with
809,993 inhabitants in Istanbul of which 126,033 were Greek (Alexandris 1983:
142). In just three years some 150,000 Greeks had left the city.

Four other political acts led to the final collapse of the Ottoman Greek "world"
there. The first was the forced conscription in 1941 of all non-Muslim men in Turkey aged between eighteen and forty-five, sent to camps in Anatolia to build roads
and work on other government projects. Death rates in the camps were extremely
high (Alexandris 1983: 213–4). The majority of deportees were only allowed to
return to Istanbul a year later.

Second and much more calculated was the government's levying of an extraordinary wealth or capital tax (Varlık Vergisi) in 1942, in the context of a serious
economic crisis caused by the Second World War. In a CHP group meeting closed
to the press the prime minister (Şükrü Saraçoğlu) explained the purpose of the tax
to the party: "This law is simultaneously a revolutionary law. It is an opportunity
for us to gain our economic independence. We will present the Turkish market to
Turkish hands by eliminating the foreigners who control our markets" (cited in
Aktar 2000: 148). Ostensibly intended to tax and deter war profiteering, the assessment boards charged with determining levy amounts targeted the businesses of
"foreigners" (non-Muslims) in particular. The major features of the tax included:

11. Personal correspondence.

- A government-approved campaign from the Istanbul press against Christians and Jews, accusing them of speculation.
- The total discretion of the (all-Muslim) assessment committees to determine who would pay the tax and how much, with no appeal mechanism written into the law except petition to the (nonelected) assembly.
- Highly discriminatory evaluations against non-Muslims (including artisans, workers, and shopkeepers), set at levels ordered by Ankara and designed to bankrupt their businesses. Alexandris provides a number of striking comparisons between the tax levied on non-Muslims and Turks. One of the most extreme was the difference between the "general merchants" Isaac Modiano (Jewish) and Vehbi Koç (Muslim Turk). Modiano is taxed 2 million lira on an estimated capital of 97,000 lira; Koç is levied 60,000 on his estimated capital of 2,000,000 lira (Alexandris 1983: 218).
- A ruthless and pitiless enforcement process, with the confiscation and public auction of property of those who could not pay the tax within 30 days of assessment, and deportation to forced labor camps in Anatolia if the price obtained from the sale did not meet the levied amount.

The end result of the sixteen-month campaign was extremely damaging to Istanbul's non-Muslim population and quarters. The tax collected from the city alone amounted to 349 million lira, of which 93 percent was collected from Greeks, Jews, and Armenians (Aktar 2000: 154). Fourteen hundred people were deported, all non-Muslims, the majority from Istanbul. Twenty-one people died in labor camps (Aktar 2000; Alexandris 1983). Notwithstanding the crippling of Istanbul's large non-Turkish businesses, the tax also resulted in a massive transfer of wealth from Christians and Jews to Muslim Turks. Aktar's study of the *tapu sicil* (property register) for the years 1942–43 in six areas of Istanbul with large non-Muslim populations (Beyoğlu/Şişli, Eminönü, Fatih, Kadıköy and the Princess Islands) reveals the extent of the change of ownership of houses, work places, apartments, land and offices. In these suburbs alone non-Muslims were forced to sell 1,202 properties in order to pay the tax (Aktar 2000: 233). Seventy percent of the sales were to Turkish businessmen, 30 percent to institutions under the control of the Turkish state (Istanbul Council, National Banks, National Factories, etc.) (230).[12] In brief, the Wealth Tax was instrumental, along with the 1955 and 1964 events described below, in destroying the multi-religious structure of Istanbul. Aktar notes that

12. *Tan* newspaper reported on the sale of the *Serkldoryan Complex* in Beyoğlu in the following way: "Indebted by the Wealth Tax, the Turkish Theatre Society has sold the Serkldoryan Buildings to the Council for 1,100,000 lire. The Serkldoryan complex includes the building that houses the Serkldoryan Club, many shops in that building, the Melek, İpek and Sümer cinemas and a printing press" (cited in Aktar 2000: 204) (my translation). All three cinemas were well-known institutions on İstiklal Caddesi (Independence Avenue), in Beyoğlu.

five years later, in the first two years of Israel's founding, thirty thousand Jews left the city (207).

The third event transforming Istanbul's urban character was the state-sponsored pogrom organized against Greek properties, churches and schools on 6–7 September 1955. Ostensibly connected to rising tensions in Cyprus between the Greek-speaking and Turkish-speaking populations, the coordinated attacks in a number of suburbs caused major damage to Greek Istanbul's built environment. Initiated by an act of provocation—the "bombing" of the Turkish consulate in Salonika by a Turkish state agent, and faked photographs published in the Istanbul newspaper *Istanbul Ekspres* showing extensive bomb damage to the Salonika house in which Ataturk was born—the final result (as intended) was another mass exodus of Greeks, Armenians, and Jews from the city. Thirty-six years later Gökşin Sipahioğlu, the editor of *Istanbul Ekspres* in 1955, said in an interview: "Of course the 6–7 September attacks were planned by the Özel Harp Dairesi (Special Warfare Unit). It was an extremely well-planned operation and it realized its aims. Let me ask you: was it not an extraordinary successful event?" (Güven 2005b: 72). According to the records of a special court in Beyoğlu established to investigate the attacks, 4,214 houses, 1,004 shops, 73 churches (29 completely destroyed, 34 badly damaged along with many Byzantine art treasures),[13] 26 schools, and 2 monasteries, as well as many factories, restaurants, and hotels were attacked and totally or partially destroyed (Güven 2005a: ix). The financial loss was huge: and according to Alexandris, two hundred Greek women were raped in the outlying Bosporus suburbs (Alexandris 1983: 257–58).

Beyoğlu in particular was targeted by the rioters, with truckloads of people carted into the suburb. Turkish nationalists had long represented Beyoğlu (Pera) as a non-Turkish space, even as a "prostitute in the bosom of the nation-state" (Yumul 2009). For example, the Republican poet Yahya Kemal viewed Beyoğlu as a foreign culture, marked in particular by its different built environment. As he wrote in a newspaper article entitled "Sayfiyede payitaht" in 1922, "After first taking Istanbul's money, Beyoğlu took its renown, its glory, its charm, whatever Istanbul had. Beyoğlu grew, it rose, it expanded, it became uncontrollable. It spread to the limits of Şişli. And this pile of buildings in which not a single stone is infused with the spirit of the past is going to grow even more . . . because newly prosperous Muslims are competing with rich Christians in developing the city. While in Beyoğlu the lights shine every night, old Istanbul is shrouded in mourning black" (reprinted in Kemal 1964: 143).

As Stokes notes, there is in Yahya Kemal's poetry a wistful nostalgia for a lost Istanbul, for which "according to the dominant logic of Turkish modernity, no more than the most fleeting backward glance could be permitted in the resolute

13. Cited in Alexandris 1983: 258.

westward march" (Stokes 1999: 122). Stokes's charitable interpretation of Yahya Kemal's "nostalgia," however, downplays the nationalist geography and history orienting his eulogizing for a missing city. Yahya Kemal's regrets are better understood when placed alongside some of his other writings, in which "*Türklük*" (Turkishness) is posited to be the source of the city's beauty and perfection. The first four points of his "Theses for a Turk Istanbul Conference" are:

1. Istanbul is the greatest of the cities that Turkishness created.
2. This city is inscribed on the imagination of all humanity and this inscription is enduring.
3. The traveler who sees Istanbul once will always remember it in wonder. Those who over their lifetime never see the city will always imagine it.
4. One event shows the creative power of Turkishness: when it conquered Byzantium, or other cities in the Middle Ages that were like capitals, it always recreated them with a completely contrasting beauty (Kemal 1964: 78).

What spatial strategies would be connected to the representation of the Ottomans as primarily Turkish, positioning non-Muslim communities as extraneous elements (or worse) in the Ottoman world, and exposing them to the accusation that the extroverted modernity of their suburbs threatened the Ottoman-Turkish essence of the city? Logically it is the practice of ethnic *urbicide*, the destroying of property and built environments whose architectural and semiotic meanings symbolize an important aspect of a minority group's identity and history, as occurred most strikingly in the 1955 pogrom in Beyoğlu and in other non-Muslim suburbs.[14]

In the (former) non-Muslim neighborhood of Kuzguncuk, where I did fieldwork in the mid-1990s,[15] contradictory stories were told about the traumatic happenings on 6–7 September. Chatting with Georgiou *amca* (uncle) one day, one of the few Greeks still living in the neighborhood, he remembered that he had stood outside his house all night to keep the rioters from burning it down. He noted that they had come on boats from the other side of the Bosporus. In a lowered voice, he also said that some local Turks had joined in. Somewhat by contrast, in a separate interview, Zehra *teyze* (auntie) claimed that in Kuzguncuk, "the Turks didn't let the looters in." Yet she goes on to say, "There was a lot of destruction . . . everyone shut themselves up in their houses. No one was killed here. Some were injured. They destroyed the priest's house. They tried to set fire to the church but it didn't burn. . . . We were afraid that they would attack again. That was when people gradually began to emigrate" (in Bektaş 1996: 148). In an interview with an elderly Muslim woman, Amy Mills (in her excellent study of Kuzguncuk) notes a similar

14. For photographs and documents concerning the 1955 pogrom, see Çoker (2005).
15. See Houston (2001).

ambivalence regarding what happened there. After first stating that the riots did not occur in Kuzguncuk, the woman later went on to describe what she witnessed: "They broke into the houses; they tied the tanks' wheels and tore fabrics in the houses. . . . *We heard sounds.* . . . They cut the rugs; they ruined things; they took the mattresses off the beds and cut them and threw the wool out of the windows. They broke the glass. One of them sat in front of the jail, wearing several layers of clothes, putting on shoes from a pile of shoes there. *What sins were committed here.* When they saw the Greeks they turned the other way" (Mills 2010: 124).

The final blow to the cosmopolitan worlds of local mixed suburbs was the 1964 deportation of Greek citizens, when the Turkish government responded to the killing of Turkish Cypriots in Cyprus by punishing Istanbul's local Rum. Unilaterally abolishing the residency rights of Greek citizens guaranteed under the conventions of the Lausanne Treaty, at least thirteen thousand people were deported and exiled, most of whom had been born in Istanbul (Mills 2010: 54, Oran 2003: 104). Another thirty thousand Istanbul Rum left with them, many of them Turkish citizens married to members of the evicted Greek community (Alexandris calls them "Constantinopolitan Hellenes"). Their few goods were loaded onto trucks— emigrants were permitted to take twenty kilos of possessions and $20—while much of their immovable property and financial accounts were first frozen and then confiscated by the Turkish treasury (Sasanlar 2006: 86–87, Mills 2010: 56). Some deportees hastily sold their properties at low prices. Education in Greek was prohibited (again) on the Princess Islands, and in 1965 many Greek properties were expropriated there to build an open-air agricultural prison (Oran 2003: 104). The end result was the rapid departure of most of the remaining one hundred twenty thousand Rum in Istanbul, leaving behind a decimated population of less than three thousand people (Mills 2010: 55).

In brief, for four decades Istanbul (along with the Kurdish areas of Turkey) was a spatial target of what Aktar calls the "*Türkleştirme*" (Turkification) politics of the Republic. By 1965 its pursuit had led to the catastrophic diminishment of Christian and Jewish minorities in the city, as well as to the creation of a Turkish bourgeoisie under the activist eye of a military-bureaucratic elite. Essentially, Turkification entails "the hegemony and domination of Turkish ethnic identity without compromise at every level and in every aspect of social life, from the language spoken in the street to the history taught in schools, from education to industry, from business to State personnel employment policy, from special laws to citizens' housing in certain regions" (Aktar 2000: 101).

When thinking about place, Tim Ingold advocates that anthropology should adopt a "dwelling perspective," "according to which the landscape is constituted as an enduring record of—and testimony to—the lives and works of past generations who have dwelt within it, and in so doing, have left there something of themselves" (2000: 189). As a general descriptive statement this is true enough, even in Istanbul today, where recognizable traces of the lives of non-Muslims remain as fragmented parts of the landscapes in the neighborhoods in which they once lived—in the boarded-up windows of a school; in a synagogue wall; in an untended cemetery; in a plaque beside a door; in a church without a congregation; or in a padlocked building.

And yet as we have already noted in chapter two, place inhabitation can be as dissonant as it is harmonious, given that the politics of dwelling gathers actors together in an intersubjective field of frictional relationships. Thus, the landscapes of Istanbul testify also to the planning and practice of ethnic cleansing and to the activity of Turkish nationalists in tearing asunder the city's historic cosmopolitanism. Indeed, the very absence of the descendants of "past generations," noticed in the silence of an empty minority schoolyard, reveals not continuity with the past but an event of rupture between inhabitants and generations. This rupture was enacted through a spatial campaign. As we have seen above, its strategic practices included the violence of urbicide, in its targeted destruction of churches, houses, and commercial properties, all of which were also "symbolic elements of the material cultural landscape" (Mills 2010: 119); through deportation orders, followed by state confiscation of immovable property; in legislation to prevent its inheritance or transferal; through the forced selling of houses at a fraction of their value to suddenly mercenary acquaintances; by the auction of goods and carpets in streets outside minorities apartments; and in the occupation of newly evacuated non-Muslim properties. For non-Muslim minorities all of this violence led to the leaching of familiars (friends, foes, neighbors, and family) from places until those remaining were left a tiny minority in neighborhoods they could no longer easily make home.

In an article on northern Cyprus, Navaro-Yashin writes that there Turkish Cypriots described their condition or inner state as being *maraz*, a mood or feeling of mental depression and unrecoverable sadness or melancholia. One cause of their *maruz* was their sense of confinement to northern Cyprus, a self-declared state recognized only by the Turkish government. A second, however, was felt to be the energy discharged upon them by the Greek dwellings they had appropriated to live in as refugees, an affect "exuded by dwellings, objects, and spaces left behind by another community after a cataclysmic war" (2009: 4). This is one way of illuminating what Ingold means in saying past generations leave something of themselves in place. Mazower (2004) discerns a similar presence in his study of Salonika. There, too, an earlier historical reality of overlapping religious devotion and coexistence between ethnic communities has been destroyed by the unforgiving politics of population exchange, ethnic deportation and (Hellenistic) modernism, which in the 1920s went so far as to build over the Jewish cemetery and tear down the city's minarets. The Nazis deported almost 90 percent of Salonika's Jewish population of fifty thousand people in 1943, to be murdered in Auschwitz. What remains of this history of habitation is a *City of Ghosts*, as the title reveals.

Ghosts also haunt Kuzguncuk. Its buildings and its objects visit melancholia upon its residents, attesting not to any enduring continuity between generations but to suffering and sin (as affirmed by the elderly Muslim woman). Mills (2010) and others (for example Bektaş 1996) show how older inhabitants in Kuzguncuk today feel an intense *nostalgia* for an earlier pre-migration time in which people of different faiths lived together in a neighborly fashion, even as they remain silent regarding local participation in state-led violence against non-Muslims designed to drive them away. Nostalgia inflects memories of the past, simplifying the complexity of lived tensions and hostilities involved in historical interreligious and interethnic relations. Silence surrounds the *intentionality* of acts that violated the rights of minorities, impairing the ability of current inhabitants to identify and condemn perpetrators, as well as to grieve or express contrition for those acts. For Mills, both nostalgia and silence serve to deflect "memory of the inclusive nation that could have or should have been" (Mills 2010: 110).

Finally, both the 1955 and 1964 events show the historical intersection of forced migration of non-Muslims out of Istanbul with massive rural migration into the city. As the non-Muslim minorities were expelled, their properties were initially abandoned to dereliction and decay. Thereafter, many were occupied by "incoming rural migrants who achieved ownership after a period of uncontested occupation. Some properties that remained unclaimed after a period of time were eventually permitted to be sold. Others were sold through unclear legal processes. In Kuzguncuk, all of the shops on the main street and many of the houses were transferred in various (and some believe through legally ambiguous) ways to Muslim Turks, some of whom had arrived in Kuzguncuk as rural migrants and worked as employees for minority-owned businesses" (Mills 2010: 57).

And yet as we shall see below, the huge academic literature on the political economy of rural migration to Istanbul, and on the growth and sociality of the gecekondu suburbs, rarely considers how those processes articulate and overlap with the events of non-Muslim emigration/deportation occurring at the very same time. Even as writers narrate the story of how the illegal squatter houses of the gecekondu were legalized (through law in 1966), they fail to comment on the simultaneous 'legal' measures legitimizing the illegal expropriation of non-Muslim land and housing. In brief, Turkish migration to non-Muslim neighborhoods from the early 1950s onward—for example, to Galata, Cihangir, Ortaköy, Tarlabaşı, Çengelköy, Kadıköy, Karaköy, Kuzguncuk, the Princess Islands, and smaller Christian and Jewish neighborhoods in the historic peninsula—coincided with state policies of Turkification against minorities, which "effectively meant a Turkification of Istanbul's urban culture" (Mills 2010: 205). Turkish nationalism's destruction of the city's cultural system of sharing urban space degraded Istanbul residents' practice of urban tolerance, paving the way for leftist/rightist urban violence.

3.4 MODERNISM

In 1974, having been turned into a theater of war by militants, Istanbul was a city structured by forty years of patchwork and piecemeal planning, transformed by decades of modern urbanism. To illuminate how this transformation unfolded, let me begin, perversely, with Ankara. Over against Ottoman Istanbul, its construction as the new capital of Turkey symbolized the rejection of one history and the creation of another. Unlike Istanbul, the relatively insignificant town of Ankara was a place "without significations, testif[ying] to the desire to locate the new project in a neutral space devoid of history" (Keyder 2003: 50). Ankara had no compromising past—although it did have a castle, whose fate became a key point of difference between architects' designs in the competition established to select the plan for the city (Houston 2008). Jansen's winning entry was characterized not by the destruction of the old settlement but by the building of a new city, laid out alongside the older area.[16] How better to showcase the distinction between the future and the past? "No building within an urban fabric is perceived in a vacuum. Invariably, its formal and functional characteristics are understood in relationship to those of other structures, both contiguous and separate" (Preziosi 1991: 104). The same logic might be applied to the country as a whole: unlike Istanbul, Ankara, famously, became a "city without minarets." Like Brasilia, then, Ankara was a city desired to *conduct* the country to the desired future (Holston 1989). Accordingly, in its early decades Ankara was an exemplary site in which the political intentions of the regime were most clearly applied in its planning arrangements and architecture.

By contrast, with the permanent transfer of government to Ankara, Istanbul in the 1920s and 1930s was a city in relative decline, its administrative functions shrinking, its population stable or decreasing. Ankara was disinclined to invest public funds there, in the form of new state factories or heavy industries. Indeed, according to some contemporary observers, parts of the older "southern" city appeared deserted. In brief, the attitude of the Kemalists was more to ignore Istanbul's urban issues than to construct in it new spaces and buildings. Its modernist makeover into a planned urban environment was impractical. Not that its total 'de-Ottomanization' wasn't fantasized about—according to the ex-mayor of Istanbul (in 1937), "In order to transform Istanbul into a contemporary city, there is no solution but total demolition, with the exception of Istanbul's monuments, and gradual reconstruction" (in Gül 2009: 81).

Nevertheless, adding to the palimpsest-like quality of Istanbul's built environment, the Turkish Republic did build a sprinkling of modernist-style new buildings in the city, particularly for state institutions closely connected to the Kemalist

---

16. See Üngör (2012) for discussion of the building of a modern city outside the historic walled city in Diyarbakır in the same years.

program. These included the 1934 Eminönü and Beyoğlu Halkevleri; the Karaköy Yolcu Salonu (built in 1937 by architect Rebii Gorbon); the Edebiyat Fakültesi of Istanbul University (built in 1938 by Bruno Taut); and the TRT building in Harbiye (1945). Other modernist structures were constructed in the city too. In the single-party period, a number of late-Ottoman factory complexes such as the Electricity Power Plant (Santral) in Silahtarağa were modernized, together with the building of low-cost housing projects for their workers (Cengizkan 2009). Like its population, the result was a mishmash of building styles and built environments, leading to a muting of the signifying power of modernist design.

More significantly, Istanbul became a site of urban planning. The most important intervention in the city in the early Republican period was coordinated by Henri Prost, chief urban planner in Istanbul from 1936 to 1950, who produced a master plan in 1938 after two years of extensive research. Prost was an expert on conserving, managing, and modifying "Islamic Cities," having worked previously as chief urban planner in protectorate Morocco from 1913 until 1923 under French governor-general Hubert Lyautey. According to Rabinow (1989, 1996), his planning practice there was best described as "techno-cosmopolitan," characterized by the building of new modern European settlements adjacent to the Moroccan medinas, a de-cluttering of the traditional city to bring to the fore its classical Islamic morphological structure, and urban provision for the expansion of the capitalist economy and for modern amenities (such as a yacht marina). Somewhat similarly, his plan for Istanbul was designed to conserve and re-present the historic grandeur of the Byzantine and Ottoman city for its imagined new inhabitant—the appreciative and mobile Turkish *flaneur*—while engineering its modernization and improving its transport and hygiene. These two dimensions of planning—preservation of cultural diversity and architectural monuments, and technical modernization—are difficult to orchestrate, as the generally unrealized nature of Prost's intentions for Istanbul illustrates.

The major features of Prost's plan included an extensive road network articulating wide boulevards to various centers of the city, destructive pruning of the urban fabric of the old city and Pera within the proximity of monuments, the making of new public spaces and two large parks on each side of the existing city, an archaeological park showcasing the city's Byzantine remains and Topkapı Palace, and the zoning of industrial sites to both sides of the Golden Horn (Gül and Lamb 2004, Pinon 2010). For various reasons, most of the interventionist operations envisioned by the master plan were not implemented during Prost's tenure. His project assumed a number of conditions, even as it maintained that adherence to the plan would simultaneously create them: one, an acceptance by inhabitants of the expertise of the [foreign] master planner; two, a rationally expanding economy; three, a positive discourse on Ottoman and Byzantine societies; four, a legislative framework that facilitated expropriation by zones; and five, a large budget. None of these prerequisites existed in

Istanbul. Although presenting little evidence for their assertion, Gül and Lamb (2004) hypothesize that the Republican People's Party's "peasantist" ideology was partly responsible for the lack of government support for Prost's plans. Much more likely was Ankara's continuing hostility toward Istanbul and its "cosmopolitan" population, for whom Prost would have modernized the city.

Despite the overall lack of implementation, a number of Prost's projects were completed, all of which by 1974 were familiar aspects of the city's urban spaces appropriated and used by activists. These included the building of the massive Atatürk Boulevard that dissects the historic peninsula from north to south; Refik Saydam Avenue separating Kasımpaşa from Galata; the opening of coastal roads along the Bosporus; the expansion of Eminönü and Üsküdar Squares; a medical zone in Cerrahpaşa; and the building of the Taksim İnönü Promenade (now Gezi Park), the Open Air Harbiye Amphitheatre, and Maçka Park (Bilsel 2010). Prost's contract was not extended in 1950.

A second phase of planning and modernizing of Istanbul was begun under the Democrat Party and its leader Adnan Menderes, whose expert committee in 1952 found Prost's master plan lacking in research and statistical study and recommended the instituting of a permanent team to upgrade and guide the city's urban renewal. Ironically, however, given the accusation that Prost's plan for Istanbul amounted to its beautification and not its modernization (Akpınar 2010), the new master plan exhibited remarkable continuity with his design. The decade of Democrat Party rule ended in 1960 with the country's first military coup, as well as with the hanging of Adnan Menderes, the elected prime minister, and two of his ministers. Wildly differing assessments of the Menderes administration's policies confirm deep-seated political prejudices in Turkey. In an article analyzing the historiography of the 1960 military intervention, Murat Belge notes that if Kemalism as implemented by the CHP (Republican Peoples Party) constitutes a revolution, the electorate's choosing of the Democrat Party in the first multiparty election in 1950 signifies its opposite, a counterrevolution. Equally logically, then, for both Kemalists and the left the May 28 coup in 1960 that deposed the Democrat Party government "possesses a positive meaning: it terminates the 'counter-revolution' and gives power once again to the revolutionaries."[17] Central to the legal case built against Menderes by the junta-appointed court were questions concerning the massive urban redevelopment program in Istanbul, in which Menderes had been personally involved. In particular, Menderes was charged with the illegal and corrupt expropriation of properties in executing his urban renewal project in the historic peninsula. Figures vary concerning the number of older buildings destroyed in the years 1956–1960, the most intense period of city reconstruction. Gül (2009:

17. "Son 27 Mayıs'ın Ardından," *Taraf Daily,* 30 May, Sunday.

152) estimates 5,000, while Akpınar claims that 7,289 were demolished "to make roads in straight lines" (2010: 192).

At the heart of the Menderes redevelopment of Istanbul was the opening up of new avenues and modern roads. Many of them followed routes first mooted in Prost's master plan. The wide boulevards eased traffic congestion and facilitated vehicular circulation through the southern city, even as they cut new lines of division between or within neighborhoods. Major projects included the building of Millet and Vatan Streets that ran east-west to the ripped-open old city walls, connecting to the new E5 motorway. Vatan Street, with its eight lanes, was the widest road ever built in Turkey. It also became the primary arena for military parades on the Republic Day national holiday. Other interventionist construction works facilitated transit around the city via an express road network. A new shore-line road (Kennedy Street) encircled the historic peninsula, connecting Florya and Yeşilköy Airport with Unkapanı, via Sirkeci and Eminönü. Karaköy Square was built on the other side of the Galata Bridge, with new roads connecting it to Dolmabahçe along the Bosporus and to Atatürk Bridge on the northern bank of the Golden Horn. According to Gül, on the other side of the Bosporus "a large avenue, Bağdat Street, connecting Kadıköy to Bostancı and a motorway between Haydarpaşa and Pendik were the major works executed in this period" (2009: 157).

As we will see in sections (v) and (vi) below, in the very years that these radical spatial changes transformed Istanbul into an automobile city, constant and heavy rural migration to it was also swelling its boundaries, leading to a housing crisis and the unauthorized occupation of state land. Despite this, government funding of mass housing remained minimal. In the 1950s the state-owned Emlak Bankası built two new upper-middle-class satellite towns in garden-city style in Levent and Ataköy, leading to the outward expansion of the city. For Baturayoğlu-Yöney and Salman (2010: 6), these were the "first large-scaled housing complexes [in Turkey], where modernist planning and architectural vocabulary are reflected in this scale, including their own sanitation and transportation facilities and environmental, social, cultural, educational, sportive, recreational and commercial infrastructure." Esen is less enamored of the Ataköy (Sea of Marmara) development, claiming it was the first step "in the deterritorialization of the north."[18] These residential apartment buildings in international style were in keeping with two other famous high-modernist buildings constructed in the same years, the Hilton Hotel constructed on a long-confiscated Armenian cemetery near Taksim, and the Municipal Palace on Ataturk Boulevard.

By 1974, Menderes' roads, squares, and apartment buildings were established features of the city, adding their site/sight lines, meeting points, scenes for action, and geographical settings to the everyday urban practices already orienting Istanbul's

18. See Esen, "Becoming Istanbul."

ever-growing inhabitants. They had also become spaces that afforded protest: activist groups occupied, paraded along, and fought over them. "The morgue was opposite Gülhane Park gates. We used to march down there from Beyazıt [along Menderes' straitened and enlarged Ordu Caddesi] to pick up a body" (Özlem, Dev-Yol). And as we saw in chapter 1, it was on Barbaros Boulevard, constructed in the late 1950s to join Beşiktaş to Levent, that Şahin Aydın was murdered in 1974.

Let me conclude by returning to relations between modernism and Turkism—in Insel's words, between civilizationalism and nationalism—in the de-Ottomanization of Istanbul. In their analyses of modern urbanist operations in the city, historians have been sensitive to the violence of planning, in particular to the huge number of buildings demolished by both Prost and Menderes to facilitate the circulation of automobile traffic and to modernize the city. They have noted, too, how modernism in planning, architecture and the arts was intimately connected to the Kemalists' desire to make a brave, new world. In her stimulating account of early Republican architectural and planning culture, Bozdoğan (2001) also interprets its rejection of vernacular ("Islamic") architecture and its adoption of modernist design as a defensive reaction to the West's deeply entrenched orientalist prejudices against Turkey. In the process, however, her emphasis on nationalism as independence minimizes the Republic's aggressive ethnic chauvinism and its own politics of ruthless assimilation, sidestepping its determination to produce a transformation not just in the country's built environments but equally importantly in the ethnicity of the people who owned, lived in, and used the city.[19]

Harder to talk about, then, has been the macro and micro spatial violence directed against non-Muslim Istanbul residents as part of that modernization. Menderes's demolitions in particular have sparked debate as to whether they targeted the properties or dwellings of non-Muslims. Keyder insinuates that they did, noting that, in the southern peninsula, new roads "cut through densely packed Christian areas of the city" (1999: 175). By contrast, in her study of the cadastral records of appropriated properties in Aksaray in the Menderes years, Akpınar (2015) demonstrates the high proportion of Muslim-owned buildings destroyed for the new avenues.

Putting aside these claims, planning histories that focus on the "bricks and mortar" of giant redevelopment projects and architectural interventions in urban space often overlook the "violence" of architecture on a less monumental scale, such as in its "micro" practice of changing the visual appearance of places. Cağaptay notes how in 1927 the "Vatandaş Türkçe Konuş" campaign of the CHP started with

19. Much more egregious is the work of Şen and Şoher, who in a recent chapter on the urban reconstruction projects of both Prost and Menderes, fail even to mention the simultaneous Turkification politics targeting the city's population, even as they claim to "shed light on the socio-political atmosphere of the period in which these reconstruction projects took place" (2015: 81).

the postering of the city. "Signs were pasted up in theatres, restaurants, hotels, movie theatres, public ferries, and streetcars to recommend that everybody speak Turkish" (Cağaptay 2006: 26). Often unnoticed, also, is the production and transformation of urban soundscapes, from the sudden enunciating of the call to prayer in Turkish in 1934, to the playing of classical Western music on ferries, and so on. There is a censorious aspect to this sound production as well, in its muting of unacceptable languages in the new urban spaces of the city, of both their spoken and sung words. In this we hear another aspect of Kemalist urbanism, in the decomposition and recomposition of the city's acoustic environment.

A third and similarly overlooked dimension of the use of space by "Turkist-modernism" has been its systematically planned "outbreaks" of acts of intimidation, in the mobilizing of nationalist mobs against religious and ethnic minorities. Rıfat Bali (2008) writes about the riots against Jews in Thrace in 1934. There has been the practice, too, of exhibitionary violence performed in newly constructed public squares in the first years of the Republic. Rather than the "sadism" of architecture, we might call this the sadistic appropriation of space. Included within this history are the public hangings of forty-seven Kurds involved in the Şeyh Said rebellion in Diyarbakır's city square, a warning to others carried out by the 1925 Independence Tribunals, as well as the twenty-seven public hangings in Menemen in 1930. That event is remembered in ceremony each year at the Kubilay memorial, the only non-Ataturk statue erected (in 1932) in the early Republican period. The missing bodies and the absent tombs of "enemies" of the Republic might be considered a related aspect of this spectacle of terror, so that the families of Şeyh Said or Said Nursi have no grave to visit or site to commemorate their actions. Juxtapose that to the monumental tombs of Turkish Prime Ministers in Topkapı, even of Adnan Menderes'.

We can describe many of these events as *performative urbanism*, intended to demonstrate the placeless status of certain urban inhabitants, with far-reaching consequences for their perception of the city. Residents subjected to these forms and experiences of spatial practice lose their trust that the public spaces of the city (or of the nation) includes or even tolerates their form of political, ethnic, or religious particularity.

3.5 GECEKONDU CITY

By the mid-1960s then, de-Ottomanized Istanbul was a place transformed by the politics of *Turkist modernism*. If government planning initiatives were only partially successful in modernizing the city—the rapid growth in its population and economy meant that Prost's and Menderes' interventions were inadequate almost before they were implemented—the nationalist and performative urban violence targeting non-Muslims and their suburbs resulted in the collapse of their populations. At the same time, growing numbers of rural migrants to the city were looking for homes.[20] One result, as dramatized in Güngör Dilmen's play *Kuzguncuk türküsü* (Kuzguncuk folk song), was the forced selling of properties for a fraction of their worth. The phrase, "Neighbor, how much is your house?" resounded in urban streets as a new local idiom (Mills 2010: 128). Of course, the vast majority of rural migrants could not move into the empty homes of non-Muslims. Further, in Istanbul there were minimal rental stocks, and migrants had little money. The result was a habitation problem, resolved only by the creative, autonomous production of small-scale "garden cities"—shantytowns, or gecekondu—on unused state land.

But what caused this mass population movement? The huge growth in Istanbul's population from the early 1950s onward articulated with a perfect storm of developments in both the Turkish and the international political economy. An extended period of global economic growth (from the late 1940s until the early 1970s) saw average growth in personal income of 3.1 percent annually in Turkey over those same years (Pamuk 2014: 248). The beginning of the Cold War between the United States and the Soviet Union led to Turkey's inclusion within the new NATO organization (in 1951), as well as its becoming one of the first recipients of Marshall Plan funds aimed at the postwar economic recovery of Europe. An expanding world economy meant a new market for Turkey's agricultural goods, whose production and total acreage sown had been boosted in the early 1950s by the importation of tractors and heavy ploughs and the building of new highways, each supported by US loans. The result was both agricultural expansion through mechanization, rapid capital accumulation (for some) and a massive influx of villagers to the more prosperous urban centers, traveling on highways built to connect farm products to market towns. For the first immigrants to Istanbul, "informal" work in services, in building construction, and in small-scale manufacturing and later in larger industrial plants provided a semblance (or better) of an urban wage. Demand for labor in Western Europe opened the way toward workers' migration there, whose remittances became an important source of foreign exchange in the 1960s and '70s.

Supported by the OECD, the turn to *import substituting industrialization* (ISI) as the new accumulation model after the 1960 coup, along with restoration of the parliamentary system and a new constitution, generated a new pull factor for migrant workers to the city. It also facilitated Istanbul's "private sector" (Pamuk 2014: 235ff) or "manufacturing bourgeoisie" (Keyder 1987: 141ff) to dominate the economy. ISI was regulated through the State Planning Office, established by the military regime in 1960. Its crucial role included allocation of scarce foreign exchange and cheap credit to approved industrial enterprises. In order both to grow the domestic

---

20. Population figures for Istanbul show that it wasn't until the early 1950s that the city regained its pre–World War One total (Pamuk 2014: 73).

market and to protect domestic industry from global competition, economic policy aimed first "to reduce, or even to completely prohibit, the importation of certain products, then to encourage local manufacturers through cheap credit, tax exemptions, and foreign currency allotment" (Pamuk 2014: 237). State Economic Enterprises (SEEs), historically established by state investment in heavy industry, provided subsidized inputs to the private sector. Along with high customs duties and a quota system on imports, ISI led to the booming expansion of the economy, as well as to an explosion of privately owned large-scale manufacturing plants producing consumer goods on the fringes of Istanbul's settled areas.

ISI did not only ensure the accumulation of profit by the industrial bourgeoisie. Smaller-scale private enterprises, too, were able to take advantage of products of state industries and of selective protectionist policy, selling cheaper replicas of products to the massive migrant populations in the country's gecekondus. In an interview I did with Fikret Amca, father of an activist from Dev-Sol, he explained how he was able to build up his workshop after arriving in Istanbul from Trabzon in 1952 when he was just fourteen years old:

> When I first came to Istanbul I worked on building sites, slept on site. We put in pipes. I carried heaters up six flights, for 6 kuruş each one, in Nisantaşı, Maçka, Beşiktaş. It had to be in the rich suburbs for them to afford heaters.
>
> I took a loan to buy the machines and opened up a small factory [atölye] in 1969, making saucepans, trays, teapots, kitchen pieces, etcetera out of aluminum. The aluminum came from the Etibank State factory in Konya. The machines came from Istanbul because they weren't complicated. To build up clients I went to Anatolia for a month, traveling on buses, to Ankara, Maraş, Erzurum, Kayseri. I was very sympathetic, young. In those towns the wholesalers took from different factories: you needed good people skills to run the business. There was no competition for customers even though lots of people opened up factories because there was a personal relationship; you would send the goods to those towns on a truck, and maybe they would pay later.
>
> We were small capital [fak sermaye]: the business went well from 1974 to 1980, when I had twenty-four people working three shifts a day [seventy-two workers]. Sometimes we couldn't meet the orders, as they were coming from Geneva, Italy, Saudi, Milan, Munich. Workers came from Anatolia, skilled workers, and we had apprentices who graduated from primary school.

Fikret Amca perceived that there was an antagonistic relationship between workers and owners. Indeed, in banning unionists from working in his factory, he confirmed Keyder's argument that ISI resulted in improved conditions and rights for *organized labor* only, including of a steady rise in real wages that allowed their full participation in the internal market. According to Keyder, by the 1970s this "labor aristocracy" (clustered in large firms and State Economic Enterprises) comprised one-third of the working class (1987: 160). The privileges afforded the labor movement by the 1961 constitution, in particular collective bargaining and the right to strike, allowed unions a legitimate place in the industrial system, leading to their growing influence in the political economy of the 1960s and 1970s (see chapter 5). Of course, such rights were not easily taken up, as Fikret Amca explains:

> I refused to let my workers join the union; if they wanted to, I scared them or showed them the door. This was illegal, but I came from the village and learned the work. I paid the workers well: if going rate was 10 kuruş I paid 11, and they were all insured. At *Bayram* I paid double salary, and once in 1974 I hired a private plane and took the workers to Bursa for a day holiday, all expenses paid. There was a police register where the workers' names were recorded: I paid every Friday afternoon, once a week, on the dot. I was a good boss: when I came to Istanbul, I knew how much I suffered, I didn't want workers to suffer the same, Allah would ask me. I still see some of the workers: one or two opened up their own places after working for me. Now no one can do this, there are only the big factories.

Fikret Amca closed his workshop just before the military intervention. "In 1980 we went broke and I shut the factory, when ten people were working there: there was huge competition, goods were coming from everywhere and the market conditions weren't good." His story illuminates interactional events experienced by many of Istanbul's early migrants—the hard move to Istanbul and his making good through skill in personal networking; changing location within a segmented labor market; political struggle over working conditions including the super-exploitation of labor; and destruction of his small-scale industrial business, due to the crisis of import substituting industrialization and its subsequent policy abandonment (in 1980).

An integral aspect of the concatenation of all these processes was the tripling of Istanbul's population in twenty years, from one million to three million people in 1970, and then to five million by 1980 (Keyder 2005: 125). This vast movement of people to the city led both to housing filling in any vacant inner-city land and to Istanbul's tremendous urban sprawl. According to the voluminous literature on the gecekondu, rural immigrants were integrated into urban life in the postwar period through employment, finding work in both smaller workshops and in the protected and rapidly expanding import-substituting industrial economy (see, e.g., Karpat 1976, Erman 2012, Şenyapılı 2004). Employment, precarious or otherwise, meant participation as consumers in the bourgeoning internal market. For Keyder, however, a more important process of incorporation into the city was through "settlement and housing" (2005: 125). This did not occur via state-funded provision of mass housing, as was the case in Singapore, for example. On the contrary, it involved informal yet organized and collective squatting on vacant state land on the periphery of the city. Residential patterns were not random but connected to chain migration from people's place of origin, leading to the clustering of certain groups like Alevi in specific suburbs. Entrepreneurs, builders, regional associations (*dernek*) and, as we will see in chapters 4 and 5, leftist groups all facilitated migration settlement through particular acts of land-occupation for people from the same village or area, strengthening existing patronage networks (see Erder 1996). Colluding with such occupation, populist policies progressively legalized the dwelling places of immigrants in the city, through politicians' promises to retroactively legitimize ownership of purloined land in exchange for inhabitants' votes.

What, technically, were gecekondu? One definition is given in the comprehensive Gecekondu Law of 1966 that begrudgingly recognized their legitimate presence in major cities. It identified its object of legislation as "illicit constructions, that were built regardless of general regulations and directives determining construction work requirements, regardless of the soils on which building is permitted or not, and regardless of the fact that the land does not belong to the builder and that gecekondu are being built without the owner's authorization (in Perouse 2004: S3).

Rival definitions stress other qualities of squatter housing. For example, Şenyapılı notes that flexibility (rather than illegality) characterizes their chief feature. Thus "in accordance with income and status obtained by the owner through mobility in the labor market, rooms, service areas, floors may be added to a squatter house, a new one may be built adjacent to it, it may be rented partially or totally, may be torn down or may be sold" (2004: S12). Very rapidly, squatter settlements, in their evolving states of transformation and legalization, became the urban rule, so that by 1975 45 percent of Istanbul's population lived (officially) in gecekondu housing (Akbulut and Başlık 2011: 22). For large-scale capitalists, this do-it-yourself dwelling strategy ensured rapid capital accumulation, not just because of low wage costs but because the state and government declined to tax private profits that might have been used to subsidize social housing production.

Perhaps most importantly, we must note that the key to gecekondu development was the *non-scarcity* of land in and around the city, an artifact of both the Ottoman land code in which land was state-owned and non-commoditized, and of the Republic's determination to expel the non-Muslim population of Istanbul (Aktar 2000). Tracts of land next to city settlements left vacant by departing non-Muslims were often nationalized, thereafter to be appropriated by squatters. Most fundamental, as Keyder points out, the prime condition allowing gecekondu housing was the ongoing decision of the Turkish state to "keep public lands out of the realm of the market" (1999: 147). This refusal to institute a comprehensive capitalist property regime incorporating land means that Erman's comment that the "development of Turkish cities was left to market forces" (2012: 295) could hardly be more misleading. It also means that land privatization after the 1980 coup is central in ending the era of the gecekondu (see chapter 7).

3.6 MODERNIZATION AND DEPENDENCY THEORY AS
EXPLANATORY PARADIGMS

Last, in the eyes of social-science researchers in the mid-70s, how was the gece-kondu phenomenon comprehended? And did these analyses seep into the perceptions of activists and revolutionaries, informing their interpretations of the shantytowns that they sought to organize and conditioning their spatial politics there? In two relatively recent surveys of the changing representations of the gece-kondu in academic studies, both Erman (2001) and Akbulut and Başlık (2011) note that in the 1970s the structural-functionalism of 1960s modernization theories were challenged by more Marxian-informed dependency paradigms. My own selective reading of this massive literature essentially concurs with their summaries. Although *Birikim*, probably the most sophisticated journal of Turkish socialism, didn't publish a stand-alone article on the gecekondu from its founding in 1974 until its closure by the junta after the 1980 coup, in more general leftist accounts, dependent urbanization perspectives were influential in making sense of squatter settlements. In them the Turkish economy's underdevelopment, rapid industrialization, and peripheral incorporation into the capitalist world economy and division of labor determined the development of gecekondu housing conditions and style. Similarly, Marxian analysis of imperialism illuminated both typologies of the third-world city and their broad urban spatial features manifested through capital accumulation. For dependency theory, the primary drama of Istanbul relates to its role as key node of economic processes that in turn constitute its urban form *and* the subjectivity of its new inhabitants.

1970s modernization theory, too, understood the phenomenon of the gece-kondu in macroeconomic terms. The most well-known study in English, Kemal Karpat's *The Gecekondu*, begins by situating migration within the *longue duree* of the economic evolution of the Ottoman Empire, before explaining that "shanty-towns appear as the by-product of rapid economic development and industrialization, of changes in agriculture and shortage of housing" (1976: 23). Karpat's work is not Marxist or socialist: his description of Turkey's economic transformation or of its political economy does not mention imperialism, nor does his declaring of "occupational change" as the key feature of urbanization (p. 38) lead on to the use of the term *proletarianization*. Indeed, the urban integration of villagers equates to their upward mobility rather than to their exploitation, and industrial rather than capitalist is his preferred adjective for the emerging economy.

As in dependency theory, however, in many modernization accounts the structuring function of the economy in creating social agents' subjectivity is assumed. In much 1970s research on gecekondu settlements and inhabitants, the village and the city, defined via the lens of the inevitability (and desirability) of the modernization of the economy and its workers, were presented as two opposed yet mutually defining ends of a continuum, with the gecekondu situated uncomfortably somewhere in the middle. Spatial and temporal location was assumed to determine the social practices, identity, and consciousness of inhabitants. Fortunately, despite gece-kondu settlements being perceived literally as half-way houses between the village and the city, in the last analysis gecekondu dwellers had embarked upon a one-way journey, even if dysfunctional or arrested development was always a danger. Poverty was an accompanying feature of living in Istanbul's gecekondus, but for Karpat poverty was also transitional, if not for parents at least for their children. Villagers' "mentality" and lack of formal education loomed large in analysts' models, even as their existing repertoires of skill and knowledge were overlooked or demeaned. Thus, for Karpat, "the city in the third world, with its incipient technological, industrial and scientific orientation, stimulates innovation and creativity and gradually increases the migrant's capacity for emotional detachment, abstract thought, and empathy and his ability to create broader ties with individual and corporate entities"[21] (1976: 40).

Accordingly, a mismatch or a time lag between location and migrants' consciousness became a focus of complaint about gecekondu residents. Given modernization theory's prevailing assumptions, the relationship between gecekondu dwellers and the "city" was therefore a key focus of study, analyzed in the main as the question of squatter transformation and urban integration. Rural-urban migration was successful to the extent that peasants' *metamorphosed* into urban dwellers (Karpat 1976: 3), or disastrous to the extent that the city *metamorphosed* into the village. Comparison with the early work of the Manchester school ethnographers on Copperbelt industrialization in Africa is instructive: by contrast, Epstein in his work on urban communities in Zambia argues that in industrial settings African identities changed situationally, not progressively.[22] "The African in the rural area and in town are two different men. An African townsman is a townsman, an African miner is a miner," was the school's famous aphorism. As with other Manchester School anthropologists, Epstein became interested in urban networks and in new forms of invented "tribalism" created in the city. Thus, his is an early critique of modernization theory and its category of urban peasants, which interprets social practices (such as hometown associations) as rural "survivals." Similarly, Ferguson's 1999 study of Copperbelt postindustrialization, in the context of Zambia's "disconnection" from the global economy, argues that squatters' cultural practices are performative, not traditional,

21. Given the necessity in modern literature for characters with capacity for emotional detachment, empathy and self-determination vis-à-vis others, could the peasant be portrayed as a rounded character in fiction? Presumably for modernization theory the answer is no, unless as representative of stock social types, including as necessarily oppressed by landlords.

22. As Epstein argued, "There is a tendency to see the urban community as a kind of ragbag, drawing its populations from different regions and cultures, but having no social system of its own; with this approach there is associated a further tendency to interpret African behaviour in the towns against the background of the tribal system. When it comes to interpreting urban political life, this conceptual approach is not merely unhelpful, but even misleading" (1964: 88).

strategic tactics oriented to (but not determined by) the collapsing Zambian economy. By contrast, when explaining migrants' urbanization Karpat writes in the passive mood: "Village culture is changed and adapted to a new political culture, while
new identities are created in the transition to a new form of social and political
existence" (1976: 36, 37). This question of gecekondu dwellers' agency is important
when in chapter 5 we consider the relationship between them and leftist groups.

CONCLUSION

Three brief points conclude this discussion. First, despite emphasizing different
aspects of the origin, characteristics, and future of the gecekondu, modernization
and dependency perspectives also shared certain procedures. Both presented the
social changes they sought to analyze as inevitable, the long-term (and long-
distance) consequence of developments in Europe, either to be replicated or tran-
scended. In the process, each tended to overlook the role of theoretical discourses
in constituting the "reality" that they purported to explain. Thus, proponents
failed to distinguish between modernization as a theory of social evolution and
modernization as a strategic rhetoric used by the state to force change or as cultural capital appropriated by the middle class to forge self-distinction. Similarly,
leftist activist groups sought to make history even while claiming that their actions
aligned with history's objective unfolding. In both cases there was a confusion of
cause and effect. A further shared feature was their agreement concerning Kemalism, which as official state practice and ideology was assumed to be both outcome
of and midwife to Turkey's very modernization. Even as socialist intellectuals were
critical of particular social outcomes assumed as inevitable by modernization theory, the political movements informed by their theorizing did not conceive the
Kemalist reforms in Turkey as constituting a serious threat to social justice or
social peace. Most commonly, it was approved as a partial revolution (bourgeois,
nationalist or otherwise), requiring completion.

Secondly, what is striking about much shantytown research in the 1970s is their
examination and representation of the gecekondu suburbs in isolation from the
rest of the city. As Erman comments, for many researchers, empirical study of the
gecekondu and its inhabitants anxiously defined it against the modern urban city
and population, with no empirical investigation in turn about how modern residents actually lived. Urban peasants, then, were compared with "an idealized
image of urbanites" (2001: 991).[23] More significantly, the economism of both the

---

23. Typically, then, most gecekondu studies failed to incorporate into their study related developments in Istanbul's middle-class suburbs. In the 1960s and '70s they, too, were under reconstruction.
See Tekeli (2009) for description of the equally informal "yapsatçı" (build and sell) strategy of the
middle class in Istanbul.

modernization and dependency approaches induced in researchers and activists alike blindness to the state and to its *political* production of space in the city, in preference to developments articulated with the industrial or capitalist economy. Core aspects of Istanbul's form and its efficacy as a receptacle for political power—for example, its sites of nationalist signification or ethnic cleansing—were either taken for granted or remained "invisible" to scholars. The ongoing nationalist intentions informing the history of modernist architecture and planning in Istanbul, the city's political architecture (including its statuary), nationalist violence that sought to rid the city of non-Muslim minorities (including its renaming of streets in Istanbul), and the banning of nonauthorized signs of Islam from the semipublic space of state institutions—note the playing of classical music on Istanbul ferries—all of these were nonissues. Karpat's analysis of Turkish nationalism is a case in point—just as Kemalism claimed, he presents it as informed unproblematically by peasant and rural culture, a synthesis that gives it its (supposed) populist character. Nationalism as state enterprise and ideology is ignored, as is its chauvinistic Turkist (*Türkçülük*) dimensions. In brief, focus on the gecekondu and its residents' assimilable difference as peasant "others" produced deafness to the "Kemalist" character of the city and to its project of Turkifying inhabitants through the ritual use of space, in its educational curriculums, and as encoded in the built environment. This is important, because it was to these processes that rural migrants and their children were subjected.

Thirdly, in the easy light of retrospection, it is clear that in the 1970s most researchers perceived the lived experience of inhabitants in the gecekondu and their spatial furnishing of their own environments through the evolutionary assumptions of modernization or dependency theory discourses. Their patches of garden, the sparse affordances of houses, even their attendance at the cinema were of intense interest to researchers, but perhaps for the wrong reasons. Along with gecekondu women's wearing of headscarves or their long flower-decorated dresses, each were interpreted as signs of their (lack of) "modernization," just as for leftist groups their listening to *arabesk* music signaled their (lack of) political consciousness. Sitting cross-legged on the floor to eat (and not at table), or partaking from a common dish bespoke a (delayed) level of civilization. Interestingly, a focus on either the macroeconomic processes that facilitated the emergence of gecekondu suburbs or on phases of its (inhabitants') urbanization obscured one of their most salient characteristics, the shantytown's emergence as self-produced.

To adapt Bachelard again, *the house we make is an inhabited house.*[24] For residents themselves gecekondu environments were interactive places of neighborliness and solidarity, intersubjective conflict, and affective intensities, as well as being gendered sites of motility and organization. They were experienced through

24. Cf. Bachelard: "The house we were born in is an inhabited house" (1994: 14).

the weather, and their understanding required a phenomenology of rain and heat: huddled around a stove; bed-sharing for warmth; walking, mud, and (precious) shoes; tea with kin and relatives on the "porch" in spring; ice in winter; marriage arrangements made at the communal water tap; threats of demolition. In her review essay on the literature of gecekondu districts, Erman stresses the middle-class nature of researchers as an important factor in their representations of the gecekondu "other," even as she presumes she can escape such class determinism by simply identifying its existence. Although class habitus may be a factor in research-ers' prejudgments, equally important in understanding the features of such writ-ing is the availability of theoretical paradigms for scholars' description and analy-sis of social relations, as well as these paradigms' articulation with Kemalism, the official philosophy of history of the Turkish Republic.

Nevertheless, despite my "wisdom" after these acts (of research and writing), one of the virtues of the studies of gecekondu in Istanbul in the 1970s is their por-trait of suburbs and inhabitants that present us with an informed if particular description of the city that leftist and rightist groups sought to harness and mobi-lize. Insightfully prejudiced, the literature provided activists with an analysis of the generation and characteristics of those places that their hope was to revolutionize.

In the next four chapters we turn to the spatial practices of activists themselves, directing our attention away from how Istanbul came to be the way it was to how militants used and transformed it, in order to better understand its recent political history.

4

Inscription, Sound, Violence

*Militant Repertoires and the Production of Space
in Istanbul, 1974–1980*

> We would often make a "küçük bombalı pankart" [banner with a small
> bomb], one not easily taken down, where we would sew the homemade bomb
> into the cloth so it could be seen, saying "'Yaşasın 1 Mayıs," or "Tek Yol
> Devrim" [Long Live May First, or One Path, Revolution]. The police couldn't
> take it down until the bomb squad came, so it would stay there for people to
> read. We would also record a tape, saying what we were doing, and then
> leave it playing so that people could hear. The cassette player would be near
> the bomb so it couldn't be stopped. The city wasn't as noisy then, a small
> sound could reverberate.
>
> —HANDE, THKP-C

Chapters 4 and 5 aim to give readers an ethnographic account of activists' spatial
practices, sensing of place, and politicizing of institutions in Istanbul from the year
1974 until the military coup in 1980. What did they make the city sound like? How
did it appear? Which tactics did they devise to *augment* its sounds and appearances, modifying its streets and public spaces as foretaste of a transformed society?
What of insurgents' creating a new political geography in Istanbul, and their use of
space to communicate, to intimidate, or to foster community action, especially in
the *gecekondu* suburbs, in factories and workplaces, and in municipal activities?
How might we describe their emerging revolutionary *habitus*—their dispositions,
ethics, and moods? And how did their educated senses perceive new affordances
for political practice in urban environments, in the process transforming their
experiences of such places? In brief, what of activists' own production of space?

To explore all this, in this chapter I present an analytic description of activists'
memories of pre-coup Istanbul, oriented to what I have called their spatial politics.
In order to appreciate the creativity of their revolutionary activism, the chapter
identifies and discusses a rich and interlocking repertoire of activists' "tactics of
space" (de Certeau 1984: 93, 94). Minimally these included the inscribing of space,

or visual politics (4.1); the generation of sound, or sonic politics (4.2); the occupation and transformation of space, including of gecekondu, urban sites, factories, and state institutions (4.3); and the performance of violence as a mode of self-defense and of intimidation (4.4). Chapter 5 continues this investigation but concentrates on the political and ethical engagements of militant groups in three more delimited regions of Istanbul, in shantytowns or squatter settlements, in factories, and at the municipal level.

In chapter 1 I noted that interviews with activists were a prime source of knowledge for my assertions about, and reconstruction of, the city. In the material below I *disaggregate* from partisans' narratives four major modes of politico-spatial practice, aware, of course, that in reality militants engaged the city simultaneously through "myriad modes of concrete action" (Casey 1996: 18), experiencing it as multisensory *interplay* of sounds, voices, visions, people, and events. This does not mean that in this interplay each of these presences was always perceived clearly. As Nuriye (THKP-C) said, "After 1977 the city was surreal, as though we were living in a novel." Militants experienced the city as chaotic, generated out of an escalating class struggle, the politicizing of everyday spaces, and the confronting experience of aggressive, interacting bodies—an "Unreal City."[1] Its efflorescing factions (even among the police), asserted their distinctive ideological programs, dismissing all others', while resembling—contradicting such assertions—many of their rivals' political practices. Given that in the city the prime "spaces" for activism were limited, it was not surprising that conflict over their affordances became endemic. Sometimes this was violence unto death, and the chapter concludes by exploring certain perceptions of death and dying expressed by the revolutionary movement in obituaries and family statements.

4.1 VISUAL POLITICS

Militants remembered a constant struggle to inscribe their groups' presence in urban space, to dominate the visual qualities of places in the form of graffiti, posters, or "wall newspapers." The result was a ceaseless "slogan competition" between leftists and extreme nationalists, and among leftist groups themselves. The hailing and educating of attention directed toward passers-by took ingenious forms, as Hande's description of a "small bomb placard" in the epigraph above shows. Marking the built environment was understood to be a vital activity, and accordingly expeditions to intervene in it were highly planned: "The organization would announce a campaign for all of Turkey, often on an anniversary or some other important date. The leadership made the decision. We would leave in a group of fifteen people each with a job. There were wall-writers—those with good handwriting skills—paint carriers,

1. As T. S. Eliot (1934) describes London in his poem *The Wasteland*.

people who would stick up the posters, brush-carriers, lookouts, and guards, everyone was carrying weapons, like sticks. Normally the campaign wouldn't be in your own suburb but in an MHP-controlled one or in the locality of a rival leftist group antagonistic to your own" (Orhan, HK).

Activists now had mixed opinions about this visual occupation of places. Tevfik, an activist from the youth wing of the TKP, described one group's covering over the posters of another group to be like a dog pissing, leaving his mark everywhere. For others, writing on walls was communication, propaganda, a method of explaining themselves, of claiming ownership of a place, of showing you weren't scared, or of saying "we control the suburb." Ex-MHP militant Mehmet noted that marked space was a sign of authority: "Slogans say, 'I exist.'" He claimed that for leftist groups, pasting notices was a good form of education: first fourteen- to fifteen-year-old youths would hang up posters, and get arrested and perhaps beaten; by seventeen or eighteen they would develop into hardened militants. But every group did the same. Fractions learned political skills and strategies from each other, adapting an international repertoire of urban protest tactics for the peculiarities of the city. "Istanbul now has no garden walls," said Nuriye (THKP-C), "nor empty lots. Advertising has taken over the city."

Many partisans could tell at a glance who controlled a place by the slogans inscribed on its walls. Although there were general slogans shared by more than one group—many factions chanted "Nazım aramızda" (Nazım [Hikmet, the famous communist poet] is with us)—there were also more specific slogans used only by certain groups to proclaim themselves and their particular political stance. Slogans delivered succinct political programs. Groups' slogans would also change over time, in response to political events or to signal historical developments.

What did militants remember about them? According to interviewees, notable slogans of HK included "Faşizme ölüm, halka hürriyet" (Death to fascism, freedom to the people). TKP partisans used the phrases "Faşizme geçit yok" (No passage to fascism), "Yaşasın Ulusal Demokratik Cephesi" (Long live the National Democratic Front), "Yaşasın DİSK" (Long live DİSK) or "Fabrikalar kalemiz" (Factories are our castle). For Dev-Yol/Dev-Sol activists the rhyming slogan "Mahir, Hüseyin, Ulaş: Kurtuluşa kadar savaş" (Mahir, Hüseyin, Ulaş: War until liberation) often signaled the beginning of some kind of skirmish. "Kahrolsun faşizm" (Down with fascism), "Tek Yol Devrim" (One path, revolution) and "Kahrolsun oligarki" (Down with oligarchy) were also popular. "Halklara özgürlük" (Freedom to peoples) signaled their willingness to support the Kurdish people in their struggle against the ethnic-nationalist oppression (milli baskı) of the oligarchy. According to Bülent, Kurtuluş rejected the DY slogan lauding legendary figures from the organization's history as not being sufficiently class based, in preference for "Faşizme karşı omuz omuza" (Shoulder to shoulder against fascism). Aydınlık, ironically described by one of my MHP interviewees as "MİT's [National Intelligence Organization] communists," changed their slogans over time, but Orhan remembered "*Dördüncü ordu Kars'a*" (The fourth army to Kars [a town in the east]), consistent with their position that the Soviet Union was the greater imperialist threat to Turkey. Then there was the flexibility of one of the main ülkücü slogans: "*Beyazıt komünistlere mezar olacak*" (Beyazıt [or Fatih, Istanbul, or Turkey, etc.] will be the grave of communists). And Ziya remembered a slogan of the Akıncı, the youth wing of the MSP: "*Akıncılar akında, zaferleri yakında*" (The Akıncılar are on the move, victory is coming). Another was the cry, "*Laik devlet, yıkılacak elbet*" (The secular state will collapse, certainly).

Visual politics took other forms as well. Ferhat (Kurtuluş) recalled draping the Turkish flag on the coffin of killed activists, to proclaim that "we are its true representatives." Partisans' bodies, too, enacted a visual politics, their embodied revolutionary deportment and style oriented toward a guerrilla war of performance. In Istanbul activists were aware of differences in presentation between supporters of the more union-focused TKP and partisans of the "urban guerrilla" factions (such as THKP-C, HK, Dev-Sol and Halk Birliği [People's Union]). "We wore olive-green parkas, and military boots. Ironically, we bought them cheap from the US army surplus base halfway between İzmit and Bursa, two hours on the ferry. Boots meant South American revolutionaries: they were like a uniform. But TKP people were more middle class; they didn't wear a uniform," explained Ali from Dev-Sol.

4.2 SONIC POLITICS

Slogans defined and divided both spaces and groups. Yet slogans were voiced as well as painted. Thus, equally important was their *sonorous* force, their ability to drown out other sounds (or slogans), their tempo that partisans used to structure time and movement, and the sometimes physically pleasurable discomfort of their loudness. Rhythmic chanted slogans constituted the distinction between a protest and a crowd. Indeed, for the purposes of a temporary occupation of place, sonic graffiti were more important than posters or banners. Sounded slogans were at the forefront of militant groups' fabrication of acoustic space. They were chanted at meetings, funerals, marches, and occupations. Slogans' aural encroachment on the city meant that often groups could be heard and not seen, their sonic presence causing excitement or dread in listeners. For militants the affective force of sounds was determined by their degree of agency in creating them—as in the difference between singing and hearing the partisan songs of others, or between firing a gun and being fired upon.

Sometimes slogans had to be managed to temper their aural-spatial efficacy, or to prevent their "sabotaging" of solidarity between groups in joint actions against fascism. Reporting on a forum organized by forty-one "revolutionary" organizations on the topic "An Independent Turkey,"[2] *Cumhuriyet* newspaper informed readers that along with the aim of formulating common actions and principles, "shared slogans were agreed upon and that apart from these, other slogans were not to be used" (2 October, 1977). The slogans awarded joint assent included "*NATO'ya hayır*" (No to NATO), "*Üslere hayır*" (No to military bases), "*NATO emperyalizmin silahlı gücüdür*" (NATO is the armed force of imperialism), "*Kahrolsun emperyalizm ve şovenizm*" (Down with imperialism and chauvinism), "*Yaşasın bağımsızlık ve demokrasi mücadelesi*" (Long live independence and the struggle for democracy), and "*Bağımsız Türkiye, bağımsız Kıbrıs*" (Independent Turkey, independent Cyprus). Slogans had to support the broad principles adhered to by the newly formed political platform, including anti-imperialism, anti-chauvinism, and anti-fascism.

Acoustic presence, then, was indispensable for the assertion of authority over place. Politics happened in sound. Alongside efforts to dominate the aural qualities of places, music, dancing the *halay*, and speeches were central to militant groups' socializing and political organizing. Indeed, participation in activist groups involved induction into a specific sonic world. Although many factions listened to and sang some of the same music, like everything else at that time (including the gecekondu suburbs), certain songs and marches were parceled out among groups. Levent (HK) noted that they listened to the legendary Turkish folk music performer Ruhi Su (1912–1985), "but not too much! He was more TİP, TKP." Ülkücü militants sang Turkist marches. Similarly, interviewees reported that genres of music and even particular musical instruments were seen as politically charged. For example, despite (or because of) its long association with the Mevlevi Sufi lodges, people who played the *ney* (end-blown reed flute) had a reputation for being cultural conservatives. Less radical leftists (CHP social democrats) perceived listening to the piano or to "Western" music as progressive, while certain militant socialist factions had a prejudice against Western rock music: "we said the Beatles were imperialist," reported Kenan (HK). He went on to say that he was hated in his organization for playing the guitar, and even thought of quitting it to play the *saz*. The nationalists disliked the piano, because of its culturally foreign overtones—indeed, for some activists in the ülkücü movement, the piano (like communism) was declared essentially non-Turkish. Non-Turkish objects (and people) were matter out of place, and merited defilement or destruction: Murat remembers how in his Education Faculty an ülkücü militant defecated on top of a piano, scrawling "*gavur icadı*" (invention of non-believers) above it on the wall.

By contrast, leftists favored *bağlama* music, and the composing of new lyrics for existing Alevi and other folk songs (*türkü*). Haydar remembered that some of the choruses were in Arabic. New verses were made about factions' famous martyrs

2. Among participating groups were Professional Chambers (Teachers, Civil Servants), People's Houses Coordinators Council, and even the Cartoonists Association.

(i.e., Deniz Gezmiş). A number of activists mentioned Aşık (Minstrel) Veysel from the East (who was blind), or Aşık Mahsuni, with his big moustache, who would play at different leftist meetings wearing *şalvar* (baggy trousers). According to Serdar (Kurtuluş), in the mid-1970s Anatolian rock emerged, with Cem Karaca playing at leftist meetings and concerts. Indeed, according to Martin Stokes (1999: 135), Cem Karaca's recording of Nazım Hikmet's poem "1 Mayıs" was the reason for his fleeing from Istanbul in 1979, after being threatened with imprisonment. For Orhan, Aydınlık members, too, sang Cem Karaca songs, as well as the 1 May March, the Austrian workers march, and illegal Zülfü Livaneli songs. He noted that the Austrian workers march in its Western key was hard to sing, as you couldn't play it with the *saz*.

When did militants sing? According to Hilmi (*Halk Sesi* journal [*People's Voice*]) they sang in groups, at public meetings at night, when going on the bus or sitting on the ferry, and at commemorations. Along with slogans, songs constituted condensed systems of knowledge. Singing possessed places while creating motivation and morale. "We needed to be ready. Singing was saying, 'I'm here.'" Filiz (THKP-C) recalls how in response to the Turizm tea garden bombing in Kadıköy, a large group of protestors marched from Kadıköy to Üsküdar to occupy the square, singing and shouting slogans all the way. Üsküdar with its Türk Ocağı was perceived to be an MHP stronghold. Ex-ülkücü Can said that three or four times a year they would arrange an evening of music, for morale and enjoyment. They would call a Turkish folk musician—"someone close to them"—either to the party headquarters or to a casino on Vatan Caddesi. Hüseyin (Kurtuluş) reported the same organizing of a "meeting with music," but used the word *halk ozanı* (people's bard or minstrel) to describe the musician.

Activists remembered that before the coup it was a time for *talking fearlessly*, in meetings and at organized events in evenings. In any particular week, one group or other would organize a "campaign" in celebration of an important figure or event. Speechmaking, then, was a valued skill. Dilek (THKP-C) explained how at high school on an important day—say the anniversary of the death of Mahir Çayan—they would suddenly open the door of a classroom and go inside. "'Pardon Hodja,' we would announce, and begin to talk. The strange thing was, next day you would stand up in front of the same teacher to do an oral exam." Members of Dilek's youth group would stand up in the cinema and give a "pirate" speech, with three or four observers watching the audience for trouble. Mehmet Metiner (Akıncılar) remembers regularly visiting the *kahvehane* (coffeehouses) in Süleymaniye, Vefa, and Unkapanı in the evenings: "'Merhaba Friends,' we would say to greet them, then turn off the television, request that they leave their games, and then begin our speech. People had no choice but to listen" (2008: 75).

Factions organized "pirate" protests or events. "We would get up and make a speech after blocking the street. Five hundred people would emerge from the side streets, cut the road. This talk was mainly directed to us, as other people were afraid of trouble" (Mahsis, Kurtuluş). Filiz (THKP-C) said the same thing, reporting that the organization would send word around that at this time and place there would be a pirate meeting. "Suddenly two or three hundred people would gather, fire guns in the air, make some speeches, shout slogans and then disperse before the police could do anything." Ferhat noted how his group (THKO-TDY [Turkish Peoples Liberation Army—Turkish Revolutionary Path]) would deliver a "shock talk" on the train from Zeytinburnu to Sirkeci. Haydar (close to TKP) claimed that unionists had to be good at making speeches, to be "big men with loud voices."

The ülkücü, too, remembered talking fearlessly, indeed remembered being the "voice of the Turkish people." In an article in the newspaper *Haberiniz* on the 1970s in Istanbul, Mehmet Sayın recalls a protest organized by Istanbul activists in response to the assassinations of the Turkish ambassadors to Vienna and Paris by the Armenian group Asala in late 1975:

> We Istanbul ülkücüler showed a sudden reaction against these two assassinations as the voice of the Turkish nation. We didn't wait for anyone's command but organized the protest on our own initiative. The first walk occurred in the evening, from Edirne lodgment to Beyazıt. The second march happened a day later and was much noisier and more crowded; we mobilized thousands of students from a number of Istanbul schools and university lodgments. Passing Sultanahmet, all of a sudden we ran inside Ayasofya. We did it so quickly that even the police didn't have time to take precautions. (*Haberiniz* 11 February, 2013)

Violating the church/museum of Ayasofya, even temporarily, was performed as a spontaneous revenge act by Turkish nationalists against Armenians and other Christian minorities in Istanbul, striking at the assumed core of that group's self-identity/being, as we have seen in the burning of Istanbul's churches in the state-sponsored pogrom in 1955. Indeed, throughout the decade the *occupying* of what we can now also identify as "acoustic spaces" (Carpenter 1960) was a vital spatial tactic, as was the violent *breaking* of another group's occupying of place.

4.3 OCCUPYING SPACE

Occupying and modifying place involved spatial, sonic, and temporal dimensions, and occurred on both a micro and macro scale. Militants might make an instant speech to passengers on a bus or patrons in the cinema; temporarily block a corridor; briefly sit-in on a busy thoroughfare; or slip into Ayasofya. By contrast, a more permanent takeover of an institution or a suburb necessitated confrontation with its occupying group: "Sometime in 1978, *Dev Sol* activists cut the main street of Gültepe off by using two *tır* [trucks]. Before then, Gültepe was under control of the MHP, and the shopkeepers were sympathizers. For three or four days there was fighting, and then the area changed to be under leftist control [*iktidar*], as they threw out the MHP. They carried sticks and beat people" (Ömer, Dev-Sol).

Both physical and symbolic violence were required to maintain the advantages associated with possession and use of territory, institutions or urban sites. Sometimes coalitions of groups would organize a major occupation of a place (perhaps on an important anniversary) or close an institution down (boycott it) by preventing others from accessing it. Şahin (*Aydınlık*) related how when you gained control of a place (*hakimiyet olduğu zaman*) you would start to clean out other groups, to stop them from organizing there. Acoustic cohabitation, both temporarily and over a longer time period, became problematic. There was a fear that militants would be enticed away by another faction and leave their own.

If members of a faction couldn't break another party's occupation of place, they couldn't enter it or use it. High schools (*lise*) were a prime example. Many students were politically active and factionalized—Hamit Bozarslan calls youth in the late 1970s "precociously politicized" (2012: 8)—and over time schools in certain districts became dominated by either the ülkücü or by leftist groups. Authority over a school did not happen by chance. Political factions and parties targeted students, in a variety of ways. Hüseyin (Kurtuluş) explained how his movement sought to organize lise students into Dev-Lis (Revolutionary High School Students):

> We rented an office in Aksaray, and then had to find a way to get into the schools so we could tell students about what we were doing. To do so I had the idea of selling badges with the name of the school on them, and bags with school name or student's name on them. We soon had access to schools and began to sell in the canteen. We were crafty. After six months we had two hundred members of the *dernek*. We taught students how to obtain student representation in school, we gave courses, one class after the other, and sold journals. In 1974 the Maoists set up their lise organization, named Mem Der.

Mebuse (THKP-C) reported that if her organization "knew a school was controlled by the ülkücü they might enroll ten students there, then twenty the next year, who'd lay low at first or quietly start to organize a confrontation." MHP ensured their control of a school by having party activists wait at the school gates and even walk around the corridors, all with the sanction of sympathetic police. Teachers would be intimidated too, afraid of being killed, although loyalty to their own political denomination might come to the fore in certain ways. One interviewee remembered being forced to march around his high school on 3 Mayıs Türkçülük Günü (3 May, Turkism Day) by the "fascists." Another claimed that because he played the *ney* his leftist literature teacher failed him, as "everyone 'knew' that only reactionaries played the *ney*. I wanted to read Namık Kemal but he made me summarize Dostoevsky." A third recalled being forced to leave Istanbul for a few months after hearing that she had become a rightist target. When she came back two friends (with guns) would pick her up to go to school.

Once a group gained control over a school, studying there became impossible for students aligned with other parties, as an interview with students from Demirli-bahçe Meslek Yüksek Okulu printed in *Cumhuriyet* newspaper shows:

The ülkücüler extort money from students and no one knows where the money is spent. Every day for an hour before lessons fascist marches are sung. The people who make us sing these marches are not from the school. And they force us to buy the book *Marşlarımız* [Our marches]. At the same time, you have five days in which to learn by heart the marches; they say that if you don't know them, then you will be beaten. Everyone is forced to wear the *bozkurt* rosette. In the corridors of the school you are forced to buy the fascist journal. Progressive students are threatened, and for this reason lots of students have left the school. Our security and our freedom to learn don't exist under these conditions. (*Cumhuriyet* 1977, October 11)

By contrast, according to Süleyman, Darüşşafaka was a leftist school, with three main left groups dominant, Halkın Yolu (People's Way); Kurtuluş (Sosyalist Dergi Çevresi); and İGD.[3] Yet despite this, "there was no possibility of separatism at school, as school gave us a place to sleep and eat and clothes. The school was in the suburb of Çarsamba (Fatih), an area of MSP influence but also with an active CHP group in the mid-seventies and a *dernek* of Halkın Yolu. For a period in 1978 we stood sentry on the *yurt* to protect students from attack."

University faculties, and equally significantly university lodgments, became prizes to be taken and held. One activist recalled how the left reclaimed Vatan Mühendislik (a student lodgment in Fatih) from the MHP in 1978—his phrase was "we broke the occupation [*işgal kırdık*]; the place resembled a field of war" (Mesut, Dev-Sol). According to activists, leftist groups controlled most of the lodgments in Beyazıt, unlike those in Zeytinburnu. Ömer (MHP) noted that in Şehremini the Trabzon Talebe Yurdu was controlled by the rightists, while on the opposite side of the street the Niğde Yurdu was under the authority of leftists: "they could fire guns at each other from the windows." Similarly, activists remembered which factions dominated which universities: ITU was controlled by leftist groups but was often the target of rightist violence, being in the center of Istanbul. Boğaziçi was not overly politicized—there were few ülkücü students there—but there were two canteens, used by normal and leftist students respectively. Istanbul University was mixed but the nationalists had taken over the literature, and for a time the economics, faculties.

The (Ataturk) Institutes of Education (Atatürk Eğitim Enstitüsü) for training high school teachers were particularly dangerous places to study, being managed by the National Education Ministry (MEB), which came under control of the MHP in the National Front Government. Ayşe remembers how after 1977 ülkücü

---

3. Darüşşafaka is a well-known nongovernment school established in the nineteenth century for children with no fathers.

students took control of the Atatürk Eğitim Enstitüsü at Marmara University, when the MEB began to enroll right-wing students there via oral exams who didn't have the required points to study. According to Faruk (Dev-Yol), these were often MHP supporters, so that the balance at the institutes changed and leftist students couldn't attend classes: "The MHP were armed with guns. They checked people's identity, and controlled the coffee houses opposite the school. The school became their castle, and they established a small *mescit* [prayer room] there. If you weren't with them, you must have been against them so it was hard to study. They would put out a *Cumhuriyet* newspaper and see who would pick it up, then they would beat them. Or they asked, 'Are you a fascist or a leftist?' If you said, 'I'm a fascist,' they would beat you. They called themselves nationalists [*milliyetçi*] or idealists [*ülkücü*]."

Things improved for leftist students in 1978 with the forming of the new Ecevit government. The space of the school was divided temporally: leftists had their lessons in the morning and rightists in the afternoon, which would be swapped around each week. Ayşe remembers that the school was bombed in 1979, killing a teacher and a student, after which the "fascists" were expelled and leftist students given accelerated lessons to graduate.

Land and suburbs were occupied, as were factories. Hüseyin, activist for a textile union, explained how if workers were unable to access rights already granted, they would barricade themselves inside the factory. For Hakan (TKP), the Black Sea town of Fatsa, where a coalition of leftist groups led by Dev-Sol members controlled the council, was a true occupation, because they had won the election. State bureaucracies or institutions, too, were parceled out and occupied by members of political parties, especially with the rapid change of governments in the late 1970s. To give just one example, *Cumhuriyet* newspaper reported on October 9 that after the MHP gained control of the Ministry of Commerce in 1977, their cadres took over administration of the state-owned Tariş factories (that processed agricultural products such as sultanas and olive oil) in Izmir.

Perhaps most significantly, interviews revealed the critical relationship between occupation of institutions and the shifting political loyalties of districts. Political factions' control over "neutral" facilities (schools, student lodgments, universities, People's Houses, factories, cafes) increased their ability to organize a political campaign in their immediate region. Thus, on the one hand, the occupation of a school, a hostel or a university campus/building and the expelling of rival groups from it influenced the character of a suburb, as did the unionization of a factory by one group or another. Hilmi (Dev-Sol) who grew up in Fatih sketched out the process there: "Fatih became more conservative after 1975. The history was like this: around that time a number of yurts (student housing facilities) opened in the district of the school. First the Vatan Mühendislik was taken over by the MHP, then Edirne Kapı Yurdu, then Erzurum Talebe Yurdu. After that, the rightists occupied Vatan Lisesi in 1977." On the other hand, the politicized nature of the suburb was reflected in the political groupings dominant in the local school. "Arrows" of political influence flowed both ways. The transformation of places that began with their occupation and continued with the militant performance of a repertoire of educational, sonic, and visual practices in them—slogans, music, speeches, marches, commemorations, graffiti and so on—made them beachheads in the urban field, starting points of attempts to make not a socialist city but a city socialist, or to unmake it.

4.4 VIOLENCE AS SPATIAL PRACTICE

According to interviewees, in these years the threat, experience, and perpetration of physical violence and even the risk of violent death became a prime feature of activists' lives in Istanbul. After 1975, even those leftist groups that did not accept the need for armed struggle began to arm themselves in response to the increase in attacks on unionists and activists. For Hüseyin (Aydınlık), the spread of guns transformed the city into a place of "civil war." Hospitals, the city morgue (in those years situated opposite Gülhane Park's upper gates), and cemeteries became well-known places, with every death turned into a political event or demonstration. *Günaydın* journalist Kadir Can, whose 2011 book *12 Eylül 1980: Akıl Tutulması* (12 September 1980: The eclipse of the mind) presents the most revealing photographs of the period, recalled that in 1975 fifty thousand people would attend the death of a leftist, and twenty people gather for the death of someone from the right. Yet later the nationalists' funerals attracted huge crowds also. His terse comment in our interview was that "the left created its own monster." Awash with threats, fearlessness, hopes, grief, and promise, intersubjective political life in Istanbul was powerfully affecting: participation in funerals, in commemorative/protest marches, in sit-ins and protests brought danger and violence to consciousness, becoming central in modifying the urban perception of militants (and their families) in their embodied encounter with the city. Here, as Bachelard puts it (1994: 67), "consciousness dominates memory."

Violence as a spatial tactic, then, was a central generator of urban space and of people's perceptions of the city. How might we account for its development? As we have seen, violence was related to the occupation and control of space/institutions. "Every organization or group had a bomb maker, educated somehow. We threw bombs to stop a group moving into a place. If they rented a flat, we would throw a Molotov through the window" (Fırat, TKP-ML [Turkish Communist Party-Marxist Leninist]). Equally importantly, violence was pragmatic. Self-defense was necessary. Leftist gecekondu established defense committees, sometimes made-up of members from different groups and local associations, to protect themselves against the attacks of MHP "commandos." Sentries were posted at the entrance of suburbs (as well as on the roof of student residences). In certain Anatolian towns, as well as in a number of suburbs in Istanbul (i.e., in Çayan), Dev-Yol/Dev-Sol established Armed Struggle Units against Fascist Terror (Faşist Teröre Karşı Silahlı Mücadele Ekibi, or FTKSME), self-authorized to check the identities of people wishing to enter in order to protect residents against MHP death squads.

Gecekondu settled by Alevi Muslims were especially vulnerable to becoming targets of anti-leftist violence pursued by militants of the MHP, who in their sectarian appeal to Sunni Turks began to associate Alevism and Alevis with leftist politics. To give just one example, in a pamphlet distributed in Sivas in September 1978 three months before their brutal massacre of Alevis in Maraş, the MHP took it upon themselves to warn residents, saying, "Beware Alevi! Do not be used as an instrument; take lessons from history. Once upon a time you used to utter, 'Shah, Shah.' Now it is not toward the Shah, but toward communism that you are heading. We will absolutely prevent this move" (Sinclair-Webb 2003: 216).

In short, much leftist violence was implicated in a defensive urban struggle waged against the MHP's para-military forces. For some of my leftist interviewees, the MHP's escalation of *degrees* of violence over the decade, as seen in the bloody killing of non-activist women and children at Maraş, or in the abduction and torturing to death of eight TİP activists in Bahçelievler, was intended to both provoke and justify a military coup, as well as to intimidate and terrify locals so that uncommitted gecekondu inhabitants became too scared to participate in leftist actions. Hüseyin (Aydınlık) attributed the same logic to the "big show killings by MIT, say of Abdi İpekçi." To that extent, rightist violence had a "rational," instrumental character, even as the targets chosen by it revealed something essential about the ideological categories and affective commitments of its perpetrators as well.

As violence increased, activists described its emotional normalization. Kadir (HK) remembered a culture of violence: "You accepted death; if a friend died you were sad but not destroyed. Once you accepted that violence could happen to you, you also accepted that you, too, could do it, because you were brave." Interviewees commented how quickly fighting became routine or was seen as natural: accordingly, when something happened, partisans were not too upset, as they accepted that activism had a cost. Reha (MHP) claimed that they weren't scared of death. This lack of fear or of self-mercy encouraged by the low-level civil war extended to opponents. Ümit (HK) remembered how he perceived enemies: "We didn't think they had a personality [şahsiyet]. We beat up people carrying an MHP newspaper," while Hilmi (Kurtuluş) reported that "it was considered a virtue to annihilate a fascist."

However, leftist groups were also violent toward each other. Sometimes the killing of an activist from a different leftist faction resulted in a bitter enmity, so that those groups would never work together or let opposing partisans enter areas under their control. At other times, even the [once] closest of leftist organizations entered into rivalry and competition with each other. For example, Ali Yıldız (2011) recounts a violent encounter in 1978 in Çayan Mahallesi in Nurtepe between Dev-Yol and Dev-Sol militants, despite the fact that both groups traced their political lineage back to Mahir Çayan and to THKP-C, and that together activists from both movements had helped establish the suburb before the split between them. Haydar (TKP) remembered an event in 1978, when a partisan left TİKKO (Turkish Workers and Peasants Liberation Army) and started to attend events in Küçükçekmece People's House, controlled by the İGD. When he was killed, "there was a huge funeral at the Cemevi, and the hardening of attitudes against MHP for the murder. Later someone confessed that TİKKO did it. So we had the same person and two murderers [*aynı insan iki katil*]! This was a political killing; its aim was to cause segregation and polarization."

Interviewees perceived that other emotions and ideals, too, were connected to violence, describing the emergence of a "hero" culture, in which fighting became a challenge between different factions. In conflicts between groups, good fighters went at the front. In an anecdote referencing his experience at Boğaziçi University, Erdoğan (HK) remembered the day Aydınlık partisans put up a poster that called Dev Sol fascist:

> Two Dev Sol students tried to take it down but were outnumbered. The next day ten Dev Sol members came from ITU to Boğaziçi, wearing black coats and carrying guns. They entered the campus looking for a fight. By chance, there was a student election that day, and political students were all in a large hall, hundreds of them. The vote turned into a fight between a coalition of Aydınlık and CHP, against others. The Dev-Sol people first went to the canteen and ripped down all the posters—we had an agreement among ourselves not to do that. They then came in to the hall just as the argument was starting. We had another agreement not to use guns. Their leader, not recognizing his enemies [Aydınlık people], grabbed someone, put a gun to his forehead and screamed, "Are you a fascist?" We understood something was wrong, and people began to run outside. The leader jumped onto the stage and yelled, "Isn't there a patriot in this room? Let them stay and fight."

The story above is revealing. In shouting out "Let's fight" (*dövüşelim*)—and not "I will beat you" (*seni döveceğim*)—the activist showed how fighting was sometimes perceived as a challenge or contest. Further, a number of activists drew attention to the gendered distribution of violence, as well as to its masculine character. Fighting occurred between young men. Akın (İGD) explained how he was shot:

> İGD hired a cinema to hold a Nazım Hikmet memorial night. We stuck our posters up all over the city. Some days later activists from SGB (Socialist Youth Association) pasted over our posters. They were the closest leftist group to us! We couldn't allow this, so we broke into their office and stuck posters on their windows, doors and tables. A few days later they attacked our headquarters, marching down the street

with revolvers shouting 'Allah, Allah'. It was nothing more than masculinity. I was shot three times. After getting out of hospital I left the group, against the consent of our leader.

Given the high possibility of a violent encounter in the city, one vital activity involved partisans in the assembling of a micro-geographical knowledge of places, and the developing of a political-spatial intuition to minimize risk. Moving around the city required its careful observation, to notice if fresh slogans had appeared or if a civil society group had opened up a new "office." Partisans commented that they knew where to walk, which way to pass, and who controlled what, a hard-earned knowledge gained from political engagements in the urban arena. In an environment perceived as a dynamic field of threats and safety, obstacles had to be evaded as often as removed. Bülent (Partisan Yolu) knew that navigating Beyazıt Square (Meydanı) was rather dangerous: "To get our credit for student support we had to walk up a nearby street. A building (billiard saloon) in that street was used by the ülkücüler, so we had to go past it in a large group, with five or six people carrying weapons in their back pockets." Similarly, according to Ümit (THKO-TDY), "We knew the city because we did research on it for our own safety. Before speaking on the train, we had carefully calculated the time it took to move between stations. If it was two minutes, we prepared a two-minute speech. It was dangerous to not finish and stay in the carriage. We would get off the train to check all the exits from a station to know how to escape, and to see which groups were in control. If something unforeseen happened, escape routes from each station had been prepared well in advance."

Despite precautions, things still did go wrong. Süleyman (MHP) recalled the time he and his friends got on the wrong ferry: "It was full of leftists. We started singing our marches, nonstop, until we reached the other side, then stayed on the ferry and went back again." In a city reverberant with the songs, speeches and slogans of rival groups, singing gathered courage even as it asserted presence. In his work with rainforest Papuans, Feld argues for the importance of their "acoustic knowing," and of "sonic awareness as potent shaping force in how people make sense of experience" (1996: 97). In Istanbul, for those with ears to hear, sound, too, revealed political affiliation, and ideology explained itself in music. Yet despite militants' acoustic apprehension of the city, sometimes their sonic expertise was of no use. Ergun remembered how a friend of his was accosted by militants upon getting off a bus: "'Which side are you on?,'" they demanded to know. Scared and unsure [of their affiliation], he joked, "'Beşiktaşlıyım' [I'm with Beşiktaş (football club)]. They shot him in the head. His mother never recovered." He stopped for a moment. "I still feel sad, and remember him fondly." And in Jenny White's (2002) recounting of an awful sledgehammer attack on a student by MHP militants, she tells how the sweating victim sensed his impending fate immediately upon hearing the opening notes of an ülkücü march struck up behind him from the bus's back seat, which informed him, too late, that he had boarded the wrong one.

Violent Times

How did writers at the time explain the rapid increase in the exposure to and use of violence while trying to perceptually reckon with its experience? In an influential article—at least for an English-speaking audience—entitled "Youth and Violence in Turkey," sociologist Şerif Mardin offered a complex cultural-cum-psychological explanation for the [apparent] explosion of violence between student groups in the late 1970s. In it he relates urban youth violence to a long-term cultural dislocation unfolding in the passage from Ottoman Empire to Turkish Republic that especially "marked" the perpetrators of that violence (1978: 235). He asserts, too, the failure of modernist Kemalism to provide a "psychological anchor" for the masses of young people migrating to or born in Istanbul's burgeoning gecekondu suburbs. There, an "ill-assorted" amalgam of values—not a successful integrating synthesis—reigned supreme, originating in the socialization of hostility to outsiders and the authoritarianism of the traditional rural family; exposure to folk culture, including internalization of the role of the epic hero; and the Republic's dissemination of a crude warrior nationalism. The sociological process can be summarized in Mardin's claim that Turkish society had become ruralized or Anatolianized (246), and that student violence emerged from this debased "culture" of the periphery.

Despite certain insights in Mardin's analysis—seen for example in the confirmation by activists of the emergence of a masculine "hero culture"—in its accounting for violence there are a number of other "differentials" that it does not consider. Mardin's attention is directed to historical mechanisms of integration (such as educational institutions and their norm-internalizing function), and to the consequences of their 1970s breakdown in the Republic's pattern of recruitment and training. Yet as we have seen in chapter 3, far from there being any failure in Republican institutions' inculcating of the "masses" with modified cultural dispositions, there is the historical role of the Kemalist state in inciting urban violence, precisely for the cause of *Turkist* nationalism. Thus, the violence of the ülkücü was in keeping with normative Kemalism, not against it.

Further and puzzlingly, Mardin does not mention male citizens' investiture in violence engendered by generations of compulsory military service. Nor does he investigate the alliance between the "Grey Wolf commandos" and sections of the Turkish state/military, as well as their support by the ruling Demirel coalition government: instead, violence is presented as a youth phenomenon, symmetrically afflicting leftist and rightist activist groups equally. More deliberately, the article quarantines youth politics from other fields of political struggle, including from the mobilization of civil society and from conflict related to social cleavages between antagonistic economic classes, seen most clearly in workplace militancy and in the murder of unionists. In the cultural universe inhabited by Mardin's youth, violence articulates with "structural survivals from the body of traditional culture" (1978: 235), but not with relative poverty, provocation, exploitation, hope, or class struggle.

Accordingly, Mardin is unable to imagine that for activists, violence was related not to cultural dysfunction or disorder but to ethical acts that sought to institute an alternative, more equal, social order. One does not have to agree with its practice to acknowledge it to be, in the "mind" of activists, a justified violence.

This last point reveals a striking dimension of his article's methodology, and of so many others. *Mardin has done no research.* His analysis is entirely hypothetical, based on selected historical processes/events given meaning by his theoretical perspective. Youth voices are thus nonexistent, and their acts and ethics are subsumed within abstract categories—"traditional society," the "Great Tradition," "core authoritarianism"—that supposedly animate and cause them. There is an irony here, given Mardin's (1997) critique twenty years later of political economy approaches and their bias against what he calls "microsociology." In that article he argues against the assumption that subjects' actions or "personal histories" are essentially derivative of relations of class and power—"colorings of social processes" as he puts it (66). Yet neither, similarly, would we wish to reduce them to epiphenomena of cultural or civilizational crisis, as Mardin does here. I make these criticisms not smugly to point out insufficiencies in his work but more to assert the integrity of a proper phenomenological perspective that begins—but not necessarily ends—with the narratives and perceptions of people themselves and with a crafted description of their social actions. Minimally, activists' violence should be apprehended in relation to the full repertoire of their embodied spatial politics, including with their nonviolent activities.

What may a more fulsome explanation for the origins and practices of urban violence involve? Were the acts of its youthful protagonists merely situationally specific, as Mardin suggests, tied in to their importation of peasant culture to the city? My research suggests we need a richer *spatial* etiology of violence than that. First, and as we have noted in chapter 1, urban violence always articulates with core processes of spatial production and place-making themselves, even as it supersedes and vastly exaggerates them. As we have seen, these include the "*violence*" of architecture, the ever-present friction between planned spatial order and users of place, and then between users of space themselves. Equally importantly, there was the pedagogy involved in militants' education and its associated modification of perception, through which certain affordances of the environment—intentional *and* incidental—were sensed, and conflict entered into over their taking-up and possessing. Urban violence, in short, was underpinned by contestation for and over the privileges of architecture itself, and was strategic in its opportunistic struggle for the ownership and transformation of the affordances of places and institutions. Thirdly, chapter 3 has uncovered a past horizon and/or template for urban violence, the spatial practices of Kemalism itself—for example, its destruction of property (or urbicide), its ethnic cleansing, and its sonic politics (music revolution and language purification campaign) used to target Istanbul's ethnic minorities—all of which constituted a legacy tactically reactivate-able by militants of both the right and the left for their own purposes.

Equally important, we have already seen above what activists themselves said about violence in interviews. One further place where organizations and their members expressed their own meanings and ethical motivations for violence, including as heroic targets (and not as victims) of the acts of violence of others, is in the death notices published for slain activists in newspapers and journals (song lyrics are another). Although obituaries are a genre of writing with their own formal conventions, what can we learn about militants' perceptions of violence and death if we also take them at their face value or word?

In militant obituaries the city is constituted as a political crucible for a struggle against fascism and imperialism (or communism), and the revolutionary cause as demanding sacrifice. Self-sacrifice required the principled overcoming of fear. As Banu remembered, "THKP-C militants believed that to be a martyr was an honorable thing and was a respected death. We said, 'martyrs never die.'" The brief notice published in *Cumhuriyet* newspaper for Reşat Oturakçıoğlu (aged twenty-one) on 2 October 1977 gives some ideas about (Maoist) militants' political cosmology: "He was a heroic personality in the struggle against imperialism, social imperialism, fascism and social fascism. His death is greater than the Altai Mountain [origin point of Turkish migration millennia ago according to Turkist nationalism]. His memory will live on in our struggle." The obituary for Kemal Karaca published in *Devrimci Yol* (newspaper) on 1 May 1977 is similar, although the identified enemy—the oligarchy—is different (see below). Printed with a black-and-white picture of the slain Kemal, the text reads: "While fighting militantly and sacrificially against the oligarchy, our heroic brother KEMAL KARACA was treacherously and deceitfully struck down. Let your memory lead our struggle, let your life be our honor! Once again, in your execution: we saw 'treason and fire.' Once again, a thousand times again, we condemn provocation."

In both obituaries we see how violence was intimately related to what Bozarslan (2012: 4) calls a "sacrificial subjectivity," through which revolutionary struggle was understood as both particular and universalistic. Militants' own (dramatic) practices of activism were connected to something wider, such as struggle for the emancipation of the working-class or, indeed, of the whole society, through defeat of the violent oligarchy.

Equally revealing is a one-page obituary for Hüseyin Aksoy published in Dev-Yol's journal *Dev Genç* (6 September 1979). How might we analyze it?

Hüseyin is first identified in a particular way: "Our comrade Hüseyin was the poor son of a worker family, a heroic friend who at a young age (15) was thrown into the revolutionary struggle and who fulfilled every duty given to him in a sacrificial manner." Then the reason for his death is declared: "The oligarchy is unable to stand the fact that the rapidly developing revolutionary movement is mobilizing

Oligarşiye karşı, fedakârca ve militanca savaşırken kalleşce,   kahpece vurulan yiğit kardeşimiz...

KEMAL KARACA

ANIN
MÜCADELEMİZE ÖNDER,
YAŞAMIN
ONURUMUZ OLSUN!
Senin öldürülmende,
bir kez daha:
"ATEŞİ VE İHANETİ GÖRDÜK"

BİR KERE DAHA   BİN KERE DAHA
KAHROLSUN PROVOKASYON

FIGURE 1. Obituary for an activist
(*Devrimci Yol* Newspaper, 1 may 1977).

as one young and old, and those seen as children." Following this, the circumstances of his murder are explained. While distributing notices about a campaign being organized by a coalition of political groups (Struggle against Imperialism, Fascist Terror, Unemployment and Price Increases Campaign), Hüseyin was apprehended and shot dead by the Kağıthane Gendarmerie commander named Erdal Görücü, despite having his hands in the air. The journal reports eyewitnesses that heard Görücü scream, "We will clear away the communists from here, their mothers and wives."

The obituary then draws out particular consequences of the act of killing. First, "The people saw once again that the oligarchy's slaughtering of revolutionaries does not terrify them but by contrast makes their hatred grow. All the terror and oppression of the oligarchy will in the end turn against it." A second consequence of the killing is also presaged. The obituary announces that H. Aksoy's martyrdom made the people realize even more that, "Katillerinden hesap soracağız. Hiçbir katil cezasız kalmaz" (We will hold killers accountable. No murderer will stay unpunished). Given that the name of the killer (Erdal Görücü) is published along-side the slogans, the reader understands a further implication: Görücü is now marked for "revolutionary justice." (Indeed, according to a more recent party history, he was "found and punished" by Dev-Sol militants some months later.[4]) The names of "sympathizers" of the oligarchy—say of MHP-aligned doctors who refused to treat a youth from a leftist group, leading to his death; or of teachers who participated in violent acts against students—are revealed (if known) in Dev-Yol publications. Fascism is given a name. Hüseyin's obituary shows how for militant groups involved in revolutionary work in the gecekondu the escalating violence of the struggle was perceived as involving confrontation not only against "civic" fascist groups (the MHP and its organizations) but also against their operatives in certain state institutions, together identified as an illegitimate oligarchy. For Dev-Yol/Dev-Sol, there was no moral authority in the oligarchy's use of, or monopoly over, violence. Accordingly, it presents its own violence committed against selected agents of the oligarchy (like Görücü) as an execution of real justice, a public punishing of the guilty, even as in the act the organization also proved its own counter-legitimate, "state-like" power. For leftists the violence of the "oligarchy" was self-explanatory, executed as core aspect of its oppressive rule. By contrast, leftist struggle against the oligarchy, including its own violent actions, was understood as defense against and resistance to that oppression, and for that reason militant groups presented activists who were killed in that struggle as heroes of the people.

Only in its last sentence does the obituary return (in a rather truncated manner) to Hüseyin himself: "He is a young soldier of our struggle and will live with us always as a martyr of the campaign." Yet in referring to him in this way the obituary partly de-personalizes his death and re-signifies his killing by proclaiming him to be a martyr (şehit), construing it as an agonistic event that testifies (şahit) to the evils of fascism and to what must be sacrificed in order to oppose it. As Tanıl Bora reminds us, the root of the two words martyr (şehit) and witness (şahit) is the same.[5] Obituaries transmute slain comrades first into one and then into the other.

One last textual genre that gave meaning to the violent "death of an anarchist" is the statement or declaration (demeç) from bereaved parents or siblings published in journals alongside more extensive accounts of murderous events, state-

---

4. His killing in 1979 was briefly mentioned in *Cumhuriyet* newspaper, but was more extensively written about in the section of a publication entitled "Revolutionary Justice against Fascist Terror," in an organization history published in 1997 by DHKP/C, who saw themselves as continuing the heritage of Dev-Sol. See 'Turkey/DHKP/C The History of our Party III.' [http://archive.apc.org/mideast.kurds /msg01886.html] Accessed April 24, 2018.

5. See Bora (2015).

ments that are less standardized than obituaries and much more affecting. Perhaps not surprisingly, these letters are conflicted, simultaneously personal and political, as well as more particular in detail. We see this in the statement of a father made in response to the murder of his son Haydar Öztürk in an MHP attack on leftist students at the Atatürk Eğitim Institute in the town of Uşak, published in the journal *Devrimci Yol*. He wrote:

> Our son was a 25-year-old young man [*delikanlıydı*]. Haydar was much loved and respected by his peers. He would always debate with young and old, explaining the dirty face of the oligarchy to people. He would inform people in particular about the fascist violence in Uşak, and called everyone to be united.
>
> Haydar often went to meetings and marches. We would say, "Son, be careful, they can kill you, they can shoot you." "If I don't go, if you don't go, who will save this country?" he would reply. "Don't be scared, they can't do anything."
>
> He would explain to us how this order was bad, and get us to listen to the cassettes of the minstrels. He would tell us that if we were unified together, the oligarchy couldn't kill us, couldn't oppress us, and that they were scared of our unity. Of course, we didn't understand all this well. But now because of what has happened to us we know and understand it very well. We saw the police and the gendarmerie attack the school where our son studied with our own eyes; we lived the event. We saw how they took away our son's corpse.
>
> We are not saddened by Haydar's death, by his dying for this cause. We raised our son for these days. We know who struggles for what cause. Every oppressed mother and father should raise their children for this path.
>
> We are no longer scared of the oligarchy's police and gendarmerie. We are on the path of Haydar and of those who have died like Haydar. If one Haydar dies then another Haydar is born. The new Haydar, his brother's son, was born three days before Haydar's death. (*Devrimci Yol Gazetesi*, 1 May, 1977, p.4)

In that same extended violent event, the police and the gendarmerie also killed a student who was part of a vigil held for Haydar at his school, when they indiscriminately opened fire on participants. A statement from the *ağabey* (elder brother) of Semiha Özakar was published alongside that of Haydar's father:

> My sister Semiha Özakar was a fresh, 16-year-old young woman who had just opened her eyes to life. She successfully completed her primary schooling in Susuz to which our village Banaz was connected, and then enrolled in Uşak Halit Ziya Uşaklıgil Middle School. After successful study there she then attended Uşak Central Lise [Mahir Çayan Lisesi]. And in a region marked by contradiction between labor and capital there she learned about the revolutionary struggle and participated in it with all her strength. . . .
>
> While we were waiting impatiently and with great hope for her to finish school and return to our village, and while she was attending the funeral at the YAYKUR Technical College of her friend Haydar Öztürk who had been brutally murdered by fascists on 17 March 1977, she was exposed to a barrage of shots fired by the police

and gendarmerie at 11.00 pm and struck in the chest, becoming a martyr of the revolution herself.

Before my sister was murdered she continuously appeared in the oligarchy's courts, who sought to place the school administrators under constant pressure. Despite this, my sister never yielded to this oppression and terror.

Of course, the oligarchy knows very well who is able to best threaten it and for this reason, . . . to feed the fascists, they printed in the press that my sister was shot by her own friends. Waiting at school for Haydar Öztürk's funeral, Uşak governor Mustafa Bezirgancı gave the order for police and gendarmerie to open fire that killed my sister, and afterwards told the press that my sister was a student at the education institute who had been taken hostage and shot by the revolutionaries. In fact, my sister Semiha Özakar was a second-year student at Uşak Central Lise, her number 1316.

The killing of my sister created deep sorrow in our family, our village and in our town, and taught us well just what the oligarchy is capable of.

CONCLUSION

Because the dead cannot speak for themselves, the living—their comrades, their families, and their organizations that publicize or write their obituaries—are faced with composing the meaning of their death. Of course, even if the dead had uttered their imagined last words while alive, we do not know for certain whether now, being "dead," they would agree with their own previously expressed sentiments or with the words of their families. As in experiencing any major event, the trauma of deadly violence may shatter one's firmly held beliefs.[6] Nevertheless, in his grief, each writer finds some solace in declaring his or her loved one to be a martyr for the greater, revolutionary cause. Perhaps less comforting is their (unwanted) new knowledge of the brutality and ruthlessness of the oligarchy, forced upon them by the death of their loved one. In testifying to this knowledge, they also have become witnesses (şahitler).

Finally, in their retelling of events, for me each statement above also registers a profound outrage at *particular* actions of the oligarchy's protagonists—in the taking away of the corpse of their son in the first letter, and in the lies told by the governor in proclaiming that Semiha was murdered by her own comrades in the second. In my interviews with ex-militants I was always impressed by how generally calm, three decades later, they were in explaining events of shocking violence

---

6. The same issue pertains to Turkish military personnel, often conscripts, killed in military action today. According to a friend, the Turkish Armed Forces makes its troops write (guided by a given template) a "final letter" to loved ones before entering into combat zones, so that the message may be read at any funeral, broadcast to the nation by state- or government-friendly private media, or published in the newspapers.

done to them and others. By contrast, in the raw family testimonies visited here writers impute something "beyond the pale" to the acts of the killers of their loved ones, which exposes the bitter nature of the political struggle between leftist and rightist forces at that time. Here, alongside ideology (see chapter 6), we sense the affects hate, love, fear, revenge, and suffering that also motivated social action.

5

Gecekondu, Factory, Municipality

Three Fields of Spatial Politics

Chapter 4 explored militants' own production of urban space, interactively generated through the performance of a repertoire of spatial tactics in different sites
across the whole city. One consequence of these "tactics of space" (de Certeau
1984) was endemic social friction as groups fought for control of the political
affordances of places, resulting in increasing numbers of activists' wounding or
killing. Chapter 5 continues this exploration of activists' constitution of the city but
attends to the political and ethical engagements of militant groups in three more
particular spatial arenas or political regions of Istanbul's urban geography: in
squatter settlements (5.1); in factories and workplaces (5.2); and in municipalities
(5.3). How did interviewees experience and transform these significant fields of
political endeavor and spatial struggle? Although leftist activists developed in
them certain sociopolitical practices specific to each field, and although for the
sake of clarity I delimit them from each other below, in reality *ideological* activism
in shantytowns, *labor* activism in factories and unions, and *urban* activism in
councils (in particular through the so-called "New Council" movement that developed in Istanbul after 1974) were core aspects of one interconnected but bitterly
factionalized, sprawling, revolutionary movement.

Spatially, how were squatter settlements, municipalities, and factories linked
together? As we have seen in chapter 3, *gecekondu*, or workers' suburbs, grew
up around new factories on the expanding edges of the city, for whom council
activists sought to improve basic infrastructure as well as to provide services
(after the act of settlement). For political and financial reasons, councils were unable to independently mobilize land to develop public housing—unlike, say, in
Singapore—providing an opportunity for socialist groups, entrepreneurs, land

"mafia," regional associations (*dernek*), and small-scale contractors to organize settlement through ongoing acts of land occupation and division. Settlements were also connected to chain migration from particular places in Anatolia, leading to the clustering of Alevi or of inhabitants from Sivas, Tokat, or Giresun (for example) in particular suburbs, as well as in certain factories (Dubetsky 1976). Last, alongside finding paid labor and serially constructing one's house, for many first- and second-generation rural migrants a third mode of incorporation into urban society involved participation in the fierce politics of either the left or the right, tying work places, squatter settlements, and political mobilization together.

5.1 MILITANTS AND SHANTYTOWN DWELLERS: SOLIDARITY AND INTIMIDATION

Gecekondu were "borderlands" that became extremely important sites of political activism, recruitment, and conflict. With their heightened sensitivity to politico-economic exploitation, leftist organizations perceived in gecekondu inhabitants a nascent proto-revolutionary consciousness, despite many residents' apparent pragmatic desire for advancement within the existing urban society. Militants were inclined toward an activist push accelerating the incipient revolutionary conditions of society. Unlike more middle-class Istanbulites, many of whom believed migrants had ruralized the city, for Guevarist- and Maoist-inspired factions the "urban peasants" inhabiting gecekondu settlements were potential co-liberators who, if rightly guided, might march upon and revolutionize the city proper. Nevertheless, as my interviews showed, this intersubjective encounter between leftist groups and shantytown inhabitants did not always unfold smoothly. On certain crucial matters, activists (many of whom were high school or university students) and residents had different interests in and perceptions of the city, despite the project of revolutionary groups to educate and activate gecekondu dwellers.

As the obituaries in chapter 4 reveal, it was in the shantytowns and the gecekondus of Istanbul that militants entered into a particularly violent mode of urban spatial production. Competition for influence over these burgeoning worker neighborhoods made them hotbeds of political struggle. Thus, relations between political factions and gecekondu inhabitants emerged as one important subject of the research. Activists attempted first to mobilize and thereafter to defend gecekondu inhabitants. Perceived by certain socialist fractions as places of revolutionary potential, by the late 1970s the gecekondu suburbs had become socio-spatial battlegrounds marked by a struggle for control of their affordances and over their autonomous organization.

One core aspect of this engagement was tension between partisans' attempted living-out of an alternative (revolutionary) ethics and their communicative relationships with residents. In the crisis conditions of Istanbul in the late 1970s, partisans'

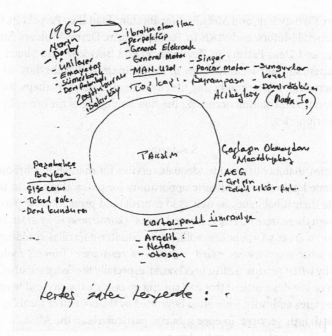

FIGURE 2. Mapping the city: gecekondu, industry, and corporation
(Christopher Houston).

performance of a radical socialist ethos sometimes drove a wedge between them and
potential supporters in the gecekondu, given its uncompromising critique of selected
practices and sensibilities of shantytown inhabitants themselves. On the other hand,
activists' ethical self-cultivation was also negotiated in interpersonal relationships
with gecekondu residents, and thus was partially oriented to their modes of reckoning with the urban environment. As we will see in the conclusion of this section, the
dilemmas faced by militants in the gecekondu are revealed in their sober personal
reflections on the political activities of their younger selves, and even in a critique of
the origins of their own ethics.

In figure 2, Şahin (TKP-ML) presents the temporal and spatial encroachment
of particular capitalist firms upon Taksim Square, here the center of the city, each
characterized by the gecekondu areas that grew up around them from the 1960s
onward. The diagram brilliantly constitutes a leftist militant phenomenology
on Istanbul, foregrounding and intertwining forces of (capitalist) production with
place.

Sahin situates Şişe Cam, Tekel, and Den Kunduran in Beykoz; Arçelik, Netaş,
and Otosan in Kartal, Pendik, and Ümraniye; AEG, Gripin, and Tekel Likör Factory

in Cağlayan, Okmeydanı, and Mecidiyeköy; İbrahim Etan İlaç, Perpektup, General Electric, General Motors, and MAN in Topkapı; Narin, Derby, Unilever, Emayetaş, Sümerbank, and Dem Factory in Zeytinburnu and Bakırköy; and Singer, Pancar Motors, Sungurlar, and Demirdöküm in Bayrampaşa and Alibeyköy. In Şahin's map, the factories and gecekondu ring the city, a visual analogy, perhaps, for a Maoist conviction that revolution occurs via the slow strangling of the center by its surrounding peripheries.

Solidarity

Municipalities' inability to provide adequate services for shanties mushrooming on occupied state land offered a historic opportunity for political groups to mobilize and educate their inhabitants, as well as to control (and protect) those parts of the city. Although there were no real "liberated zones" (*kurtarılmış bölgeler*) in Istanbul, in the sense of areas where police, soldiers, or counter-guerrillas could not enter, there were what interviewees called "districts of resistance" (*direniş mahalleleri*) controlled by leftist groups.[1] Leftist gecekondu, especially the "edge suburbs" (*kenar mahalleleri* or *varoluş semtleri*) that had sprung up outside the city and temporarily beyond the state's authority, were often boycotted by the council or local capital and provided with little services. In edge suburbs, particularly in the Alevi ones, youth became heavily organized into radical groups.

How did leftist groups initially order gecekondu settlements? Vacant state land was valuable. Different leftist groups were able to extract both a form of land rent and political loyalty once they were in control of an area. For a small sum of money given to the organization, people could buy land, or a subdivision. There had to be no state presence for socialist organizations to confiscate and distribute public land. If there was no state authority, then occupation happened extremely quickly. Alternatively, settlement was much slower if there was council authority. Militant groups were aware, of course, that in many cases an informal "land mafia" was already organized to speculate on land or to facilitate chain migration from a particular region to new gecekondu areas. Illegal political groups joined in this older, well-established pattern of land appropriation and allocation. Thus, although some scholars claim that in the years before the coup new migrants to Istanbul found it impossible to build shanty housing because "radical groups" controlled land that they exchanged for political loyalty (see Tekeli 2009b), it is more likely that gecekondu growth ceased with the formalization and commodification of the housing market in the decade after 12 Eylül.

---

1. In his excellent study *Türkiye Solu (1960–1980)*, Ergun Aydınoğlu makes the point that the *kurtarılmış bölgeler* declared by DY, DS, HK, Kurtuluş, TKP-ML, and others were also zones that had been cleared of the militants of rival groups, so that they were unable to pursue political activities there (Aydınoğlu 2007: 405–6).

Nilgün remembered being present in a field where militants from HK divided up land using a thread. Ergün (Maoist TKP/ML) explained how his organization did it: "I went to 1 Mayıs, and to Nurtepe [to Enternasyonel Mahallesi: now just a pub name]. We went to do political work (*siyaset calışması*), to win the masses (*kitle kazanmak için*). We helped make houses: the more houses you could make, the more supporters you could win. Thus, wherever we could we commandeered land. I went with others to Kağıthane Demircilik (near today's Bilgi University): we called a meeting and said, 'Is there anyone here who has no house?' We took them to Nurtepe and said, 'Here, your houses.'"

Crucially, however, not all leftist political parties or factions were equally involved in attempting to organize squatter-housing dwellers. Based on their interpretation of present conditions, factions constructed their own revolutionary practice (see the "Conclusion" below and chapter 6). Some believed that radical change could come through winning control of the municipality, or through the takeover and politicization of professional associations; others through armed propaganda that would hasten revolutionary conditions without "waiting" for the working class or the conjuncture of the "right" time; others asserted that the industrial working class should lead any revolution, supported by the revolutionary energy of "proletariat-izing" "villagers."

This interpretive politics had an effect on the way different leftist factions addressed and interacted with the gecekondu. According to interviewees, the TKP, for example, was more focused on the workers' movement and factory organizing through their links with DİSK. As with radical unions in other countries, DİSK sometimes asserted the efficacy of a "revolutionary strike" (*devrimci duruş*), a strategy for bringing the country to a transformative crisis through stopping production. Somewhat by contrast, for Maoist- (i.e., HK, TKP-ML, or HB) and for Latin American–inspired anti-imperialist groups (for example, Dev-Yol), both relatively more interested in poverty than in class, the attempted organization of gecekondu residents was intended to conscientize the urban poor to the causes of, and solutions to, their present conditions. Maoist militants from both the gecekondu itself and from the city's more established working- and middle-class suburbs perceived the shantytowns as the abode of "urban peasants," and the slogan "from the slum (or periphery) to the city" (*varoştan kente*) informed their practice of revolutionary work there. Indeed, district work (*semt calışması*) and consciousness-raising (*bilinçlendirme calışması*) in the gecekondu was a logical aspect of their partisans' revolutionary practice, including for their university- and even high school–aligned students.

The pedagogical training of the groups themselves also modulated militants' intentions toward the gecekondu. Militants recalled how their perceptions of the gecekondu derived from the study practices of their factions and from their political education concerning global history and the city, guided by the purposive act of revolution. Sponsored perceptual (phenomenological) modifications involved more than activists' grasping of theoretical information about underdevelopment and class struggle. Alongside militants' reading of revolutionary material, organizations insisted upon their practical work in the gecekondu. Partisans' attempted building of relations between what they called the resistance districts (direniş semtleri) and themselves became a rite of passage for tens of thousands of leftist students. For student-militants, visiting, working, and staying in informal settlements, perceived as sites of unfolding revolution, was a duty as well as a process of character formation. According to interviewees, student work in squatter settlements (i.e., in Kocamustafapaşa, Fikir Mahallesi, Topkapı, Alibeyköy, Ümraniye, Nurtepe) involved a huge range of practices, including selling the group's journal there, teaching literacy classes, protecting the gecekondu from attacks on its sites of solidarity (for example, on its coffeehouses), and providing services (holding health clinics, bringing medicine, giving legal advice, building roads and stairs, digging house foundations, organizing piping and public water taps, and pouring concrete). "I took a woman to have an abortion—I was 16!" said Özlem.

In the gecekondu suburbs, especially those initiated and organized by leftists in the "resistance suburbs" (direniş mahalleleri), activists and residents were involved in their own projects of spatial production, from the actual generation of material environments (building of roads, stairs, and houses; subdivision of vacant state land and the distributing of plots to families; laying down of cement barriers at entrances to suburbs as defense of the area against attack) to the recruitment of potential members and the organization of protests, boycotts, and various forms of local self-governance (i.e., the election of a muhtar), including consciousness-raising education directed at inhabitants. According to Sen (2013), in the suburb of Çayan (named after Mahir Çayan) developed in 1977 by Dev-Sol, activists pursued a form of centralized planning, including the naming of streets/parks, and the regulation of house type and house height. Furthermore, in a struggle against capitalist relations, the organization banned the constructing of pillars in houses that would enable the adding of extensions or of further stories, each of which might be used in commercial activities. The selling or renting of houses was discouraged, seen as a form of speculation or a source of alienation.

Somewhat similarly, in order to facilitate gecekondu collective life and to cultivate feelings of social solidarity, organizations established consumer cooperatives in the suburbs under their control. (People who were members in different groups ran some of the cooperatives.) Activists would track down and buy food and materials directly from the factory—olive oil, butter, sugar, sunflower oil, salt, pasta, and shoes—and sell them at cheaper prices to members. According to Omer (İlerici Lise Derneği [Progressive High School Students Association]), the logic of the cooperative was demonstrated in the saying, "üretici'den tüketiciye" (from producer to consumer). In short, activist groups sought to develop, administer, and regulate an informal anti-capitalist political order through these uses of place and daily practices.

Many student activists themselves were from some of the first, more established gecekondu suburbs settled in the 1950s. As part of their "people's war," students from different groups devised their own curricula of small novels and books to teach reading. For those from Turkish People's Liberation Army (THKO) and Turkish Revolutionary Path (TDY) for example, it included Leo Huberman's *The Socialist Alphabet* and Stalin's *Anarchism and Socialism*. Students would go to a house meeting with people they did not know to talk to them about politics, visits organized by a sympathizer living there who would invite local people to come. They would go to factories to support workers on strike. Other groups sent students to areas perceived as ripe for organizing, renting a house for groups of six or seven activists to stay there, in solidarity with the residents. Work in the gecekondu was also part of increasing the influence of the organization, so that they could gain people's support for their activities (i.e., marches, strikes, protests).

Intimidation

However, alongside narrating these practices of solidarity, ex-militants also reflected upon their practices of violence and intimidation. For example, when a group was dominant in an area (*hâkimiyet*), it collected money (called a tax) from local shopkeepers and small businesses, and could even make an identity check for strangers in the suburb. Militants would say that they were collecting donations for a friend in hospital or in prison, or for a cause. Organizations would announce that today because of some event, perhaps a commemoration of a "martyr" or a strike, the shops would have to close, to pull down the steel guards on their windows. According to militants, this was also "a show, saying, 'look at how strong we are,' as well as evidence for which people would disobey them." As Emre, ex-militant of HK argued: "They [locals] understood it was a command: they were scared of us, that we would make trouble for them." Sometimes local shopkeepers were killed, said to be a leftist or a rightist. Reha (MHP) said that his group even took money off the local mafia, who were afraid of them.

These narratives reveal the fact that the "belonging" or loyalty of a particular neighborhood to a certain group was less than clear. To the extent that poor suburbs, or different parts of them, were under control of the rightists (aligned with the state) or of the leftists, militants used the term *dual authority* (*ikili iktidar*) to illuminate the polarized situation. Suburbs could also change their affiliation. Gaining control or authority over an area facilitated establishment of informal political order and the attempted organization of its youth into the faction. Control was tenuously maintained through establishing associations/clubs, coffee houses, or party quarters there. A different facet of the intimidation of organizations was expressed in the colloquial idiom that they were tough guys or bullies (*kabadayı*). Thus, Hüseyin

(Aydınlık) noted how political groups in the gecekondu also acted as economic patrons, their militants often being unemployed youth in the suburb, given jobs such as selling journals or collecting "taxes." That was "better than them sitting in the *kahvehane*. . . . There they couldn't marry. They would win some status, being a member of a party, with the hope that 'maybe I will find a girl.'" Political groups took on the role of the neighborhood *kabadayı*, which in popular films both dominates and protects its weaker members.

For Istanbul, interviewees mainly agreed on a common political geography.[2] For example, according to Erdoğan (Dev-Sol), the "fascists" controlled Beyazıt, Fındıkzade, and Zeytinburnu. The rest of Istanbul—excluding the rich suburbs— was mainly leftist. For Ergun (Maoist TKP/ML), Bakırköy was leftist, because Dev-Genç (Revolutionary Youth) was very powerful there. Aksaray was leftist, Fatih mixed, and Beyazıt "cosmopolitan," with its thousands of students from all over Turkey studying at Istanbul University. According to Ümit (*Birikim* journal), Mecidiyeköy, too, was mixed. He was less sure of its political geography, but he thought that Şişli was leftist because of its various university faculties. According to Ertuğrul (Dev-Sol), Bakırköy was a mixed and less polarized suburb, but sympathetic to the left. The same applied to poorer suburbs like Bağcılar, Güngören, and Yeni Bosna, where Kurds lived, and where there was not a very militant leftist movement. For Şahin (TKP-ML), the right controlled Zeytinburnu and Tatar Mahallesi, whose resident Tatars had been organized by the MHP, whereas for Mustafa (TKP), Güngören was a mixed, cosmopolitan suburb, majority populated by people from Mardin but hardly any rightists.[3] Interestingly, in the main the spatial sense of MHP activist Serdar conformed to the general political topography sketched out by left activists: for him Beyazıt, Üsküdar, Mecidiyeköy, Şişli Cami Cizgi, and Beykoz were under control of the right, while the left controlled Kadıköy, Büyükdere, and Paşabahçe. For Mehmet, a member of Genç Ülkücüler (Young Idealists), the first high schools in Istanbul targeted for organizing were Pertevniyal and Vefa Liseleri.

2. In February 1980 *Aydınlık* newspaper began publishing a now notorious series of articles, under the title *İstanbul'da paylaşılmış mahalleler* (The shared suburbs of Istanbul), or *İstanbulda hangi semtler kimin elinde'* (Which groups control which suburbs of Istanbul?), detailing leftist activities even down to the level of specific streets and coffee houses. In 1978–1979 the same newspaper had published another series titled *Bilinmeyen sol* (The unknown left), surveying the political left and sometimes even publishing the names and pictures of leaders of rival leftist groups.

3. University student hostels (*yurts*) were divided too. According to Reha (MHP), at Istanbul University Atatürk Yurdu was controlled by the left, and Sivas Yurdu by the right. In Fındıkzade, Niğde Yurdu was leftist and Trabzon Yurdu rightist. For Ergun (Halkın Yolu), the student hostels in Fındıkzade and Topkapı had been taken over by the *ülkücü*(-s). According to Şahin (Vatan Partisi [Fatherland Party]), Beyazıt was a place of conflict, but leftist groups generally occupied its hostels.

More widely, the violence in poorer or newer suburbs generated a new political structure for the city, as well as an experiential difference for city residents: rich suburbs were "quiet." One activist who lived in Teşvikiye said no events ever happened there.

Activists' spatial perceptions of the city were only partially "objectively" true. They reflected personal experience, hearsay, or the circulation of rumors and knowledge about the killings of an activist from one group or the attack on another in a certain suburb or place. Militants discerned the changing authority in a place by their tracking of its environment, taking note of the whitewashing of slogans and new locutionary acts. The political hegemon in gecekondu areas, or even over particular streets or coffee houses, could change, leading to factions' constant concern to shore-up their occupation of places. In such a situation, the transport hubs and the lines that crossed or joined up suburbs became particular spaces of danger.

Interviewees noted that around 1977 the gecekondu became much more violent, and that activists began to carry guns to protect themselves from attacks of the right-wing *ülkücü*. Cars or even pedestrians would go past a coffee house and open fire, which meant that people needed to be careful in choosing which street to walk down to get to their homes. Accordingly, solidarity work in the shantytowns was often perilous. Councils and the gendarmerie occasionally sought to demolish illegal housing, and people tried to defend themselves. Suburbs attacked by the *ülkücü* required student militants to go there and protect them. According to Bülent (Dev-Yol), students and youths of the suburb would wait at the entrance to the suburb with weapons, constructing cement speed bumps there to stop cars going in fast to attack the coffee houses. More senior members of the factions would sleep in the organization's houses, in trying conditions: "We lived very poorly; the homes were freezing, but we didn't notice much; we slept back to back sometimes to get warm. We must have smelled, as water was often cut but we didn't notice. Now I notice people smelling," Hilmi (Kurtuluş) remembers.[4]

There was half-control over the coming and goings into the suburb. For many militants after 1978 a feeling of being caught up in civil war emerged, and in a sort of internal migration or political expulsion activists started to move out of a suburb if they were not of the same group as those who controlled it. Interviewees felt that the escalation of violence resulted in an erosion of popular support and that the intense factionalism and competition between groups made it easy for the state to infiltrate them. Around that time the more radical settlements organized their defense committees from members of different groups and locals. One of the most famous settlements in Istanbul was 1 Mayıs Mahallesi (The May First Neighborhood), a suburb in Ümraniye built up from scratch by the non-aligned Dev-Yol

4. In winter central heating systems facilitate the spread of individuals throughout the house: a single heating point like a *soba* (stove) forces people into a common room.

group.[5] Some degree of cooperation appeared between leftist groups in their different areas, at least in agreeing to leave each other alone.

The Intersubjective Ethics of Revolution

One way of thinking about these practices and perceptions is to consider their relationship to militants' developing ethical sense. As seen above, learning to be an activist involved an apprenticeship in spatial and aural perception, developing practitioners' awareness of the dangerous urban environment and of its affordances for action, including of the particular affordances offered by (gecekondu) people. Activist organizations were communities of practice, modifying militants' ethical perceptions as much as their relationship to places. For example, leftist groups' educating of militants involved cultivating in them a *mood* that would enable them to sense and be affected by particular aspects of shantytown existence—for interviewees, this was a fostered sympathy that perceived its misery as an artifact of exploitation. At the same time, their work there unfolded among the maelstrom of intersubjective experience and personal interaction with people in the gecekondu, which sometimes came into friction with other explicit intentions of socialist class struggle, in particular their politicizing of the urban crisis in Istanbul. Here leftists were caught between trying to solve the problems of the poor and seeking to educate them and to incite a revolution.

The recent interest in ethics in anthropology (for example Zigon 2009, Faubion 2010, Lambek 2010) can be useful here for better understanding certain moral dimensions of this revolutionary awareness and intent. An important feature of this literature has been its critique of sociological models that conflate the cultural with the moral, in which morality as a system of shared values, sentiments and procedures of judgment is presented as congruent with society (or with its classificatory and disciplinary domains). By contrast, Laidlaw (2002: 315) claims that in anthropology a renewed focus on ethics should begin by describing ethnographically the possibility of human ethical freedom. This entails an understanding of ethics in everyday life as involving the exercise of actors' critical reflexivity vis-à-vis culturally socialized norms, involving their ability and effort to decide between possible actions.

Yet how might this reflexivity come about? One useful aid to understanding leftist activism in Istanbul is Faubion's distinction between what he calls the dynamic/inventive, and the homeostatic/reproductive dimensions of the ethical

---

5. See Aslan (2004). A second, more famous experiment in local democracy was the case of the Black Sea village of Fatsa in Ordu, also mobilized by Dev-Yol. In Fatsa, Dev-Yol organized an elected people's parliament and health committee, with an elected mayor who was a member of the faction. There were even people from MSP in its Resistance Committee. Both places were targeted for "special" treatment after the coup, including for forced changes of name. For Fatsa, see Aksakal (2007).

field, and their generation and reinforcement of ethical subjects. For Faubion (2010), awareness of the distinction appears most clearly in periods of *social crisis* in which the disruption of the normativity of everyday routine entails a lack of fixity in the process of system maintenance and an expanding of humans' ethical imagination. Ethical transformation here arises from a crisis of subjectivity, from a *rupture* with social practices and their associated modes of reproducing moral capacities. Similarly, Zigon analyzes how *moral breakdown* (in the ex–Soviet Union) brings into view the "everydayness of being moral" (2007: 133), while making visible the operation and particularistic interests of perception-constituting institutions and public discourses that structure the moral field. Caroline Humphrey's research on the consequences of what she calls *decision-events* is a third illuminating starting point, decision-events being brought about by crisis situations that enable a transformation of individuals' previous political sentiments, visions, and practices, recomposing them in the process as transformed subjects. In Humphrey's (2008) own discussion, one of the three decision-events at issue includes an attempted socialist revolution in Inner Mongolia, China, in the 1920s.

All three models are helpful for understanding the modified ethical perspectives of revolutionary subjects in Istanbul. Place breakdown as experienced in the urban context incited a questioning of spatial order and its hierarchical divisions, as well as sensitivity toward existing conventions of urban engagement, bodily movement and comportment, and socially gendered relationships. For both male and female student militants from Istanbul's more middle-class suburbs, successful propaganda and solidarity work in the gecekondu required conscious performance and mastery of a new embodied style. Serdar (*Halk Sesi*) remembered the Yılmaz Güney film titled *Arkadaş* (Friend), where someone asks the hero why he has long hair. "He cuts it. I cut mine. We didn't want to do anything that would separate us from the people."

In the squatter settlements talking, eating, sitting (on the floor), and even smoking were intuited as ethical performances and as props critical for the success of communicating the organization's message. For example, militants perceived that to smoke Marlboro cigarettes would set them apart from the people. "Revolutionaries smoked Birinci, with no filters. There were two other more expensive filtered cigarettes brands, Samsun and Maltepe. Sometimes we even took off the filter, as it was seen as a luxury" (Özlem, THKP-C). In the process of intense social interaction with shantytown inhabitants, activists sought to exhibit exemplary behavior according to certain existing normative practices and ideals, as well as to add fresh meanings to them. Banu (TKP) told me the story of a university student who came to the union building for lunch where she was a lawyer: they were all eating together, and she noticed him hardly touching his food. "Why aren't you eating?" she asked him. "I am trying to get used to being hungry," the student said, "like the workers."

Revolutionaries' distaste for overt displays of cultural distinction and wealth—a politics of anti-consumerism—also resonated with certain circles in the broader society. Indeed, Mebuse (THKP-C) described the desire not to make people want what you have (*özenmesinler*) a Republican value. "It [Kemalism] didn't share but it tried not to make people jealous." An activist explained what it was like in his house in the middle-class suburb of Nişantaşı in the late 1970s: "If a friend from a poorer family came over, I might have said, get a cola from the fridge. But my grandmother didn't like that to happen, because she thought that if the boy saw the stuff in our fridge it would shame him."[6] We might say that although class differences rooted in ownership of productive forces and professional qualifications/ wealth segregated Istanbul's city-space in the 1970s, overt distinctions generated through styles of consumption were frowned upon. Nevertheless, Hüseyin (TKP) mentioned that in the 1970s workers couldn't easily come to İstiklal Caddesi, unlike now. Ethical self-cultivation was also fostered through the politicization of gendered and sexual conduct, which simultaneously became a spatial tactic and an embodied politics. Marriage and relationships took on political meanings, as Şahin (*Birikim*) recounted: "I married in 1979, partly so I could set up another activist house. For a wedding present I asked my Mum and Dad for eight *divan* [sofa beds]. Ten or eleven people would stay and eat every night: I remember doing lots of dishes with two, three other people. We shared everything: even the money I was given at the wedding disappeared!" Şahin's account shows how women were needed as camouflage to help set up a safe house in a gecekondu area, especially if guns were to be hidden there. Thus, it was usually a couple that rented, even if they weren't married. The couple would seem to go off to work (they would say they were working in a factory in Topkapı), so that after a few months the house could be used as a meeting place until it was too risky.

Female militants would sometimes stay overnight at the organizations' houses in the gecekondu with other males. "That's why the newspapers said things about our morals, but no one thought of having sex in that time," noted Dilek (Dev-Yol). "We said 'sexual relations were bourgeois.'" Indeed, factions also strongly discouraged sexual relations between activists, and displays of affection were policed. "If you so much as touched a hand, it meant you were together, married. Only if you were engaged could you hold hands, otherwise it was shameful" (Levent, Dev-Sol). A number of interviewees mentioned Dev-Sol's establishment of a "Revolutionary Vice Squad" (Devrimci Ahlâk Zabıtası, or DAZ), who frowned upon student activists holding of hands in parks. "Of course, we all held hands secretly," said Hilmi.

6. Intended or otherwise, many of my interviewees felt that the new economic policies initiated after the coup fostered a change in people's economic ethics and in neighborly relations. See chapter 7.

Purely by chance, I interviewed two people (from Kurtuluş) months apart, who independently told me the same story:

Ferhat (male): There was a situation when we placed a young man wanted by police in the house of a married couple. After a month or so the young man and the wife began an affair. Some groups might have killed them in punishment but we expelled them for lack of honor.

Mebuse (female): I was once given the task of giving a decision to a married woman [who had been above me in the organization] who had another relationship: "We're cutting relations," I said to her. The woman started to weep. "You're right," she said. "It happened. But I loved him." We judged the woman more critically.

Similarly, organizations jealously supervised the interaction of activists with members of other groups. Having a relationship with someone from another group was prohibited, and members would be brought before the party committee for doing so.

According to interviewees, nearly all the females who visited the gecekondu were from middle-class Istanbul families, which was not necessarily the case for male students. Female students and activists tried to politicize squatter settlement women, but to do this they felt that they could not be very different from them, and so tried to present themselves as similar. The longish skirts worn by female activists conformed to the sexual ethics of both gecekondu residents and of militant groups, who discouraged flirting between members. Certain phrases summarized the "techniques of the body" (Mauss 1973) demanded of female activists: "revolutionary girls don't use make-up"; "revolutionary girls don't dress up." Coming to a meeting in high heels was not approved of. For Filiz, activists could not draw attention to their body: "We never wore dresses showing our shoulders or breasts, but parkas. Plus, we wanted to resemble the people and not to make ourselves distinct from them."

In retrospect, activists in interviews were aware of how their political strictures and moral practices partly reflected broader gender models, as well as the masculinist logic of the leftist groups. "There was no feminist discourse then. Only two groups had a women's section, the TKP and Dev-Sol" (Orhan, THKO-TDY). According to Arzu (Aydınlık), "Maoists were involved in a sort of project of populism. We had a picnic once, and a girl swam in the sea in a bikini. 'How shameful,' everyone said." In organizations' attempted production of moral subjects, discourse on obligations to the sacrifices of martyrs, and on the importance of conformity to the values of the people came together. Taner Akçam (2013) remembers an announcement distributed to students at Middle Eastern Technical University (Ankara) that declared how shameful it is to witness activists "sitting on the grass with their boyfriends and girlfriends engaging in disrespectful and unauthorized relations and behavior at the same time as a forum is held to condemn fascism and to increase our determination and knowledge of the struggle, as well as to remember our friends who have been slaughtered by fascism."

Yet, ironically, despite the performative and embodied ways in which activists sought to resemble gecekondu inhabitants, female students could still experience a disconnect in their encounter with shantytown residents, rooted in locals' perceptions of distinctions in class and gendered lifestyles, including practical expectations around schooling:

> I went to the gecekondu for two weeks to do some research for the wall newspaper I was working on in Lise (in 1977?), to Alibeyköy, a place where most of the migrants couldn't speak Turkish [they were Kurds]. One of the women had sewn "*Halk kurtuluşu engellenemez*" [People's liberation can't be hindered] on a pillow cover. We invited the unmarried women to a meeting, some of whom were older than me, and the men weren't happy.
>
> "But I'm doing stuff," I protested. "You're a student," they answered back. "They're girls."
>
> At dinner, they gave me all the meat from the chickpeas. (Filiz, HK)

Interviewees also acknowledged that male domination of unions and political factions was taken for granted at the time. In the gendered division of political labor, women did intelligence and support and were barred from violent actions—robbing a bank; using a gun; "nationalizing" (stealing) state factory products like pipes from depots—although they sometimes carried a gun to a protest for the designated male firer. Even when women worked full-time as revolutionaries, for example, joining a factory workforce to organize workers, they were subservient to the male leaders of the faction: women were significant in organizing women workers, but men as professional revolutionaries organized the organization. The word used for women in many political factions was *bacı* (sister), which, according to Ebru (THKP-C), revealed in the idiom of kinship a concern to constitute female activists' domesticity and sexual unavailability: "There was a secret and unacknowledged male hegemony to protect women's honor [*namus*]. Women were perceived as weak or unsuccessful and were excluded from the higher echelons of group decision-making." For socialist groups, analysis of the "woman question" concluded that women suffered from a dual oppression, dominated by both their husbands and the capitalist system. Banu remembered that in *Kurtuluş*, "it was said that a revolutionary man couldn't oppress a woman. We shared domestic duties, I cooked, and my husband did the dishes. However now I notice that I was doing all the housework." Ayşe (TKP) noted that of more than a hundred lawyers in union confederation DİSK less than five were women. She reported that workers would sometimes call her "Avukat Bey" (Mr. Lawyer). Even in the textile factories union representatives were men.

On the other hand, Omer (MHP) simply noted that the MHP was a male party. "There were no female activists. We didn't think there was a 'woman's problem' in

Turkey, we never debated that. We were very isolated from women; we didn't address them." Similarly, in his autobiography Mehmet Metiner notes that the Akıncılar did not accept that women could be involved in politics, and thus that in the 1970s the Islamic movement was a male movement (2008: 98).

All these accounts point to a vital issue regarding the modified ethical percep- tions developed by activists through the moment of crisis, and it concerns the efficacy of the performative work and the influence of militant groups in the gece- kondu. Did their service; consciousness-raising; and attempts to fit in with, mobi- lize, and change local inhabitants meet with residents' support and approval?

This is a difficult question to answer given the complexity of forces interacting in and through Istanbul's newly created edge "suburbs," including both leftist and rightist violence that simultaneously coerced residents into certain supportive actions while scaring them off from further participation. Two brief examples will have to do to show how this strict ethical project sometimes came into conflict with the life-world and ethical perceptions of gecekondu residents themselves. In most gecekondu suburbs neighborly ties were strong, rooted in reciprocal rela- tions necessitated by the solidarity of the common migrant struggle to make a livelihood in the city, as well as in a history of ongoing regional sympathies and networks. Thus, even when families (or their children) were recruited by opposing political groups, this did not necessarily mean the end of their neighborly rela- tions. Can remembers his ülkücü neighbor (in Hürriyet Mahallesi, settled in the early 1960s) warning him that "police were waiting for me on the corner. Years later, that same person visited the houses of leftists when they came out of prison to say 'geçmiş olsun' [my sympathies]. Again, one night when we were attacked by the gendarmerie while writing slogans on the walls, I remember we took refuge in the house of a rightist family" (in Mavioğlu 2008: 84).

In these examples neighbors of different political persuasion refused to endorse the ideological zeal and separatist project of revolutionary groups (leftist and rightist) that would undermine existing relationships. Their decisions reveal how the requirements or experiences of everyday sociality between neighbors back- grounded—to use the phenomenological term that describes how intentions change the aspects of things for us—such divisions. Indeed, political rituals/performances and political rhetoric often project relations between rival groups to be more adver- sarial than their different members are in actual, face-to-face neighborly interac- tions. This is in part because the word-worlds imagined in political ideologies are more intense than real-life situations.

Secondly, as we have seen, music was a central aspect of both leftist and rightist political organizing and sociability. Yet according to interviewees, one particular type of music was intensely disliked by all revolutionary groups, as it was by the Republic's cultural and political elites: the genre of music named arabesk. TRT didn't play it on television or radio. The sound world of the Kemalist music revolution had long rejected so-called eastern music and its modal structure—and more particularly Ottoman music—and *arabesk* was perceived as similarly sonically foreign (see Stokes 1992, Özbek 1991).[7]

Unfortunately for the left, arabesk was also the "music of the gecekondu," and thus rang out loud and clear as a point of aural difference between the acoustic styles of militants and non-militants. One activist remembered gecekondu dwellers in Alibeyköy listening especially to singer Müslüm Gürses, whom he described as making songs of "rebellion with no hope" (*isyan var ümit yok*). Another felt that arabesk's defeatist lyrics and Arabicized style fostered "revolt with no organization" (*isyan var örgüt yok*). According to informants, militants' encounters with arabesk music in the shantytowns were characterized by disapproval and censure. Indeed, arabesk music elicited powerful embodied and affective responses from leftist hearers. In a perceptive comment, Bülent (Dev-Sol) noted how activists had "no reasoned argument against arabesk, but a state [*hâl*), and a position [*tavır*]." Hilmi reported that in Kurtuluş "we were violently against arabesk as opium music, it was understood to be the same as religion, created by the bourgeoisie to distract people from politics. We revolutionaries thought that listening to arabesk was shameful, as it encouraged a focus on personal feelings and distracted people from politics." Clearly there was a link between the demand to curtail one's use of and interest in "luxuries" and wasteful pleasures (TV watching; games; sitting in the *pastane*, visiting the brothels), and activists' dislike of arabesk, which they felt incited the wrong type of excessive emotion.

Nuriye (Dev-Sol) remembered how "for us, arabesk was low-quality and apolitical, and we thought it was connected to the rightists. It also wasn't from Turkey." For Mehmet (HK), because young people in the gecekondu listened to arabesk, it was hard for leftist groups to establish a relationship with them. "They wanted to 'turn the corner,' not listen to politics." Sonic sensibility being significant in generating and hearing political discourse, leftists' negative reaction to arabesk affected their ability to mobilize slum residents. In brief, arabesk music revealed not just a difference between the musical preferences of militants and gecekondu residents but stirred up a critical leftist judgment of shantytown inhabitants' sentiments and tastes. Revolutionary ethics could not appreciate such "minor" opposition to the cultural order of things.

7. For this reason a classic anthropological model that might privilege "society" as the ultimate producer of the "soundscape," or assume an homology between the natural landscape, social organization and the phenomenological experience of inhabitants, needs supplementing in Turkey by analysis that takes into account the Kemalist State's cultural revolution in the 1930s, including its music revolution aimed at reconstituting the nation's "cultural acoustemology" (Feld 1996: 93). Feld defines *acoustemology* as "local conditions of acoustic sensation, knowledge and imagination embodied in the culturally particular sense of place" (91). In both the era of revolutionary Kemalism and in the 1970s revolutionary city of Istanbul acoustemology was plural, and thus sounds were often heard antagonistically.

Accounting for the Past

Four decades later, today the built environment of the 1970s gecekondu no longer exists. Through the extension of the *yap-sat* model of housing to the once small garden houses of the shantytowns, and then with the full commodification of land and the huge expansion of the real estate sector and market, Istanbul has become a city of "*apart-kondu.*" Of course, the political mood of the city, too, has changed, as have the lives and social practices of its 1970s militants. How, then, did ex-partisans interpret the politics of their youth? In asking activists to attentively describe the event and ethics of their engagements with shantytown residents in the late 1970s, the interview process facilitated a perceptual modification as well, providing narrators with an opportunity to re-signify memories in the present. In reflecting upon a time in which there had been "no time to reflect," activists also reconceived aspects of their historical relations with inhabitants in the squatter areas. Decades later, Bülent, ex-Dev-Sol member, appreciated now how "in the gecekondu, listening to arabesk was an act of assertion for girls. They would put the cassette player on the windowsill to broadcast to the street, not to listen for themselves: 'Look,' they would say, 'I'm here; I'm listening to Gencebay.'" Many militants understood that their own sound and fury in the city had been similar: their visual and aural production of space, in slogans, graffiti, marches, music, speeches and protests announced that they, too, "were there."

Further, in their reassembling and recontextualizing of the past, activists often expressed a modulated criticism of the actions, logic, and assumptions of their own parties in the years before the coup. For leftists, often this involved a reevaluation of their relations with shantytown inhabitants. Indeed, the fact that in certain gecekondu local residents "betrayed" activists by identifying militant organizations' houses to soldiers after the 1980 coup was a distressing reality for many of my interviewees, and contributed, some thirty years later, to a sober assessment of the character of their historic political activities in the informal settlements, as the following comments make clear:

> Filiz (Kurtuluş): We called it *bilinçlendirme çalışması* [consciousness-raising]. I think it was effective up to a point. Now I think what a strange thing to do, I'm against it. It was an attempt to establish authority. This was the left's biggest mistake: you can't organize/politicize someone through economic support, as there is no knowledge. They became your activists for their own interests. The people showed the police which houses the *örgüt* made for themselves.

> Dilek (TKP): I gave education about their rights to workers, men and women. But now I think that I was arrogant in my dealing with those women. I used to get them to tell me their daily schedule [children's breakfast, work, cleaning, etc.], then tell them that they shouldn't give their salaries to their husbands, or they should make him help them at home. We aimed to change them [*müdahale yaptık*]. Now I wouldn't do that, but I was twenty-three when I started working for the union.

Our attitude was connected to our politics: the Communist Party was at the fore-front, so like the Communists, I knew better. Communists know better, we know what is right and wrong. Today I think that idea is wrong, an attitude of superiority, I think it wasn't democratic. I was working for the people, so I would make the deci-sions [*ben karar veririm*].

Orhan (HK): Now I think: those people didn't talk about revolution. Why did they accept a relationship with us? They wanted someone to listen to them, to support them, to protect against suburb demolitions, or help with money. Because we did this, this gave us the right to be listened to.

Deniz (THKP-C): We tried to solve problems. Ironically this created a space for us to become redundant or replaceable [by the state or someone else]. We wanted to replace the existing order: the gecekondu people wanted to create an order.

Serdar (Aydınlık): We were interested in a world that had no relevance for the people in Cuba, China, and so on.

Did these measured criticisms of their younger selves constitute a rejection of their radical politics, and a disowning of its embodied knowledge that had been so hard won? Yes and no. Ex-militants often expressed how the years immediately before (and after) the coup were a time of extremes, and thus that they, too, by implication had been "extremists." Yet at the same time, ex-militants indicated that the modification of their political, spatial, affective, and ethical perceptions caused by their participation in radical factions continued to partially orient their lives in the present, as it did for hundreds of thousands of other still politi-cally active ex-activists in the city. Here we notice one further dimension of their revolutionary ethics and its dispositional capacities: its *transfer* into new social contexts and its *translation* through time, *accruable* into new political struggles of the day. As phenomenology notes, to some sure extent the consequences of past intersubjective relations continue in the present despite their completion as discrete events. Thus, the research with ex-activists has shown us something significant—pedagogy is rarely wasted. The historic modification of apprentice militants' ethical attention through education in activist practice has become a past horizon, liable to be redeployed or foregrounded in ex-activists' perspectives in the present.

Clearly, then, ex-partisans' memories of Istanbul have been dynamically and ceaselessly constituted in the relational context of their ongoing intentional engagements with its social and political worlds. We have already cited Lambek, who notes that people's judgments about the ethical qualities of specific incidents or actions are located "within the stream of particular lives and the narratives that are constituted from them, changing its valence in relation to the further unfolding of those lives and narratives and never fully determined or predictable" (2010: 4). These past incidents may be re-judged in different ways, including a realization of their collective dimensions. Thus, in hindsight—some thirty years after their failed attempt to make an urban revolution—ex-activists identified a number of other historical horizons that had animated their perceptions of the gecekondu in the late 1970s and mediated their political tactics there.

We have already considered a number of them in chapter 2—leftists' ideological Kemalism, as well as their convictions concerning the inevitability of a socialist revolution. Reflection on their gecekondu relationships identified a number of others, each connected to particular aspects of Kemalism. According to many interviewees, nearly every leftist group in the 1970s believed that historic Kemalism was a progressive force for change, even if it still required *completion*. Thus, from their revised perspective of the present, activists acknowledged the *affective* legacy of Kemalism, attributing it to the Republic's success in inculcating embodied dispositions in activists through their schooling and in its generation of political memory.

Militants perceived, too, how two other preexisting schemas germane to the official history of the founding of the Republic also moved them in the 1970s. The first was the virtuous legitimacy of political violence done in the name of establishing a new, independent Turkey, freed from the machinations of imperialist powers. The justifying myths of Kemalism authorized a continual liberation struggle. Right-wing nationalists and leftist socialists alike shared this conviction, even if their imperialist enemies and their internal co-conspirators were different. Furthermore, Atatürk's famous address to youth that positioned them as the preservers of the Republic meant that, as Çağlar (1990) points out, "the Greywolves were not alone in seeing themselves with a mission to save the country; all youth groups gave themselves the same mission, the Left included" (97).

Kemalism's second legacy, adapted by activists of all political persuasions, concerned its validation of a ceaseless civilizing project originating from the enlightened "center" and directed at the transformation of the periphery. Most groups thought that the periphery had come to the city. Even if, for the Marxian left, "culture" was understood as a feature of the superstructure conditioned by the infrastructural forces of production, ex-militants noted that no one doubted the continuing need for "cultural revolution," core feature of 1930s Kemalism. Rightists and Islamists, too, were dedicated to the disciplining and (re)educating of prospective cadres. Indeed, given that official Kemalism historically described itself as "revolutionary," and denoted various of its reforms from above in exactly the same way—hat revolution, alphabet revolution, music revolution etc.—the legitimacy of revolution directed at the masses was taken for granted, even if in this case it was justified as a revolution "from below." The sanctioned word *devrimci* (revolutionary) was everywhere, affixed to civil society and party organizations alike.

In a sign of the post-12 Eylül times, this has not been the case since.

5.2 LABOR ACTIVISM AND ITS MODES
OF ENGAGEMENT

Alongside militant organizations' ideological and political activism in the squatter settlements of Istanbul, their workers, too, became a target of leftist groups, sometimes, perhaps, rather cynically in the competition for revolutionary hegemony. Above we noted how militants' spatial practices in the gecekondu were connected to the hopeful perception that their inhabitants constituted a (potential) proto-revolutionary subject. Similarly, union work, labor organizing, and solidarity with workers in factories were also key strategies in political groups' agitating for radical political change, predicated on the (potential) revolutionary class consciousness of a new, imagined subject: *the proletariat.* As the phenomenological insight shows, workers are not simply there, but emerge as the chief agents of revolutionary change as militants perceive and embrace a materialist history. Yet unions and labor had a longer history in Turkey than radical leftist or rightist organizations, and they retained their organizational autonomy throughout the decade. Indeed, the first organized confederation of unions had occurred in 1952 with the establishment of Turk-Is. According to both Mello (2010) and Berik and Bilginsoy (1996), in the 1950s and 1960s the leadership of the Turk-İş confederation was closer first to the Demokrat Partisi and then after its closure to the Adalet Partisi (Justice Party), each of which had a more pro-labor image than the CHP and were willing to develop "clientalistic" or corporatist relations with union leaders who sought to trade improved working conditions for workers' electoral support.

Worker-focused activism also included the forming of large organizations for and by state employees, who after the 1971 military intervention had lost the right to unionize, bargain collectively, or strike, each of which had been granted by the 1961 constitution and confirmed in 1964 legislation (Kutal 2003). Thus in place of prohibited unions, public sector workers such as teachers, engineers, police, medical personnel, and others established new politicized mass associations (as noted, often qualified by the word *revolutionary* in their title) that sought both improvements in the conditions of their own specific areas of work, and a reordering of the wider social relations of the day. Relations between mass associations and unions were strong yet fluid. According to Faruk (CHP), administrators or clerks in the state-owned Sümerbank for example, whose functions included owning and developing textile factories and loans or advice to firms in carpet production, were barred from joining unions, even as the forty-five factories owned by Sümerbank were all unionized by Teksif Sendikası. Faruk recalled how as an accountant at Sümerbank he used to join strikes at their factories and speak at union meetings. Further, while working for Sümerbank in Hereke he also reported on his founding with other members of the local CHP of a foundation there named the Hereke Kalkındırma Derneği (Hereke Development Association), organizing a library, theater productions, tree plantings, and marches in support of local strikes. Left-left and left-right rivalry entered into the creation of these mass associations as well, as seen in their fiercely fought elections, or in the simultaneous existence of Pol-Der and Pol-Bir, two rival groups established for and by the police. Teachers, too, were split between leftist and rightist associations. According to Ümit (*Halk Sesi*), organizations that used the word *dernek* were leftist, and those that used the term *birlik* were rightist.

As with the mass public sector associations, the trade union movement in the 1970s had also fractured, both among a number of confederations characterized by different ideological currents, in particular between Türk-İş (Confederation of Turkish Labor Unions) and DİSK (Confederation of Revolutionary Labor Unions), and also along party or faction lines. Union participation was huge. According to Mello, membership in DİSK and Türk-İş had increased to five hundred thousand and seven hundred thousand respectively by 1980 (2010: 12). Two other smaller confederations of unions also emerged during the 1970s, MİSK (Confederation of Nationalist Workers Unions) connected to the MHP, and Hak-İş (Confederation of Right Workers Unions), tied into the more pious religious politics of the MSP. The breakaway of more radical unions and unionists to form DİSK in 1967 led to more than a decade of intense competition in factories and work places between unions affiliated to DİSK and those loyal to Türk-İş. DİSK, which was initially close to the Workers Party of Turkey (TİP) and then for a period in the mid-1970s to the TKP, pursued a more political unionism, advocating for workplace action, including strikes by rank-and-file members, as a valid means of addressing issues of workers' rights. For Mello, the DİSK alternative was predicated on its belief that "current social relations were better understood through a socialist interpretation of the salience of socioeconomic injustice and class antagonism on the one hand, and the belief that active political action could address these injustices on the other" (2010: 11).

What constituted the contested "opportunity space" for militants in unions and in factories, enabling leftist political groups to intercede in workers' activities? One major enabling factor was the dispute over and evolution of legislation concerning the legal status and rights of unions. To give one example, in 1972 the Constitutional Court struck down as unconstitutional the AP (Justice Party) government's 1970 labor law revisions that had given Türk-İş exclusive right to represent labor, as well as restricting the right of new unions or confederations to legally organize unless their membership exceeded one-third of workers at the work site. The amendments sought to control the labor movement by privileging the more right-wing Türk-İş confederation. The new situation allowed local workers to form local unions that were entitled to negotiate a collective agreement, with no minimum size of workforce. Enterprises affiliated with unions rose dramatically. One result of legislative changes was both a destabilizing of existing unions and the flourishing of new ones in both large and small work places all over the Istanbul-Marmara region, linked to an easing of the period a person must work in a place before becoming legally eligible to join/form a union and to vote or stand in their elections.

These developments encouraged the TKP and many other militant groups (some Maoist) to engage workers by assigning members to factories and workplaces, with the expectation that they would organize them there. Gün (TKP) told me how he entered the *tershane* (shipyards) in 1976, after graduating from the trade high school in shipbuilding. He won entry to university, but on advice of the party decided to become a worker and went to work in the factories on the Golden Horn. Indeed, the illegal TKP became influential in the workers' movement after 1975 through their alignments with or control over unions affiliated to DİSK. Ayşe (Kurtuluş) committed herself to a similar event. Leaving medical school at Istanbul University in 1979, she went to labor in a factory in Ortaklı near Topkapı that made blankets. "It had five hundred workers, four hundred fifty women and fifty men in higher positions. Kurtuluş had decided to target textile, food, and metalwork industries for organizing. To enter the factory, I had to lie about my education [needed only to be primary school graduate] and marriage status [had to be single]. We saw that it was difficult to organize from outside; we had to do it from inside."

Laboring in a factory in order to mobilize workers was extremely hard. It involved working for the minimum wage, and living in the gecekondu. It was expressive of a time of great idealism, when militants left everything, including family, to become revolutionaries. Organizing workers for industrial militancy was a struggle. Ayşe remembered how the first task was to be accepted: "To do that you had to be a good worker, work like the workers, and live like them (or live even worse: not to spend money we ate potatoes, walked everywhere, also we gave money to the organization). It was hard for me, because I was someone who had never picked up a needle in my life. We made friends there, visited each other, attended the *kına gecesi* [women's celebration on the eve of a wedding] and *sünnet* [circumcision] celebrations, went to the factory together." Yet Ayşe's commitment also cost her dearly. She explained how her mother had died in 1979, upset after visiting her at the police station, and falling under a train. "My brother and Dad met me at the police station and we went home together. 'How is my mother,' I said as we went. 'You'll see at home,' they said. As we arrived home my *teyze* [mother's sister] came out, screaming. 'Ayşe, what have you done?' she shouted. Things that would destroy me now didn't wreck me then," she concluded. "It was very hard, but sacrifice was easier if you believed that a revolution was coming."

A second, more economic structuring of political opportunity involved what Berik and Bilginsoy call "the two-tiered labor market structure" (1996: 45). The modern, import-substituting industrial sector (private and public) constituted the first tier, including massive state-owned industrial plants such as Petkim, Lastik,

Tekel, and others. Certain state-owned factories made primary products, selling their steel, refined petrol, mining products, and manufactured goods (such as tires) to both the private sector for further development and to the state itself—that is, cars to the police and weapons to the military. Tekel for example employed sixty-eight thousand workers in Istanbul alone, producing in different factories cigarettes, *rakı*, matches, and salt, as well as managing large tobacco leaf depots.

The second tier involved smaller, private firms subject to intense competition and characterized by low wages and poor conditions, as we have already seen in chapter 3 in the example of Fikret Amca's business. Labor activism there was harder, given the ability of employers to prevent outside workers from entering the production sites.

According to Berik and Bilginsoy, in the 1970s, fully one-half of the industrial labor force was employed in the public sector, including clerks in state banks and other such positions. State economic enterprises were heavily unionized, and conditions in their factories (paid holidays, salary increases, and sometimes facilities such as a theater, a salon for meetings, an eating hall, etc.) made workers in them a "labor aristocracy." Further, unlike in private plants, workers did not lose their jobs for participating in strike actions. The (mainly) Türk-İş-affiliated unions that represented workers in them were not particularly militant. Yet it was possible for workers to vote for which union to join, and unions (if their delegates voted to) could leave Türk-İş and join DİSK. Thus, more militant unions were able to exhort workers to vote their way, just as more militant workers were able to try and radicalize Türk-İş unions.

However, state-owned enterprises had less "positive" effects on labor activism as well. First, the sector was subject to political nepotism. When the party in government changed, so did the factory's administration. This employment pattern extended to workers themselves. According to Mustafa (TKP), who was working as a technical expert and union representative for the Türk-İş affiliated union Dökgen Iş in the state-owned Golden Horn civilian shipyard (Tershane), a new group of unskilled workers—he called them a *lumpenproletariat*—would enter the factories with each general election, often in a group (from Rize or Samsun, etc.). He reported that by the time the shipyards went bankrupt in 1995 there were three hundred workers in the factory and fifteen hundred on the payroll! Workers would vote in union elections as a bloc, related to the exchange networks of party affiliation, kinship, regional origin/solidarity, religious-denominational, or ethnic ties that they had mobilized to gain entry-level jobs. For Mustafa, new workers, therefore, were far from possessing a working-class consciousness or identity, although as the writing of the Copperbelt ethnographers on African miners and workers in Zambia have long shown, people are quick to adapt to the situational context of class conflict, unions, and wage-labor that characterizes an urban-based industrial economy (see for example Ferguson 1999).

The "non-socialist" character of many workers required activists to demonstrate a special range of performative and embodied skills in the actual practice of union work. Unionists had to be crafty or cunning in establishing relations with workers—indeed, according to Mustafa, in order to get elected they had to be like "anthropologists," finding things in common with them:

We had to be very strategic. "How can we represent you," we would ask. A huge strike was unreasonable. Union work was as much social as directed to factory conditions, as state factories would make a new collective agreement very two years, not just because of inflation but in order to stop DİSK. Union elections happened every two years, and in that period a collective agreement was signed for two years. It meant a lot of elections! There was a real democracy.

What did we do? In 1977 there was no yağ [oil] or tüpgaz [LPG]: we organized a truck of olive oil with the council to be sold at the factory. We organized a consumer cooperative at shipyards: a small amount of money was taken from salaries, and we began to buy and sell stuff. We tried to organize a housing cooperative. Most DİSK factories were doing this, collecting money monthly from members and using it to build a block of flats for members. We nominated a unionist to take workers to hospital.

Even embodied appearance was an important mode of engagement with workers. Gün (TKP) noted that he never saw a small unionist. "They needed to be big men, good speakers, with a loud voice: in a meeting, or in a conflict, the more you could shout the more successful you would appear." Perception of a person changes according to the perceiver's understanding of their power: years later, Gün remembered that someone met him and said, "Wow, you used to be a more imposing figure."

Activists' commitments to unions and to workers also involved slightly easier duties than joining the factory floor in order to politicize workers from below. A number of interviewees from different political organizations had worked as educators and/or as lawyers for unions, representing workers in court who had been sacked for their political activities, most noticeably for striking. Legal work included informing union members about their rights vis-à-vis the state and their employers. Further, unions were legally empowered to educate workers about the details of a collective agreement (i.e., about severance pay arrangements or wage increases), with some activists taking an opportunity to explain their version of Marxism-Leninism. Others saw it as a chance to do propaganda for TKP, using the Soviet Union as a model. Mehmet recalled saying to workers "Over there everyone has a job, house etcetera." Self-critical, he wondered in our interview at his desire then to make all workers TKP sympathizers. "Now I believe a union shouldn't be connected to a party."

Likewise, Haydar remembered his work as an education officer with Basin İş (Print Workers Union), one of the founding unions of DİSK. Basın-İş had nearly ten thousand members, including employees in the state Malzeme (Stationary) Office. He was a member of the legal Vatan Party (founded by the older communist Dr. Kıvılcımlı), which was "more radical than the TKP but still rejected armed struggle." His comments indicated how even after 1975, when for a period DİSK was dominated by the TKP, many of its individual unions also had relations with other political groups.

For student members of revolutionary groups, solidarity with workers was shown through joining workers at picket lines, or in guarding the strike tents put up outside factories at night. In her student days, Özlem (Dev-Yol) recalled going to where a strike was happening, even if coordinated by some other group or union, to stay on duty in the tent, collect money, write placards, recite poetry, dance the *halay*, and so on. "Strikes were a rehearsal [*prova*] for the revolution," she remembered feeling. Bülent (İGD) recounted how they had a theater group from a number of different student groups who went to strikes to perform for the picket line or protesters. "Workers used to look at us as we performed, very stereotypical characters in the plays, the worker, the bourgeoisie, the police, etcetera. Even then, I wondered what they thought watching us," he told me. Indeed, militant industrial action, including strikes to stop production, became widespread in Istanbul after 1974, some in solidarity with other strikes, some for more pay, for fewer hours, or for safer conditions. Strikes would also happen on important anniversaries. According to Mehmet Salah (1984), in 1976 there were more than two hundred official and unofficial strikes, and May Day was celebrated by tens of thousands of workers in Taksim Square for the first time in fifty years, despite an official ban.

Last, and just as we have seen in other fields of urban political practice and discourse—in universities, in the gecekondu, in public spaces, and so on—ideological differences and political conflict between unions was widespread, both between MİSK and leftist unions, and among different leftist groups themselves, derailing any attempts to make common cause in the slow and difficult task of organizing the new proletariat. For Samim, after 1975 the TKP leadership acted as a virtual police force within DİSK "to prevent all other socialist 'infiltration'" (1981: 79). The threat of violence against labor activists was also a constant companion of union work: as we saw, on July 22, 1980, MHP militants assassinated DİSK Chairman Kemal Türkler in front of his daughter outside of his house in Üsküdar, one among many other killings. Sometimes to break a strike, police or ülkücü would open fire on protestors. According to MHP activist Hüseyin, their aligned union group MİSK was a militant organization with weapons, called in by the bosses to break a strike. "It wasn't a group from below," he noted. By contrast, TKP-aligned Omer thought that MISK did have some workers connected to it looking for work, but that it wasn't that strong. He remembered that Harp Iş was a union controlled by the MHP, organized in Kırıkkale in a state-factory producing weapons, which was both dangerous work and very heavy industry. Yusuf (Sürekli Devrim [Continuous Revolution]) confirmed both claims. He thought that MISK sought to get work for its own members, even as bosses used it to stop leftist groups organizing in factories. He also remembered "patron" or employer unions set up by the owner of the factory, into which everyone who worked there had to pay dues.

Severe disagreements over the *intent*, *method*, and *end* of labor activism fractured leftist politics as well. Thus, despite Mello's conclusion cited above, where he asserts that DİSK pursued a *socialist* political unionism in contradistinction to the moderate or state- or business-friendly unionism of Türk-İş, for some other leftist groups both confederations were suspect in the light of desire for a more radical unionism. For example, in a long article in the fortnightly *Devrimci Yol* newspaper covering a miners' strike in Aşkale, the unnamed writer accuses both Türk-İş and DİSK of "*reformism*," of providing an "apparent" alternative to the policies of the bourgeoisie while actually obstructing the creation of a genuinely revolutionary unionism that represents the working class:

> Today in Turkey there is a working class that has reached 5 million, of which some 1.5 million are organized in unions. A variety of rightist and reformist unionists dominate Turk-Is, the biggest confederation by numbers. Reformist and revisionist unionists control DİSK, separated from ordinary workers and managing things from above. Neither confederation is doing revolutionary unionism. In general, the working-class movement is obstructed by the oligarchy and, under the *wing* of DİSK, by a section of the bourgeoisie. The clear result is that in Turkey the working-class movement and the socialist movement have not yet been able to become a united whole. Socialists have not yet been able to lead the economic-democratic struggle of the working class. . . .
>
> The duty of socialists involves organizing and giving consciousness to the *spontaneous* and unorganized opposition of the masses to the system and directing it into a struggle against the ruling power. . . .
>
> Today socialists must play a leading role in every struggle of the working class, organize its opposition against the present order and break the influence of the reformists-revisionists. Today the reformists and revisionists have an influence over the working class. This influence is not sourced from the masses. It has no cadres and is empty. The influence of the reformers and revisionists over the working class lasts only as long as the respect gained by a health worker who goes to the village where a doctor never visits. (1 May 1977 *Devrimci Yol*, p. 5) (my emphases)

If Dev-Yol's criticism here of the two main labor confederations in Turkey has a textual and ideological genealogy, it is surely to be found in Lenin's similar identification and critique of what he calls "trade-union consciousness" in *What Is to Be Done?* There Lenin asserts that the "*spontaneous* development of the working-class movement leads to its subordination to bourgeois ideology . . . for the spontaneous working-class movement is trade-unionism, and trade-unionism means the ideological enslavement of the workers by the bourgeoisie. Hence the task of Social-Democracy [communism] is *to combat spontaneity, to divert* the working-class movement from this spontaneous, trade-unionist striving to come under the wing of the bourgeoisie, and to bring it under the wing of revolutionary Social Democracy" (emphases in the original).[8]

For Lenin, as for Dev-Sol, "trade-union politics" seeks alleviation of the suffering caused by the workers' condition, but not the abolition of that condition itself. Further, Dev-Yol's conviction that the spontaneous resistance of workers to their exploitation requires the direction of socialists to transform it into a political revolt against the oligarchy (or regime) is also to be found in Lenin's pamphlet. In it he cites approvingly the "profoundly true" words of Karl Kautsky that "socialist consciousness is something introduced into the proletarian class struggle from without and is not something that arose within it spontaneously." Dev-Yol's assertion above of the inadequacy of class struggle alone in developing workers' consciousness of their position and task makes sense in the light of other of their strategies, including armed propaganda and guerrilla struggle by a select militant elite that might "shock" the proletariat-bystander into action (see chapter 6). Phenomenologically, the political problem for Dev-Yol here was to change workers' class-conditioned perceptions into revolutionary ones.

5.3 URBAN ACTIVISM AND THE NEW MUNICIPALISM

Let me continue this chapter on the ethical and political engagements of militant groups in Istanbul by discussing a third vital arena of political practice there, the maelstrom of council activism. Municipalities were the formal state agencies charged with "servicing" a rapidly expanding city. They were also democratic institutions, their mayors voted in and out of office. As with labor activism, among revolutionary factions there was intense disagreement over the *intent, method,* and *end* of municipal politics, much of which revolved around the issue of legalism.

For Dev-Yol and for many other revolutionary factions, the "parliamentary" or electoral road to socialism was only viable if legal arrangements allowed a truly independent political movement or party of the working class to emerge. As this was not the case, the question concerning the "attitude" revolutionaries should take toward elections was pressing. Further, given their analysis that within the legal confines of the existing power arrangements the CHP was a party that merely appeared to be progressive and democratic while serving the interest of the bourgeoisie, the question of how revolutionaries should relate both to it and to the working class organizations and professional associations that "erroneously" saw in it an effective solution to the fascist danger was also of great practical and

8. See https://www.marxists.org/archive/lenin/works/1901/witbd/ii.htm, accessed July 2, 2018.

theoretical importance. In the same edition (1 May) of the *Devrimci Yol* newspaper cited above, an article on the upcoming June elections in 1977 concluded that even as revolutionaries must critically explain to the working class the bourgeois content of CHP policies, they should not campaign for people to vote against the party.[9] The reason was twofold: first, parties like the MHP and AP whose foundations were truly fascist should be the primary critical target. And second, although the CHP's administrators and leadership were suspect, its working-class activists and supporters were potential allies in the broader anti-fascist struggle, and thus joint actions with them were to be encouraged.

Was Dev-Yol correct here in distinguishing between the political sensibilities of rank-and-file supporters of the CHP, and those at the party's national level? In one way they were. According to both Andrew Finkel (1990) and İlhan Tekeli (2009a), one primary feature of council work in the years 1974–1980 was relentless conflict between local councils and national governments, particularly over financial and institutional resources controlled by the central authority which local politicians needed to fulfill their political programs. In short, municipalities lacked financial, political, and administrative autonomy from the state. This conflict was exacerbated when city mayors and national politicians originated from different political parties. For example, in Istanbul, candidates representing the CHP handsomely won both the 1973 and 1977 local (*yerel*) elections, displacing the Adalet Party and reinforcing the party's move to a national left-of-center political stance under the leadership of Bülent Ecevit during the same period. Their victory led to a chronic dispute (from 1973 to 1980) with right-wing National Front coalition governments. At the same time, however, the existence of factions within both the CHP and the AP themselves, representing different interests and ideologies and advocating for different urban policies and funding arrangements, led to conflict, too, between local (popularly elected) mayors/administrations and rival leaderships, officials, or politicians from their own parties.

For both Finkel and Tekeli, this was part of the context in Istanbul and the Marmara Basin (and in Ankara as well) in which a significant "new council movement" (in Turkish, *yeni belediyecilik hareketi*) began, which, although "created in the wake of the Republican People's Party move leftward, was not part of the strategy of the national leadership" (Finkel 1990: 205). As a prominent contributor to the movement, Tekeli describes it as "social-democratic" municipalism, which in the face of frozen or even declining funding from the central government developed two new defining practices: that of creating new financial sources and simultaneously becoming a direct factory manufacturer of scarce commodities—asphalt, bread, etcetera—themselves ([1988] 2009a: 273–74). For Finkel, a "political faction (indeed, it housed competing factions) in search of popular urban sup-

---

9. See "Seçimlerde devrimcilerin tavrı ne olmalıdır?," *Devrimci Sol Gazete*, 1 May 1977, pp. 1–2.

port" (1990: 190) initiated this municipal movement, similar in its mobilizing intent to the more radical political groups abounding in the city, and to the union activists discussed above. The activists, planners, technicians, administrators, and politicians of this new "democratic" municipalism—itself an amalgam of different political tendencies with grossly insufficient resources with which to solve the massive urban transport, housing, and infrastructural deficiencies of gecekondu city—were also forced to take account of, and sometimes to act in cooperation or competition with, some of the more radical political groups vying for control there (see below).

What political features emerged from and informed this new municipalism? In a separate article Tekeli summarizes its main operating principles as democracy, productionism, resource creation, organization of mass consumption, and inter-council unity and cooperation ([1998] 2009b: 128). For Selahattin Yıldırım, general-secretary in the late 1970s of the innovative and influential Union of Marmara and Straits Councils (or MBBB), "at the start of the 1970s the general characteristic of the understandings of local authorities was state-focused, passive, and turned in upon themselves" (1990: 25). Conditions were ripe for a progressive new program and ideology, oriented to innovative forms of service to local residents and to the democratization of municipal administrative practices. Citing a 1977 edition of the main journal of the Union of Marmara Councils (*Marmara ve Boğazlar: Belediyeler ve Kent Sorunları Dergisi*), Yıldırım summarizes the new municipal movement as involving "a productive, consumer protective, and resource creative council that enables the people to govern themselves, to participate in decision making and implementation processes at every level, a *Democratic Council* that recognizes the primacy of the interests of collective groups, that facilitates the production of public goods and services in direct ways, that breaks the power of monopoly and institutionalized profit taking in urban areas and redirects these to the people, that enables a cheaper, healthier and more direct urban consumption and that expands the opportunities of resource creation" (1990: 27).

Alongside its classic council functions (rubbish, water, electricity, etc.), this democratic municipalism initiated a number of novel spatial policies and services. In keeping with the incredible creativity of political movements in these years, and despite their financial penury, Istanbul municipalities established projects in a huge number of areas: in consumer rights (new local markets or *halk pazarları*, official sales of basic foodstuff to guard against price rises, bread factories and sales); in mass transport (Metro, roads allocation); in new institutions (suburban representative councils, consumer and producer cooperatives/companies, inter-council association); in educational facilities (professional and trade courses, adult education); in programs directed to youth (cultural centers, peace and freedom festivals, book campaigns, etc.); and through policies protecting Istanbul's historical and cultural sites and environment. Many of these initiatives continue as normalized aspects of council services today.[10] Selahattin confirmed this in our interview, explaining that the new council movement was simultaneously a civil society movement, based in the left wing of the CHP. For him, "the success of the movement was that it introduced a new language or discourse into council politics that by 1977 had entered into every political party's program [CHP and AP], and that has continued ever since, particularly in the rhetoric first of the Refah Party and then of the AKP. The language brings together service [hizmet] with democracy, its new element."

We must mention the new municipalism's interest and work in the area of mass housing and settlement too. To spite the massive problems municipalities faced in accessing central state land, two vast ambitious "modernist" housing projects were planned and one (partially) completed, Batıkent in Ankara. The other, ultimately unrealized, was the İzmit New Settlements Project (İzmit Yenilikçi Yerleşmeler Projesi) in greater Istanbul, a huge public housing development of thirty thousand dwellings (for one hundred twenty thousand people or more) oriented toward low-income working-class families, to be built on land "expropriated" by the council. In an article published in the journal Mimarlık (Architecture) in 1978, Tuncay Çavdar, one of the project's chief architects, describes its practice of participatory design, which included a series of mass surveys completed by likely inhabitants before any building was begun, discussion meetings with them in coffeehouses, workplaces, and union rooms attended by planners/researchers, and the incorporation of (potential) residents' feedback into "mobile" design plans.[11]

For Çavdar, "the İzmit New Settlement Project affirms the political principle of the participation of users in planning decisions, . . . and its aim is to connect social, economic and technological issues within a framework of participation" (1978: 55–56). The İzmit project's broader political vision may perhaps be best discerned in the title of Çavdar's article: "Toplum bilinçlenmesinde araç olarak katılımsal tasarım" (Participatory design as a tool for raising community consciousness). Finkel notes another of its goals, to deflate land speculation by providing mass cooperative housing stock (1990: 208). Minimally, we see how its spatial politics contrasted with the earlier urban interventions of both Prost and Menderes in Istanbul (chapter 3), which were guided by a pristine modernist conception/conviction of the expert knowledge of space technicians who brooked (in theory) no compromise with their monumental design.[12]

10. See Öz and Eder (2012) on the implementation of neoliberal urban policies and the partial closure of the periodic (halk) bazaars in Istanbul established by the new municipalism.

11. See also Kandiyoti (1977) for discussion of her research for the İzmit Municipality into the housing needs of potential residents in the settlement project, in which she draws attention to the difficulty of planning for a population undergoing rapid social change.

12. Holston critiques the planning principles of both Le Corbusier and of CIAM (International Congress of Modern Architecture), the most influential advocate for modern urbanism between

In the end, the project was never physically begun. Keyder registers but brusquely dismisses the attempts in the late 1970s by "social democratic and statist platforms" to institute cooperative or public housing, which were "brought to life in a few small projects, [but] realized only minimally" (1999b: 147).

The participatory method and consciousness-raising ambitions of these spatial projects and services raise two vital questions: first, how did relations between factions involved in the new municipalism and the community unfold; and second, what dialogue (if any) did the new council movement establish with illegal political groups that also sought to educate and mobilize Istanbul's gecekondu inhabitants and workers, as well as to mimic or even to preempt council activities? Answers to the first question are difficult to hazard, given 12 Eylül brought the experiment in alternative municipalism to a premature end. Nevertheless, Cavdar writes in his conclusion (1978: 60) that the close attention given to the İzmit project by local people and their high level of participation disproved prevailing assumptions about participatory planning, especially the claim that its greatest obstacle is the reluctance or unwillingness of people to become involved.

What of relations between rival political factions in their competitive gecekondu engagement and mobilization? Above we noted how Dev-Yol recommended the possibility of working with the grass roots "anti-fascist, progressive" elements within the CHP during the general election to resist fascism. Beyond that, however, the false hope engendered in working people by the reformist and non-revolutionary nature of the CHP made opposing it imperative. Exactly where the CHP's municipal consultants and professionals were positioned in this tactical politics of Dev-Yol would have to be worked out on the ground. Other leftist writers (e.g., Murat Belge) were more open in principle to cooperation with the legal local government movement, arguing that socialist organizations should participate in the council institution, even to the extent of forming city government if the possibility arose. However, because this may give rise to the risk that ameliorative reform of workers' and squatters' conditions merely render local exploitative capitalist arrangements more palatable, and given Turkish municipalities' constrained institutional situation, Belge recommends that socialists and socialist groups should work independently "alongside but outside councils" (*belediyenin dışında ama yanında*) (1979: 18), seeking ways to solve problems of people's daily lives while agitating to increase municipalities' political and financial autonomy from the central state. He notes, also, that over time such greater political autonomy may also weaken the capitalist state. Crucially,

---

the two world wars, arguing that "One of the social effects of modernist master planning is the depoliticization of those who are not planners, since their political organization becomes irrelevant if not obstructive in decisions about urban development" (1989: 8). However, he describes, too, how Le Corbusian planning was also directed against land speculation and untrammelled private interest that deregulated the urban development.

for Belge this weakening was equally important for any future socialist administration, to prevent it, too, from becoming despotic. Here the title of his paper makes more sense: "The importance of municipalities as the organizational nucleus in the transition to a socialist society" (Sosyalist bir tompluma geçişte örgütlenme nüvesi olarak belediyelerin önemi).

By contrast, how did activist-professionals from the new municipality movement itself experience relations with revolutionary organizations and militants? According to Selahattin (interview), despite the similarity of their final aims, "the perspective and approach [yaklaşım] of the revolutionary groups were different to ours. We worked to transform things from within: ours was a more concrete [somut] approach, theirs more abstract or theoretical [soyut]." Despite their efforts, for Selahattin, their political and spatial practices had no permanent impact: "Their struggle endured as a symbol but not their actions."[13] Yet, despite his perception of the lack of lasting "urban" success of leftist revolutionary groups, he conceded that in Istanbul they had "helped" in the occupation of state land, something the new municipal movement had also sought to legally achieve, with little success. Indeed, as we have seen, its giant project at Izmir, to be built on expropriated state land, was first postponed when internal political conflict in the CHP led to the de-selecting of its championing mayor, and then abandoned after 12 Eylül. It was later developed privately.

Selahattin also reported that the professional planners, consultants, and employees of the progressive municipalities "didn't really engage with such groups or oppose them." Further, being unconvinced of the efficacy of the urban and spatial projects of illegal and/or revolutionary organizations in the gecekondu, he doubted that they could have built roads or been in "administrative" control of a suburb. "Perhaps they put stones down in muddy places?" he wondered, noting that the municipality made roads after gecekondu settlement, and that the Istanbul councils shared bulldozers. His opinion is at odds with the memories of other of my interviewees, who recounted their activist involvement as both university students and as young (engineering, architectural, planning, cartographic) professionals in the establishment, management, and protection of squatter suburbs. Batuman's interesting discussion on the role of such urban experts in the politics of housing in the period 1960–80 illuminates this disagreement, as his research indicates that there was a "clear differentiation" between the 1960s and 1970s generation of urban professionals. As he says, "While the generation of '60s was reluctant to directly involve themselves in the building of new settlements, younger generations did not hesitate to undertake this mission as a political duty" (2006: 71).

---

13. Yet, interestingly, for Selahattin, the Black Sea town of Fatsa, where a coalition of different groups led by Dev-Yol won elections and ran the council, was an exception: "They did what we did, but with more bravado/shine." The mayor was arrested and died in prison after 12 Eylül.

In sum, aggravated relations between rival factions working in the gecekondu, including the new municipal movement, revolved around a number of contrasting political aims. Should groups seek to mobilize workers for revolutionary action to change the system, or concentrate mainly on improving the living spaces and material well-being of inhabitants? What combination of local autonomy and political authority should prevail? Could "socialist forms of organization" coexist alongside capitalist ones, so that spatial politics in the gecekondu might open up a beachhead pointing the way to a socialist future? Would electoral participation in the system of "bourgeois democracy" lead to progressive social change? As we have seen, answers to these debates animated political activism in Istanbul, accounting for partisans' varied sense of place and spatial politics in the city, as well as for radical groups' contrasting relationships with Istanbul's shantytowns, factories, and municipalities.

CONCLUSION

Let me conclude by taking a step back from militants' narratives and prompted memories of their own activities and multisensory perceptions of the city as presented in chapters 4 and 5 to construct an overview of the results of their "production of space" in Istanbul. As already mentioned in chapter 1, activists themselves had shown an interest in the question about the generalizable nature of their own local experiences, given their insights into the segregated character of the city and of activists' distributed experiences within it. Below I construct a more synthetic model of revolutionary Istanbul through reflection on aspects of individuals' perceptions and experiences of everyday activist life.

The research has shown, seemingly paradoxically, that activists perceived the city as both differentiated and homogenous at the same time. In terms of the *variety* of their urban experiences, members of competing factions had different memories of the city, as did individual members even within particular factions. These distinct memories occurred for several reasons. First, within factions there was a division of organizational labor—in every group some people were professional revolutionaries supported by the party, while the vast majority of activists were not. Secondly, different factions were connected to distinct parts of the city's political and spatial field, even as they competed with each other for influence over and within territory. The reason so, as we have discussed already, is because different groups established (or were able to establish) particular relationships with particular segments of the broader society. Thus, according to interviewees, Dev-Yol partisans fostered linkages with both students and intellectuals and people living in the slums—and were therefore over-exposed to paramilitary violence from the extreme right in the struggle over the gecekondu—but they were not particularly close with workers in large factories. By contrast, the TKP (through DİSK) sought and forged a strong relationship with unions and through them with those work-ing on the factory floor, while CHP leftists zeroed in on the municipal system.

As we will see in the next chapter, these relationships were partly related to the different ways in which political factions analyzed Turkey's historical situation (or the "social structure" of the country), from which a revolutionary methodol-ogy or strategy was devised. Distinctions between groups hung on a word: did conditions favor a "national-democratic revolution," a "socialist revolution," a "progressive-democratic," or a "democratic-popular" one? (see Lipovsky 1992: 131–47). Did Turkey's economic and political context make national developmen-talist, anti-imperialist politics more necessary than anti-capitalist or socialist ones? Similarly, would radical changes in social life come through local electoral pro-cesses (for example, as asserted by CHP activists in the "New Municipalism" movement)? Or did it require the mass organization of workers through revolu-tionary trade unionism? And what would bring about a revolution: a progressive coup, a popular front led by the working class, or a vanguardist armed struggle that might break open the artificial balance of power generated by the imperialist center and its local oligarchic-comprador confederates? Who might spark a "'peo-ple's war"?

In other words, different groups, characterized by different ideologies, leaders, and historical narratives, generated different and particular spaces for their work. As a generalization, Soviet-aligned socialist groups targeted the spaces of workers; anti-imperialist and nonaligned groups sought to organize slum dwellers and students (although every major group established student wings); some Maoist groups were concerned with building a "national front" of progressive forces (including between radical army officers, bureaucrats and radicalized villagers), others with "direct action," or in fomenting a popular uprising spearheaded by a worker-peasant revolution.

Another reason for the variegated quality of activists' experience of Istanbul—according to some activists themselves—was that certain groups attracted mem-bers from different class backgrounds. In an interview with Nicolas Wroe (2004) in *The Guardian*, Nobel Prize winner Orhan Pamuk says that the idea of writing a "Dostoevsky-ian political novel" was in his head while working on his novel *Snow* (published in 2002). "This idea had a long gestation. In the late-70s, I tried to write a political novel about people like me: upper-class or middle-class students who went with their families to summer houses but [in term time] also played around with guns and Maoist texts and had fanciful ideas about throwing a bomb at the prime minister." Note that Pamuk says "Maoist texts" rather than texts produced by the TKP, whose activists in the main did not "play around with guns." Other activists noted that some groups were more middle class—the term at the time was *petty bourgeois*—or had different combinations of intellectuals and skilled worker members.

At another level, however, activists' perceptions of and experiences in the city were, in fact, rather similar. The interviews revealed the significance of the struggle for control over particular sites or arenas; spatial fields that through this collective assertion of a repertoire of militant embodied techniques and actions were transformed, on a smaller scale and over an increasingly regular duration of time, into *theaters of war*. Dramatically, the power deposited in urban spatial arrangements and reinforced in the orchestrating of events that take place within them is threatened with irrelevance when social movements themselves produce a multiplicity of opposing spatial events in response. Torre (1996: 249) notes how "bodies produce space by introducing direction, rotation, orientation, occupation, and by organizing a *topos* through gestures, traces and marks. The formal structure of these actions, their ability to re-functionalize existing urban spaces, and the visual power of the supporting props contribute to the creation of public space." We have seen how, in addition to their orchestrated concatenation of political techniques of the body, political activists perceived, generated, and sought to dominate space through their visual and sonic strategies too, employing musical practices like crescendo, staccato, dissonance, timbre (tone color) and rhythm in political performance. Similarly, slogans/silence, marching/motionlessness, and choreographed movements such as the ritual of mass *namaz* in public places made powerful interventions in space; these micro-practices were performed repeatedly all over the city, in the process characterizing and partially re-creating public space. Yet clearly there was nothing "public" about the places produced by revolutionary bodies in Istanbul in the late 1970s, given groups' drive first to expel others from them, and then to occupy and monopolize them. Violence inscribed itself on places and bodies, reconfiguring and fragmenting urban space in the process.

In brief, the interviews showed that the *same* spatial strategies were carried out in different *places* over the whole city—for example, the *korsan* (pirate) meeting and enforced listening was enacted at the school, in the street, in the cinema, on the train, at the *kahvehane*, on the picket-line, and in the square; the violent occupation of similarly resounding acoustic spaces was replicated in the factory, in the university lodgment, the slum and even state institutions (namely police stations, or the semi-official People's Houses). Accordingly, activists generated and experienced homogeneity of space across the city despite the varied geometrical, architectural or semiotic dimensions of the built environment. These particular activist performances stitched diverse places in the city together into a single urban field. In the process, and contra Lefebvre's emphasis (see chapter 2), the *tactics of activists constituted space more than spatial organization and arrangements conditioned practices*.

The same domination of frictional spatial practices over the power embedded in the concrete arrangements of buildings can be discerned in the physical violence against "architecture": activists directed regular destructive force against buildings, often through their bombing, in order to stop a rival group's advance into an area, or in order to retaliate against an earlier outrage. This destruction of the built environment—a micro *urbicide* of shops, chemists, coffee houses, tea gardens, meeting houses, and even state institutions—was not an assertion of a desire to be free of the roles projected by buildings so much as an attempt to retard or expel their current occupiers and controllers. According to Humphreys, the term *urbicide* "describes the double project of the destruction of communities, their habits and cultural heritage as an integral part of warfare" (2002: 55). In this definition the semiotics and spatial design of the built environment is read symbolically as representing a cultural/religious group. By contrast, violence against buildings in Istanbul in the 1970s served a more strategic and pragmatic function, as Mustafa's account below shows: "In 1978 or 1979 Metin Yüksel was murdered outside Fatih Mosque. He was a famed figure, carrying two guns, and wasn't scared of anyone. His MHP attackers came from Nevşehir Student Lodgment, which was in the street behind the mosque. In retaliation his Islamist group attacked the lodgment and burnt it down. The building stood empty until after 12 Eylül."

Post-coup social pacification of Istanbul can be understood as an attempt to reverse this feature of social life. That is, the targets of pacification were, first, activists themselves, and then second, their place-constituting spatial practices and performances, and not the destruction and redesign of the geometry of places per se. To achieve this, the army also occupied space—schools, universities, public places, gecekondu, factories, streets and municipalities—and conducted propaganda in them through their own repertoire of spatial, visual, and sonic strategies, from the silencing of places and their desertification through curfews, to pasting "wanted" posters of activists on the walls, the broadcasting of speeches and martial music in public spaces, and by changing place names. For example, following the coup the name of the Ümraniye suburb, 1 Mayıs (May 1st), was changed to Mustafa Kemal (after the founder of the Republic) (Aslan 2004). One of the most powerful symbols of this new authority (*iktidar*) was the junta's occupation of the DİSK building in Ankara, to be reused as the Constitutional Court.

In the face of that ruthless assault, activists could offer only the most fleeting of resistance, as we will see in chapter 7.

6

Militants, Ideologies, (F)actions

What Is to Be Done?

Competing ideologies. Political factions. Activist ideologues. In previous chapters we have explored the creative work of these subjects in devising a huge suite of revolutionary practices, tracing out these practices' transformative spatial force in a variety of urban arenas. In this chapter, we attend more closely to their interrelationships, which revolved around two inseparable concerns: in order to make a revolution, what is our situation, and how is this to be done?

In the social sciences, ideologies, theoretical traditions, and philosophical paradigms that purport to explain the world do not easily run out of explanatory steam. Their perdurance—while the world changes and individuals die—suggests that as much as theories *discover* and *illuminate* certain realities about their objects of explanation, in part they also constitute the *quality* and *meaning* of those objects for those who think through them. For activists in Istanbul in the mid-1970s and later, political ideologies (Kemalism, nationalism, Marxism, socialism, etc.) performed the same role, informing and mediating their perceptions of the city—of the meaning of its environment, the significance of its events, the intentions of its inhabitants-interlocutors, and the political relevance of its global history.

Yet as much as ideologies "spoke" through individuals, individuals gave them particular and uneven vocal tone. To understand that dialogue, we might again find useful certain claims of phenomenology, in particular its insight into how people (for example, activists and intellectuals) inject theories or disciplines into the world as modes of perception, making it as if this is what the world is. In the process, along with providing "mere" meaning, social theories, ideologies, and historiographies also enable "doing" in the world. Thus, they can be examined not only for their arguments but also for their contribution to the shaping of their proponents' moods and actions. Put differently, a phenomenological approach to ideology and theory helps us to value the potential for collective empowerment and personal authority—for expanded agency—that interpretation of texts and discourses provide. More fundamentally, phenomenological anthropology encourages us to consider how political "writ" is "referred to and acted upon in daily [political] life" (Knibbe and Versteeg 2008: 51).

To the extent that political ideologies such as nationalism, socialism, communism, or Kemalism required education to master them and to perceive the world they posited, they were indigenous both to the *habitus* of parties, factions, activists, intellectuals, and political movements in Istanbul, and to state institutions such as schools, universities, and military colleges.[1] Thus pedagogic edification in, and personal adaptation of, political ideologies were complementary processes, as organizations and institutions sought to have novices "think" with their take on the world. Moreover, factions also wanted militants to "feel" the world through their political categories as well. To note just one example, given their commitment to the virtue, defense and enlargement of *Turkish* ethnicity and the *Turkish* state, one core objection of the *ülkücü* and of the MHP to socialism was not only that it would collectivize the means of production and redistribute private property, but also the equally grievous affective fact that Marx, Lenin, Stalin, and Mao were foreigners, or non-Turks. As Ahmet Kabaklı, *Tercüman* newspaper's chief political columnist and MHP supporter, wrote in a mood of heroic yet chilling nihilism, "Both communism and socialism are a creation of Western imperialism. Similarly 'humanism' is another imperialist lie. Cosmopolitanism is dead, as is Westernization. The only thing left is that Turkey becomes itself [*kendi kendisi olacak*]. The future belongs to the Turk-Islam [*Milli-Islam*] synthesis" (*Tercüman*, 10 October 1977).

In brief (and to rephrase a point made in chapter 2), political organizations and political ideologies, which were an intimate aspect of activist life in the late 1970s and early 1980s, did more than model and analyze the world with concepts that constructed a complex reality—through specialized terms like comprador bourgeoisie, feudalism, oligarchy, imperialism, counterrevolutionary forces, Turkishness, state capitalism, national democratic revolution, sharia, nation, and so on. They sought also to generate the moral significance of the world for the activist self, bestowing meaning and value on the entities, histories, and people that they brought to activists' attention. Directing activists' feelings had ethical implications,

1. Further, in an urban age of mass literacy, compulsory schooling, pedagogic and informative state television/radio production, partisan newspapers, apologetic and exegetic journals, and of powerful institutions such as courts of law, much of the population may also be considered "local theorists or ideologues," taking up and adapting to their own purposes other people's contentions or narratives about work, politics, national culture, and the international world.

as ideologies provided an alternative understanding of the self and of others—a new expressive language that allowed people not necessarily to know themselves better but to know themselves (and others) differently. As Sartre notes, emotions transform people's relations to the world "in order that the world may change its qualities" (1976: 61).

This chapter attends to a single broad theme with at least two dimensions—activists' perceptions of their factions and of their factions' ideologies. Minimally, factions and ideologies presented militants with particular accounts of the urban environment in Istanbul, as well as with the causes of the broader theater of conflict in Turkey and around the globe. Attention to activists' experiences of political ideologies and of radical political factions—to their "appearance" or meanings for militants and to the affordances and constraints that they engendered—must take into consideration that revolutionary language and groups are particular kinds of things. For Husserl, different spheres of being (i.e., objects, places, people, or ideas, for example) possess their own specific "mode of being an object of consciousness" (Levinas 1995: 127), and thus what he calls their own "regional ontology." For example, as we have already seen, in the (pre-political) natural attitude, our perception and use of *place* involves the practical utilization of its affordances according to one's wishes, which involves a certain obliviousness to the place's constructed nature and to the efficacy of its builders' intentions embedded in them, in terms of their attempted conditioning of our actions and relationships. Somewhat differently, in our acts of consciousness relating to interactive relations/judgments concerning the *actions and character of other persons*, we presume the meaning of others' utterances and actions derive from their intentions, naively overlooking our own responsibility for partly constituting their comprehensiveness.

What "regional ontology" or ontological specificity was revealed by militants' encounters with factions and even more so with their ideologies? For activists, each appeared or was experienced as making a new and radical truth claim about the world that they inhabited. Thus unlike, say, activists' perception of a table, which referenced their practical immersion in the world, the living of which directed attention to specific dimensions of that table, ideologies and factions were encountered by listeners/readers as making upon them a demand to action, if militants accepted their call or "transcendent" claims to truth. Why does this feature of ideologies emerge for revolutionaries and for theorists? In understanding the nature of our anthropological theories about people's cultural practices, Michael Jackson recommends "setting aside questions concerning the rational, ontological, or objective status of ideas and beliefs" (1998: 10), in favor of a phenomenological method that explores what systems of thought accomplish for those who invoke and use them. By contrast, however, fieldwork with activists in Istanbul confronts how militants and factions themselves pursued exactly those epistemological questions, because they conceived that the truth of ideologies' descriptions of the world was vital in assessing their potentiality to revolutionize it.

Nevertheless, despite their best intentions, not all interviewees felt that they had mastered the complexities of their group's Marxist-Leninist, socialist, Islamist, or nationalist theory. This being so, it would not be faithful to the experience of partisans to present a description (or a reading) of the ideologies of political factions as total, rival, or closed systems in themselves, as might be pursued by political theory, even if their visions and bits and pieces of their language and schemata were vital in inspiring activists' practices. Thus, the chapter moves back and forth between two phenomenological foci: description of how partisans (personally and collectively) constituted or applied ideologies while wrestling with their factions; and analysis exploring how the political/spatial actions, experiences, and decisions of militants were guided by the varied historical narratives, political claims, and economic models of leftist and rightist ideologies.

Last, and briefly, we should remember that the activist recollections of movements and ideologies presented here were (in the main) composed retrospectively—in 2011, 2012, 2014, 2016, and so on. More precisely, militant insights reference a double temporality: the period thirty-five years earlier that included its own a sense of duration, for example when an activist reflected upon the difference that particular events made in their perception of the city at that time; and the present "now" from which they are reflecting. Sometimes interviewees explicitly invoked this double temporality. Thus, in speaking about the sincerity of their convictions, many ex-activists perceived, from their perspective "today," that in the late 1970s factions asserted the absolute truth of their own political ideologies, and discerned suspicious causes in those who thought differently. In other words, reflecting in the present, they understood that three decades earlier they could not hold the position that they held a point of view (and that others held one too). Rather, they bore the pressure of ideologies' truth claims, as well as of political factions' dogma that they alone possessed the correct analysis of the situation.[2] At other points in the interviews ex-militants were less careful to clarify whether their retold anecdotes, stories, and evaluations about the past also reflected their feelings at the time. Sometimes activists commented that that was just how it was then.

---

2. Accepting that others hold a different, equally plausible, point of view reminds us of the recent claim made by Charles Taylor that the most important phenomenological feature of a *secular age* is its creation of a context in which believing in God is just one possibility among others, so that we live "in a situation where we cannot help but be aware that there are a number of different construals, views which intelligent, reasonably undeluded people, of good will, can and do disagree on" (2007: 11). By comparison, the refusal of Istanbul activists to accept the relative truth of the convictions of others makes me wonder whether Taylor's assertion applies only if/when actors depoliticize religious feelings and assertions, quarantining the "transcendent" from politics.

6.1 MILITANT PERCEPTIONS OF FACTIONS
AND IDEOLOGIES

Factions propagated specific ideologies at the same time as ideologies characterized and defined particular factions and parties. Similarly, activists made up and
constituted factions and ideologies, even as factions and their ideological contentions shaped and informed partisans' perceptions. Who or which had agentive
priority—militants, factions, ideologies, or ideologists? Disinterring activists, ideologies, political organizations, and political practices from each other without
dwelling on their entanglements is misleading. Consider Emre's (İGD) experience
below:

> In 1977 I went to France for a visit and came back after a month with a number of
> books in French on Euro-communism. (I went to the French High School.) I showed
> them to a leader of the İGD, who wanted to borrow them. I couldn't get them back
> for a long time. I said something to a friend about him taking my books when he
> could hear. He said to me, "*Senin ne okuyacağına ben karar vereceğim*" [I will decide
> what you will read]. Every *örgüt* had a list of books etcetera that people should read,
> and they didn't like you reading other groups' stuff. They were not the original texts
> of Marx, but material written by the party's leading intellectuals or founders.

Emre's account reveals certain memorable experiences of belonging to these
large and powerful political organizations, as well as insights into how activists
encountered their ideologies and theories. On the one hand note his ardent incli-
nation toward accessing political ideas and theory, of seeking to engage with its
meanings, to apply and to use it. Following Guenther, we might call this his pursuit
of "epistemic agency" (2017). On the other hand, notice his perception of being
forced to submit his explorative reading and theoretical understandings to the
direction of others, and to the "official" ideology of the organization, a curtailing
in turn of his hermeneutical freedom. Here his experience of being simultaneously
both a political actor and of being acted upon by others involved not just intersubjective interplay and conflict between himself and one of the group's leaders but
also between himself and texts/ideas.[3]

A number of other preliminary insights into militants' perceptions of factions/
ideologies emerge in Emre's narrative as well. First, organizations were encountered as places of learning, both for student activists, workers, and for *gecekondu*
inhabitants who were recruited into the party. But like all (effective) education this
involved a guided pedagogy, a reading of vetted, recommended texts and of party
programs. To give just one example, in an education program presented to readers

---

3. For Michael Jackson, this dialectic between the experience of being an agentive subject and of
being a passive object of other forces (people, circumstances, cosmic powers, illness, etc.) is also understood as a central feature of the human existential condition.

in the newspaper *Devrimci Yol* on the fateful morning of 1 May 1977 (p. 15), the reading list contained the following twelve items:

1. *Diyalektik ve Tarihi Materyalizm* (Stalin) (*Dialectical and Historical Materialism*)
2. "*Marksizm Üzerine*" (Lenin) ("*About Marxism*")
3. *Ütopik sosyalizm ve bilimsel sosyalizm* (Engels) (*Utopian and Scientific Socialism*)
4. *Komünist manifesto* (Marx-Engels) (*The Communist Manifesto*)
5. *Yakın çağlar tarihi* (Yeliseyeva) (History of the recent ages)
6. *Emperyalizm* (Lenin) (*Imperialism*)
7. *Devlet ve ihtilal* (Lenin) (*State and Revolution*)
8. *Leninizmin ilkeleri* (Stalin) (*Principles of Leninism*)
9. *Yeni demokrasi* (Mao) (*New Democracy*)
10. *Ulusların kaderlerini tayin hakk* (Lenin) (*Right of National Self-Determination*)
11. *Ulusal sorun ve sömürgeler sorunu* (Stalin) (*National Question and the Problem of Colonialism*)
12. *Kesintisiz devrim* (M. Çayan) (Ceaseless revolution)

Yet prior to this experience of hermeneutical apprenticeship, in the main it was not possible for activists to read, study, or to "shop around" so as to choose in a considered manner a preferred faction for its appealing ideas. Rather, in the first place, militants cast their lot in with a political party or organization—usually because of friends, family ties, or links with place of origin—and thereafter developed their deeply felt ideological convictions. There was, then, a certain intersubjective history to people's exposure to specific groups and ideas. Filiz recalled how she became involved with Kurtuluş because her brother was already an activist with them. Can commented that "our being leftists was inherited from our father" (Mavioglu 2008: 82). Mustafa (TKP) claimed that Alevi from Tunceli were often affiliated to TİKKO; that Samsun leftists were all Kurtuluş; and that activists from Hatay were strongly connected to Acilciler (Urgent Revolutionaries), given the leader was from there. More generally, Mahsis (MHP) thought that children whose fathers voted for the Demokrat Party became rightists and MHP; children whose fathers voted for the CHP became leftists. But there were (comprehendible) exceptions too: Mehmet Pamak explained how he became a leader of the MHP in Çanakkale, despite being of Kurdish descent:

After the infamous "Zilan" massacre [of Kurds] by the Turkish military in 1930, those of my family who survived were exiled to Çanakkale. We were met with great hostility and derision in the village in which we were settled—I can well remember being derided as "Kurds with tails," as well as the threat during my childhood that "you came from the East wearing one shoe, and we will drive you out of this village in the same condition." Yet despite all this oppression, my family never embraced a Kurdish identity. In fact, forget Kurdishness, we tried to prove that Kurds were Turks; we even became Turkish nationalists. My family became leading lights in the Çanakkale Turkish nationalist party. (Pamak 1992: 331–32)

In brief, activists were first friends, sisters, sons, cousins, and locals before they were fascists, socialists, Islamists, or communists.

Second, Emre's experience indicates that political groups were perceived as exclusivist, indeed as censorious of other groups' ideas and as prohibitive of militants' fraternization with other activists (even if at times organizations or parties worked with allied groups on particular campaigns or events). Militants were valuable, and thus factions were experienced as both jealous and as controlling, anxious about the wooing away of members by the partisans, theoretical insights, or more radical actions of other groups. Ömer (CHP) remembered the spatial politics at work while staying at a lodgment in *Dördüncü Levent* for the children of military officers with students from different universities: "the *yurt* was controlled by the left, with different leftist groups eating among themselves and cooking their food in their own kitchens." Bülent (Dev-Sol) recalled how "we had a passion for justice, but we were merciless to ourselves; we couldn't have a relationship with someone from another group." Exclusivity, spatial segregation, and shared political action produced deep camaraderie, expressed and generated in groups' possessing of their own ideological interpretations and keywords, of their own songs and slogans, and of their carving out of their own segregated spaces, even in prison wards. Before the coup, different groups prepared their own food in their own kitchens in prison, just as in the student lodgments. Organizations marked their differences through minor distinctions in style: Orhan (TKP-ML) described it as an "accent" in small details of hats, beards, boots, and coats. Factions also propagated their own histories about why or who split off from whom, or about who truly followed the theoretical and political lineage of earlier influential or charismatic figures or organizations. Samim rather cynically describes them as "gathered around their theories, which in reality functioned as emblems or perhaps trademarks, . . . which represented the "honor" of the group and thus were inevitably petrified" (1981: 82–83).

Reflecting upon this particularistic solidarity, a number of interviewees described factions, in an interesting turn of phrase, as being like "*tarikats*" (Islamic "sufi" groups) united by a "*cemaat duygusu*" (feeling of solidarity of a congregation). Similarly, Yusuf (Sürekli Devrim) described the existence at the time of a "*sekt duygusu*" (sect sense or perception), so much so that groups were like "*mezhep*" (Islamic denominations). What might these expressions mean? None of them were said as complements, regardless of whether their makers had any firsthand experience of participation in Islamic groups (some may have). For leftist ex-activists, perhaps the imagining of resemblances between leftist and religious groups sought to capture their experiences of "blind" commitment to their faction. Yet contradictorily, the analogy also worked to illuminate the proliferation and wild variety of groups, and of their members spinning off to follow someone else. Ahmet (Kurtuluş) posited a different set of religious likenesses: "there was a book and a leader, and the disciples [*müritler*] look for the best interpreter or most knowledgeable person. This accounts for the factions. It isn't surprising, given the hundreds of years of religious organizing/culture." Samim wrote that for leftist militants, "there was an appropriation of Marxism which transformed its theory into closed ideology, even a faith" (1981: 81). With these metaphors, political factions were reimagined as religious-like places of members' willing submission to more knowledgeable leaders, even as they were also experienced at the same time as places of "companionship in conversation" (as mentioned in chapter 2). The religion metaphors suggested one last feature of faction life, a sense of the dependency of inexperienced militants upon factions and their leaders and thus of their predisposition to guided yet premature "actionism."

Third, political factions were experienced internally as both authoritarian and as hierarchical. According to Fatih (THKO-TDY), every group had a "constitution" and a manifesto, its foundation stone (*temel taş*). These were un-debatable, at least by most cadres: if you disagreed, you would become contrary (*aykırı*) to the party's line. Deniz (Kurtuluş), too, remembered that there was little room for debate within a party—insistence upon an alternative position meant that suddenly you were told that you had been expelled (*kovuldun*). For her, this was an organizational problem, and factions' lack of internal democracy or any platform for debate was partly responsible for members' traffic from one group to another. Despite the slogan "democratic centralization," most groups were much more centralized than democratic. Of course, Turkish socialists have not been the only people to struggle with the difficulty of reconciling common group action with the ongoing freedom of individual members. MHP militants experienced the same authoritarian rule even more explicitly—Ömer commented that at the time he couldn't see any contradiction in the ülkücü saying, "*Fikirde hür, emirde robotuz*" (Free in ideas, robots on command). Whereas for leftist militants the experience of hierarchy and authoritarianism stood in theoretical contradiction to many groups' professed ideals of democracy and egalitarianism, for MHP activists, sayings such as "*Üstler tenkit edilemez*" (Those above cannot be criticized) were asserted to reflect core features of Turkish culture and conduct such as absolute obedience and military discipline. Similarly, Metiner (2008: 85) notes that at Erbakan rallies, the Akıncılar saw no problem in crying out in a single voice, "*Vur de vuralım. Öl de ölelim*" (Tell us to strike and we will strike. Tell us to die and we will die).

But a number of interviewees also insinuated that personal rivalries (or a belief among rival leaders in a group or party that they could do it better) led to the defection or transfer of people from faction to faction as well, even if after the act of separation ideological disagreements were often posited as the cause of the rupture.

Alongside loyalty and faithfulness to political creeds and to the charismatic leaders that articulated them, militants experienced chronic instability and improvisation, a mixing and making up of things on the spot to pin down events, people and circumstances in flux. Mehmet Metiner tells of a memorable meeting he attended in Maraş, organized by a group within the local Akıncı association:

> On the table there was a Koran and a Turkish flag. The leader pulled out a gun from behind his back and placed it on the table, saying that now we must swear an oath upon them. I can't remember the oath exactly, but it included promising that we would never renounce the cause, and that even until death we would pursue war [*cihat*] with our whole souls and resources. We swore upon the Koran, the flag and the gun. It was the first time any of us had ever encountered such a ceremony.... Until that day our organization had never held such an oath-taking ritual. (Metiner 2008: 67)

Metiner concludes his account by saying that at the time it was not known that Salih Mirazbeyoğlu and his group (in Maraş) had initiated a campaign from within the Akıncı association to foster a more militant Islamic politics—its members later broke away and formed the IBDA-C (Greater Eastern Islamic Raiders Front).[4]

Here we might consider the significance of what some ex-activists identified as a dominant mood shared by militants in the late 1970s. Kenan (HK) thought that they possessed a "subaltern arrogance" (*küstahlık*), an attitude of "I'm oppressed, so I can do anything." Similarly, Levent (Kurtuluş) attributed their mistakes and lack of respect to their youth, and felt that militants had "swelled heads," as if drunk on their own power (*çok şımartıldık*). He recalled being in prison before the coup, and shouting at the guard for not bringing him watermelon! Mustafa (TKP) remembered that there was a belief that "we could do anything." Although such comments appear to criticize militants' personal ethics, it is also the case that ideologies relate, as Michael Jackson reminds us, to matters of existential agency as much as to issues of theoretical coherence or to economic and political advantage (1998: 21). Thus, in internal group rivalries we can divine the political and personal *utility* gained by political actors via their mastery or radicalization of ideology, say by creatively applying a narrative of historical materialism that understands the present as a stage in an unfolding process of transformation, or by painting a rival's position as inappropriately passive.[5]

---

4. Salih Mirazbeyoğlu was a member of the Akıncı who had started a second journal in the name of the organization in the late 1970s. He was famously arrested in 1998 and imprisoned until 2014 for being the leader of an illegal Islamist terror organization (IBDA-C).

5. Similarly, Kemalist elites have long indexed their own personal authority to manage and restructure society to exposition of how their reforms conform to a purported universal socio-evolutionary progress.

Last, Emre's narrative above reveals a core related facet of the pedagogic, exclusivist/introverted, and authoritarian qualities of organizations: activists' experience of their defensive, hostile and/or disputatious relationships with other parties and fractions. To engage in politics meant to join a party, group, or organization—most of which were in defensive positions against other groups. All interviewees commented upon the high degree of factionalism experienced by leftist militants, so much so that union organizers might pressure employers to sack workers from rival unions or factions. In an interesting re-interpretation of the past, Ömer (HK) noted, "Although they didn't use the term at the time, certain leftist groups were like 'blood enemies'" (*kan düşmanlar*). According to this analogy, political factions resembled not religious organizations so much as kin-groups, their solidarity and violence articulated with affective sentiments of family honor, loyalty, and revenge. Dropping out equated with the betrayal of one's (political) lineage. Emre finished his account above by describing his anxiety about giving up political activity, after he had been shot and wounded in a feud with another leftist faction: "After getting out of hospital I left the group, against the consent of the leader. For weeks I was watching out of windows in case they attacked me. There was an ülkücü saying: 'Strike the one who leaves the cause: strike me, if I leave.' [*Bizi terkedeni vur: terkedersem beni de vur*]. I was worried that the same principle applied in the left."

More generally, socialist groups inspired by the Soviet revolution and perhaps part supported by the Soviet Union (i.e., TİP, TKP, TSİP [Turkish Socialist Workers Party) competed for influence with those animated by the Maoism of the Chinese revolution (i.e., PDA [Proletarian Revolutionary Enlightenment), HB, TKP-ML-TİKKO, and HK).[6] In that rivalry, the *orta yol* (middle way) or independent groups (i.e., THKP-C, Dev-Yol/Dev-Sol; MLSPB [Marxist Leninist Armed Propaganda Brigade]; Kurtuluş) were useful, at least according to interviewees from those organizations, as they had no *defining* ideological opposition that disallowed their supporting certain actions of the leftist factions oriented to either Chinese or Soviet communism. However, as we have already seen, ideological rivalries were over-determined by spatial politics, so that even groups with similar theoretical positions could become rivals and refuse common cause. Indeed, as the select rollout of groups' names above show, within each of these three general groupings—pro-Soviet, pro-Maoist, and nonaligned—there were influential contending factions. And as my interviewees have already revealed, in the 1970s there were many more legal and illegal organizations, groups, journals, and political "tendencies" than those listed above.

---

6. During the Sino-Albanian split HK abandoned official Chinese political positions and became followers of Enver Hoxha in Albania.

While the left was a fractured yet growing mass movement, Yaprak (TKP) felt that antagonism between leftist groups existed partly because people "perceived a revolution would happen, so there was a struggle for power. Who would be more powerful, who would earn the right through doing more than others?" Haydar (DİSK) said something similar: "You believed a revolution was coming, you needed to get your place. Thus, if there was a revolution in which the workers were to be at the front, each group tried to organize the workers. There was a leftist sickness, all energy devoted to fighting against other groups." Interviewees confirmed that as the conflict between factions intensified, less-politicized people started to cool on the left, so that by 1978 the mass movement had begun to lose popular support.

The fate of the people's houses (halkevleri) was a case in point. Reopened in 1963 by civil society groups independent of the state/government, by the mid-1970s the many halkevleri in Istanbul were active in music courses (saz), theater, and mathematics lessons for high school students, as well as in educational seminars on a wide range of topics (photography, arts, etc.). Managed by various leftist groups that had won control of them in elections, including by a leftist current in the CHP, in poorer suburbs the halkevleri, too, began to be caught up in the violent "anti-fascist" struggle taking place all over the city. Thus Mustafa (İGD/TKP) remembered that in 1979 a bomb was thrown into the garden of the large halkevi in Bakırköy, killing three people and scaring parents so that they stopped sending their children there. Similarly, Hüseyin (DİSK) recalled how in 1976 the Küçükçekmece halkevi congress was so large it had to be held in a cinema. Thirty participants came in 1979. "The people left, the militants stayed behind," he commented wryly.

To summarize, how did activists experience factions and ideologies? Over and above their particular arguments and claims, political ideologies possessed powerful agency for activists: exercising a force to segregate space; creating or fracturing relationships; and generating amity or enmity. Partisans perceived that ideological positions constituted political groups, being narratives told by members to bind themselves together. At the very same time, however, ideologies were also experienced as efficacious doctrines that sundered one group from another. For novices, revolutionary language appeared as a sort of gnostic knowledge that reinforced leadership and hierarchy within the group. Ideologies caused things to happen, through their stirring of emotions and by their declaration of allies and enemies.

However, militants also recalled how ideologies were useful for reckoning with their options, for the project of revolutionizing the city; and perhaps for short-circuiting history itself by providing guidance on the correct strategy for taking power. Thus, for activists, the content of ideologies did matter, despite intuition of the similarities of factions' use of them, and indeed of the similarities of factions' organizational habits. Below we see how for militants the truth or "end" of ideologies/concepts was important because it preceded decisions concerning their adoption as means of revolution.

6.2 WHAT IS TO BE DONE? IDEOLOGICAL ANALYSIS AND REVOLUTIONARY STRATEGY

In a final arresting comparison, Serdar (Aydınlık) proposed that "factions were like feudal groups, trying to collect members." Like the other similes noted above, here *feudal* is a loaded word, given the heated debates in the late 1960s and 1970s among the left, both in Turkey and internationally, over the political and economic characteristics of agrarian production. But why was such a simile or debate bitterly controversial, apart from reasons of scientific accuracy?

Leftists perceived that analysis of the structure of the political economy was inseparable from identifying the proper revolutionary tactics for seizing power. Thus, if the form of production dominant in rural areas was feudal or semi-feudal, then political struggle to destroy landlordism and feudalism must take priority. If capitalist relations had already penetrated and transformed the agricultural structure, then socialist struggle should seek the destruction of capitalism. "Ideologies," then—in this case, contrasting claims about the structure of the economy and of the class relations existing in the country—led to the pursuit of different political strategies.[7] The reverse became true as well: polemics over political analysis reflected disagreement over revolutionary practice and commitments. Before exploring how activists themselves remembered and recounted the links made by their factions between interpretation of the society/state and revolutionary strategy, let me recreate in the language of the day two short and antagonistic case studies, one leftist and one rightist, to show how contrarily social conditions might be described and then articulated with political tactics.

First, what spatial politics should follow if an oligarchic landlord class, aligned with a "comprador" bourgeoisie, dominate society and the state in conjunction with international centers of imperialism, particularly American? The existence of a comprador class demands an anti-imperialist politics; the existence of a landed

---

7. Stalin's definition of Kemalism in 1927 is a good example of how a description of Turkey's class situation is intimately associated with a "failed" political program. For Stalin, "The Kemalist revolution is a revolution from above, of the national mercantile bourgeoisie, which was created during the struggle against the foreign imperialists and, in its further development, was directed essentially against peasantry and workers, against the very possibilities of an agrarian revolution.... The characteristic feature ... of the Turkish revolution is that it is stuck in the 'first step,' in the first phase of its development, the phase of the bourgeois-liberation movement, without even trying to proceed to the second phase of its development—the phase of the agrarian revolution" (in Ter-Matevosyan 2019: 188–89).

oligarchy means peasants must be organized (and might represent the base for a mass opposition). If an earlier military coup had punctured hopes in the "leftist" or nationalist faction in the army and state, then that disappointment leads logically to the founding of a replacement *people's* army (of liberation) and, if necessary, to urban guerrilla war and armed struggle.

Yet what happens to political strategy if we vary the diagnosis of social conditions, even slightly? Assume that precapitalist feudal relations organize Turkish agriculture in alliance with a "*collaborationist*" (*işbirlikçi*) bourgeoisie under the hegemony of US imperialism. Together landlords and capitalists dominate subordinated classes such as workers and peasants through a parliamentary mechanism, which is also seen as obstructing the developmentalist and nationalist principles of the early Republic. Should not the logical consequence be an adaption of the revolutionary potential of Kemalism by creating a national alliance—that is, an alliance between student militants, radical/young military officers, the *national* (noncomprador) bourgeoisie, the progressive state bureaucracy, and civilian intelligentsia (who should become its leading vanguard)—that might modernize the economy, including conducting land reform?[8] The first analysis (made by Dev-Yol/Dev-Sol, MLSPB, etc.) led to rebel guerrilla struggle; the second (MDD [National Democratic Revolution]; Aydınlık-TİKP; Denge Kawa) to attempts to constitute a national front and ferment a "revolutionary" officers' coup.

On the political right, organizations developed their specific ideologies in disputatious terms as well. Disagreement over the nature and extent of imperialism, and thus controversy over the oppositional tactics that its character merited, was not reserved for the left. The "fascist right," to use Keyder's term, also sought to understand Turkey's underdevelopment, positing a "chauvinistic explanation that defensively glorified the history of Turkish states but at the same time identified a culprit in western attempts to subjugate the Turkish race" (1987: 211). Equally powerful within it was a pan-Turkist current, which saw in the Chinese and Russian oppression and diminution of ethnic Turks (Uyghurs and others), a *communist* imperialism that threatened communal self-determination and national sovereignty.

By contrast, Islamist religious parties and activists were anti-imperialist in a different way (to the MHP), despite a common background in the ideology of the

---

8. Latin American socialists were caught up in similar debates over social analysis and political program. According to Carlos Fuentes, given that agrarian feudalism was the basis of the wealth and political domination of the governing classes in Latin America, the "political conclusions drawn from such a conception involved the elimination of feudalism through a revolution in which the bourgeoisie was to play a progressive role" (in Seddon and Marguilies 1983: 4). It was that diagnosis that led Gunder Frank to ask in response why the "national" bourgeoisie would want to solve the issues of imperialism and feudalism, and thus why political radicals would seek to join a "national front" to support them (4). See also Keyder 1987: 209ff.

Turkish-Islamic synthesis.[9] As relations between right-wing Turkish nationalists and emerging Islamists soured in the late 1970s (especially after the 1979 Iranian revolution), Islamists challenged the anti-communist and thus (occasional) pro-American sentiment of the MHP by critiquing Western colonialism in Muslim countries for its establishing of puppet anti-Islamic regimes that were accused, like the Kemalists themselves, of seeking to destroy religion. In response, in Istanbul the ülkücü accused the Akıncılar, with their anti-American and anti-Republican stance, of being "yeşil komünist" (green communists). As in the first case above, contrasting social analysis issued in rival and opposed anti-imperialist political conduct. Turkists pursued civil war/militarism that would eliminate non-Turks and/or "racially degenerate" leftists from the Turkish nation.[10] Islamists worked for the establishment of a şeriat state that would reorder Kemalist society. According to Müfit (MSP), these differences meant that their youth wings did not like each other and rarely held joint events, especially after the killing of Mehmet Yüksel in the courtyard of Fatih Cami (see chapter 1).

In what ways did other ex-partisans, in our spontaneous and performative interviews, describe groups' rival interpretations of political realities, and how did they extract an activist or revolutionary method from them? As a learner, I was impressed by ex-activists' sociological acumen concerning their own factions, their defining theoretical positions and related spatial politics, as well as their knowledge—sometimes partisan or conflicted—of the genealogies, ideological positions, political strategies, and alliances (both practical and theoretical) of other groups. Their insights into the variety of concepts of revolutionary strategy held by different factions were part of their broader knowledge of political viewpoints, as well as of reasons for leftists' lack of unity. Indeed, they recounted this knowledge three-and-a-half decades after the destruction by the military junta of their own parties and organizations.

· For example, in response to my query about antagonistic political programs amongst leftist groups themselves, Kenan (ex-TİKP) sketched out the synoptic diagram below, identifying three dominant circles of political "prejudice" (or

9. In his autobiography, Mehmet Metiner claims that in the late 1960s and early 1970s the position of the MTTB, the first youth organization of the MSP, was not a "Turkish-Islam" synthesis so much as an "Islam-Turkist" one. In it, both Turkey and the wider Muslim world were presented as needing the "nation chosen and saved by God," or a Turkish-led Islam (2008: 36). By the late 1970s, an Islamist critique of both syntheses had emerged, captured in the slogan-like saying of the Akıncılar: "Ne Sağcıyız ne Solcu, İslamcıyız İslamcı' (Neither Rightist nor Leftist, we are Islamist Islamist).

10. Orhan explained to me why he "chose" to be a rightist (sağcı): "I loved Turkish values, Turkish identity, Turkish music, and Turkish national culture. I played the ney. I was a 'cultural nationalist' [kültür milliyetçisi] or a 'conservative nationalist' [muhfazakar milliyetçi] or a 'religious nationalist' [dini milliyetçi]. We didn't like Ataturk for changing Turkish culture. The Muslims were weak, so in Istanbul it was mainly the communists versus the nationalists. According to us, differences in left factions didn't matter; they were all communists, and we wanted to stop communists and defend Turkish culture."

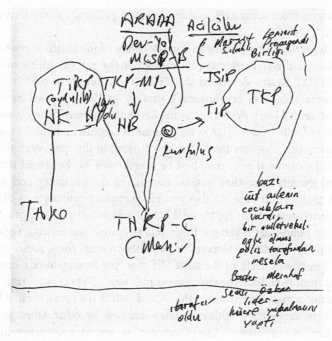

FIGURE 3. Leftist groups' family tree (Christopher Houston).

prejudgment) and practice in the second half of the 1970s, as well as traces of their predecessors from earlier in the decade.

On the left of the diagram, growing out of the THKO (Turkey Peoples Liberation Army), he situates a "Maoist" cluster, including HK, TİKP (Aydınlık, for whom in the 1970s he was an organizer), TKP-ML, and HB (Peoples Brigade), seen as a breakaway or development from it, and HY, whom he presents as also issuing from the THKP-C. In the center he inscribes the acronyms of three other groups—Dev-Yol, MLSPB, and Acilciler. He traces their ideas and strategies back to another influential organization, the THKP-C and (in brackets) to Mahir (Çayan), one of its founders, shot dead in a siege with nine other partisans in Kızıldere village after their kidnapping and killing of an Israeli consular official in 1972.[11] On the right-hand side is a socialist circle around the TKP, seen as aligned

11. For activists or political groups emotionally connected with the original THKP-C, Kızıldere has become a site of specific memory and meaning, a symbol of heroic resistance to an oppressive order. A number of leftist bands have composed songs titled "Kızıldere," including Grup Yorum, Grup Munzur, and the singer Selda Bağcan. Accompanied prominently by the *bağlama*, the songs affirm that "Kızıldere unutulmayacak" (Kızıldere will not be forgotten).

in some way or, more accurately, as sharing certain political assumptions with the TİP and the TSİP.

Interestingly, Kurtuluş (Liberation) in the center of the sketch is positioned as moving closer to the TKP orbit despite its origin in the guerrilla ideals and actions of the THKP-C. Kenan described the THKP-C as *focoist*, in part inspired by Che Guevara's successful revolutionary strategy in Cuba, as well as by Regis Debray's influential work *Revolution in the Revolution? Armed Struggle and Political Struggle in Latin America* (1967), his critique of Leninist and Maoist theories of "timely" revolution that was translated into Turkish in the same year. According to Debray, the capitalist state may best be overthrown by the armed struggle of a vanguard guerilla force that "resists" mobilizing the peasantry and separates itself from their self-defense. In that process exemplary military acts of guerilla bands, by providing a *focus* for popular but suppressed discontent, can catalyze, speed-up, or jump-start a general insurrection against the existing regime. For Debray, popular support of workers or peasants *proceeds from*, rather than *precedes*, the insurgency itself, in the same way that "the formation of a broad anti-imperialist front is realized through the people's war" (Debray 1967: 125). Turkish *focoism* gained a mass dimension in the second-half of the 1970s, even as it developed different tendencies. Although often accused by other leftist groups of "adventurism" or of anarchy, "[Che] Guevarist," or focoist, movements in Turkey (THKP-C, Dev-Yol/Dev-Sol, MLSPB etc.) appeared to agree with Debray's claim that "*the people's army will be the nucleus of the party, not vice versa. The guerilla force is the political vanguard in nuce and from its development a real party can arise*" (115, italics in original). "Armed propaganda" became one of its key practices, constituting both a mode of revolutionary action and a mode of relationship with the people, even as its pursuit necessitated distance from them as well as organizational secrecy.

Armed propaganda also potentially facilitated the onset of a new relationship with one's self. According to Hamit Bozarslan, and as may be discerned in Frantz Fanon's work as well, in the poetry of Mahir Çayan there is a personalization of revolution as creating a "New Man." For Çayan, "the responsibility for slavery also lies with the slave himself and it is only his resistance that will allow him to become a free man. Violence is the main key to reach this goal" (Bozarslan 2012: 6). Thus, the guerilla movements' general accusations of passivity against, say, the TKP is best understood from this *foco* actionist perspective. If we take this accusation metaphorically rather than literally—TKP cadres were just as politically active in their own way—we can identify in both leftist and rightist activisms multiple and contrasting *temporalities* of revolution, as well as a variety of moods connected to different strategies for social and self-transformation. Factions disagreed over the *time* or *tempo* of revolution. Guerilla groups who pursued acts of revolutionary violence and armed propaganda did so in a mood of impatient hyper-agency, whereby they calculated such acts would crack open both existing social relations and the selves constituted and oppressed by them.

Some of the more spectacular *focoist* actions in the late 1970s included the robbing of the Ankara-to-Van train in 1977 and, in 1979, Dev-Sol's "confiscation" of both an oil tanker and the Migros supermarket bus for distribution of their resources to the people. But militants from rival groups were also familiar with *focoist* presumptions. Ümit (TKP-ML) described the Acilciler as arguing that you shouldn't wait for the proper conditions for a revolution: "With your propaganda connected to your actions, you sought to bring the revolutionary process to a head. You don't wait for the working class but can bring things to a sharp point [*keskinleştirelim*]. You might assassinate some retired judge, and leave a note saying why you did it—'the man-made corrupt decisions.' The problem was that the other side had more powerful means of propaganda. It would be reported next day about his children being left fatherless, for example."

Last, in the bottom corner of the diagram I record a comment of Kenan, in which he reported that in the group MLSPB, famous for what he called its "Baader-Meinhof" type of actions, there had been a number of members from upper-class families, including the son of a Parliamentarian who was killed by police. He also mentioned the name of notorious police informer Şemsi Özkan, who was in the organizing committee of the group. In the superimposition of my notes upon Kenan's sketch we see a tension between the language of communalism that characterized leftist and rightist theorizing—as encountered in their use of terms for groups such as the petty-bourgeoisie, the peasants, Turks, Muslims, the people, and so on—and a language that referenced the individuals that made up such collectives, personally notorious for their particular actions or fate.

Kenan's sketch bears comparison with another diagram, titled "Family Tree of the Turkish Radical Left" (unfortunately too big to print). Sometime after our interview, Bülent, who had been a partisan of TKP-ML, sent it to me. Certain differences and similarities between the two diagrams are worth commenting upon.[12] Bülent's family tree of the radical left presents an even earlier "ancestor" for the THKP-C and THKO, each seen as originating in the Dev-Genç (Young Revolutionaries) movement. In turn, TIP is drawn as an earlier forebear of Dev-Genç itself, although the tree also sketches in a number of organizational or ideological ruptures in its identified chains of transmission. Bülent's leftist family tree also reveals much more clearly (than Kenan's) the profusion of groups and fractions that blossomed in the years after the 1974 amnesty, as well as their rapid fragmentation. In it at least forty-eight different groups appeared in the years between 1974

---

12. Neither visual representation includes the Republican People's Party among the leftist lineages, despite its moving in the 1970s to a more social-democratic position, and the forming of a leftist faction within it partly inspired by a program of "reformed municipalism."

and 1980. Interviewees were not convinced that this burgeoning of leftist factions necessarily equated with overall growth in a pan-leftist movement. Şahin (THKP-C) noted that "every split meant the groups got smaller and smaller," an apt analysis for his experience in groups inspired by the legend of Mahir Çayan.[13]

However, common to both diagrams are the three concatenations (or clusters) of political groups with their somewhat similar—if not to their partisans—ideological tendencies. In Bülent's tree we see fractions branching out from TIP and sympathetic to the "Soviet" socialist model, those inspired by the Cuban experience and the THKP-C (the diagram shows four major revolutionary groups developing from it), and a congeries of hostile groups galvanized by THKO and animated by different types of Maoism. There is also something slightly misleading about each diagram that arises from their visual method, or from the objectivist genealogical tracing of descent lines and founding dates. Groups did not become "anachronistic" or replace themselves quite so cleanly, meaning that they continued to have multiple simultaneous existences.

A number of activists were similarly informative about certain empirical landmarks of the political landscape. Hüseyin recalled that Aydınlık held its first congress in 1980, in which ten thousand members joined, with maybe three thousand from Istanbul. "We weren't very strong in factories, but in 1978 HY joined us, and they had connections to the *tershane* [dockyards]." Mustafa (Vatan Partisi and unionist) described how the three biggest groups in Istanbul were Dev Yol, TKP, and HK. "Dev Sol's journal sold seventy to eighty thousand copies. TKP's theoretical journal was *Ürün*, and its political strength lay in DİSK and the newspaper *Demokrasi.*' Ergun (TKP) reported that in 1978 there were "five hundred members of the Communist Party, 50 percent of whom were professionals, being supported salary-wise by the party. The others had their own jobs. Members were seen as elite." Filiz (TKP) confirmed that "to become a member you needed to be invited, and recommended. (This "new" Communist Party only started after 1973.) That is, membership came from the party, not the other way around. Members were assigned a place to work, in İGD, in a union, a big factory, professional chambers, or in a halkevi."

More subjectively, how did other leftist militants talk about group formation, revolutionary strategy, and the ideological features of their own and rival groups? Mehmet (Partizan Yolu) said, "We saw ourselves as leading and organizing the

13. More than those people who were involved in its everyday dynamics knew about this complex dividing of political organizations. For example, I was surprised to read in the rightist newspaper *Tercüman* an interview published with an unnamed officer from the Politics Bureau of the police, who reported that after the death of Mahir Çayan the THKP-C had split into five groups, each struggling for influence and to take the initiative in actions as urban guerillas influenced by South American history. It even named the leaders of one of them (Dev-Yol), Gülten Çayan and Taner Akçam. See *Tercüman,* 19 October 1977, p.10.

working class [*işçi sınıfı*]. We thought that the TKP was too passive/pacifist and we believed in armed struggle, as in South America. We agreed with the ideology of Dr. Hikmet Kıvılcımlı, who is buried in Topkapı" (died 1971, see chapter 8). Somewhat similarly, Mustafa (TKP) remembered that "everyone attacked the TKP, from left and right. We were accused of being pacifist by more radical leftists—'we're fighting fascists,' they said—yet we too were attacked by the ülkücü." Mustafa thought there was a jealousy from smaller leftist groups toward the TKP, at the same time as a worshipping of violence and weapons. By contrast, Haydar remembered that "even in the TKP there was a serious debate in 1978 around the issue of violence. A group called TKP İşçinin Sesi [TKP Workers' Voice] argued for opposition through weapons."

Filiz (Dev-Sol) explained the clash of perspectives on violence succinctly: "There were a couple of key areas of distinctions that distinguished groups from each other. Everyone wanted socialism, but believed in different methods to achieve it. Thus, one big difference [*ayrım*] was between those who believed in armed struggle, compared to those who sought a parliamentary road, or peaceful means (like TKP), who believed in educating the workers (conscientizing them) as their first duty." Bülent remembered that militants in Dev-Yol, caught up in a violent conflict with the ülkücü, would say, "What peace? They are attacking us!" In a like vein, Hüseyin (TKP) recollected that "there was ideological resistance to the idea of winning the council and then making changes. For proponents of a National Democratic Revolution, this was seen as a form of opportunism, and was looked down upon in revolutionary terms. If you argued about entering elections, you would be seen as an agent. "'That isn't a revolutionary approach,' you would be told."

Alongside debates concerning the efficacy of armed struggle versus popular mobilization, political factions also staked their political strategies and futures on different groups within society as the locus of revolutionary (or counterrevolutionary) force or hope. For unionist Haydar (TKP), Marxism aimed at a modern society, and the working class was the target for politics. "For the TKP this meant the industrial workers, city youth, city women. The TKP wanted a revolution but a progressive democratic revolution first, then a socialist one. You win a space for yourself by working to win the workers. The aim was to lessen exploitation; but to *abolish* it a revolution was necessary." Gün left HK for Kurtuluş, seeing in its political practice a more conventional Marxism that similarly assumed the importance of the industrial working class in the establishing of any new society:

> Maoists were more interested in poverty than in class. I was more interested in class struggle. That's one reason why I left HK to join Kurtuluş, which was half pro-Soviet but also oriented to the workers movement. After a while I didn't want to be in a group thinking about peasant movements. Kurtuluş split from Dev-Yol in 1976. Dev-Yol didn't have links with workers. Kurtuluş's intention—a good intention—was to

be closer to the working class; it wanted to do class struggle. I went to Cevizli, where they made Maltepe cigarettes, to teach workers about Marxism. When I left [with some others] they called us CBS, which was also a well-known paint brand. It was short for *çizgisi belirsiz sosyalistler* [Socialists whose line is unknown/don't know their line].[14]

By radical distinction, Bülent (TİKP/*Aydınlık*) reflected upon changes in his group's position in the mid-1970s, on their "discovery" of outside forces as the paramount players in Turkey's fate and prime source of its internal contradictions, and thus on their downgrading of the importance of political forces and fractures at a national level:

> Initially we were very hard, but Doğu Perinçek devised a new strategy after 1975. We called it "*real politika*." We didn't agree with armed struggle. We supported China against the Soviet Union, and began to forget about *iç çelişkiler* [internal contradictions] in the name of attributing everything to international forces. In that process we began to separate from all the other groups, and we proclaimed the Soviet Union a bigger threat than the US, saying it wanted to interfere in Turkey. We even had a new slogan in 1980: "*Dördüncü Ordu Kars'a*" [The Fourth Army (based in the Aegean) to Kars (in the East)]. All of that was wrong [I think now].[15]

Bülent's last comment—his critique of his party's minimizing of the relative autonomy of local fields of struggle and domination—is illustrative of the circumspect tenor of many interviewees' reflections. Reporting their ideological assessments in the past tense, nearly all activists conveyed that this was what they believed then, but that they didn't think in the same way now. This thoughtfulness included finely considered judgments about ideology, made in the light of the 12 Eylül coup and its bringing to a shocking end all expectations and hopes of revolution. To give just one example, Faruk (TKP-ML) acknowledged how "dogma led to *deformasyon*: people couldn't see properly, like they were looking through spectacles that distorted reality." Yet Faruk also noted that the left had had little time for

14. Although the period 1974–1983 is not known for its humor, in fact comic political word play was common. To give one more example, according to Ali (Dev-Yol), they used to mock Maoist groups (such as HB, HK, HS) by referring to them as *Halkın teferrüatı* (People's incidentals/miscellaneous).

15. Here Bülent is referring to Aydınlık's assent to the "three-world theory" attributed to Mao Zedong, in which the globe is divided into three political blocs, including the *imperialist* United States and the *social imperialist* USSR in the first; Europe, Canada, and developing powers in the second; and exploited third world countries (including Turkey) in the third. The import of the theory is not the global divisions per se but the political strategies that emerge from them. For pro-Chinese Maoist groups in the third bloc, principal political tactics involved struggle against the first world superpowers and solidarity with the underdeveloped third world (if necessary, with Pinochet in Chile), and only secondarily struggle against "minor contradictions" such as that between state oligarchy and workers within Turkey itself. Thus, for Kurdish Maoist groups such as *Denge-Kawa* the three-world theory enjoined support for Kemalism and the Turkish state. See also Jongerden and Akkaya 2018: 276.

the development of "scientific thought," as it was only since 1961 that a leftist politics in Turkey had begun to form. "To think about politics—the armory was weak. There was no time to say, stop, let me think a bit. Life didn't wait." Despite this realization, Faruk was also able to appreciate the rapid generation of ideas and practices by political organizations: for him, "activists were productive" (*verimli*), even as that productivity became sectarian and intolerant of other "creeds."

Last, let me conclude this section by briefly summarizing a number of *written* accounts by former activists who (at a different remove from events) have also critically engaged with factions' answers to their urgent question, "What Is to Be Done?"[16] Wise in retrospect as befits the more comprehensive thinking that writing allows, activists' accounts are also somewhat more sociological and historical than those referenced above. Written almost immediately after the coup in 1981 under conditions of martial law and published in *New Left Review*, Ahmet Samim (a pseudonym) accuses leftist factions and activists in the 1970s of being obsessed with power. He notes the result was bitter debate over revolutionary lines of action, so that groups' theories and actions were divorced from the real situation and concerns of workers, peasants, and others. For him, the left approached the question of strategy "as one takes up a cookery book to produce a marvelous dish—in which both the structure of the country and the masses were no more than ingredients. The fetishization of 'immediate' power and 'total' struggle drew the left further and further away from reality" (1981: 82). Writing some three years later, Mehmet Salah (also a pseudonym?) argues that the young revolutionaries who opted for guerrilla warfare in the 1970s seriously misjudged political and social circumstances, given that conditions that might license such struggle did not exist in Turkey: "There was no stagnation in mass mobilizations, neither was there powerful reformist-syndicalist control over the workers' movement, nor was the left movement stuck in the limitations of parliament" (1984: 98). Three years later again (in 1987) Çaglar Keyder discerns a similarly drastic misdiagnosis of Turkey's social conditions by leftist groups, but this time on the grounds of an erroneous analysis of its political economy. Because "the agrarian structure was not characterized by the existence of a landed oligarchy, and the internal market-oriented, state-supported bourgeoisie was hardly comprador," any political strategy based on such assumptions "was also misdirected. . . . The left's analysis of underdevelopment legitimized its departure from more customary socialist aims and shifted the emphasis towards national development within statist anti-imperialism" (1987: 209).

16. In Lenin's *What Is to Be Done? Burning Questions of Our Movement*, published in 1902, he sets out the relationship between the working class and a revolutionary socialist party. As with Debray's *Revolution in the Revolution*, widespread dissemination of its Turkish translation(s) in the 1960s and '70s made it an influential text.

In his more narrowly focused study *The Socialist Movement in Turkey 1960–1980* (published five years later in 1992), Igor Lipovsky devotes his last two chapters to the question of the lack of unity (in both ideas and action) between four legal socialist parties (TİP, TSİP, SP [Socialist Party], TEP [Turkey Workers Party]) in the second half of the 1970s. Animosity between their leaders played a part, but Lipovsky identifies three besetting weaknesses in socialist politics. The first was an inability to connect socialist theory with the labor movement. The second was its inability to found any mass political party. And the third was its inability to move beyond its origins in the intelligentsia and labor aristocracy. His summarizing conclusion is quotable: "It was impossible that all of the above would not affect the socialist movement in 1960–1980, a period generally characterized by splintering, organizational weakness, insufficient political maturity, the absence of ties with the masses and the constant tendency to split" (1992: 166).

Ergun Aydınoğlu takes a more organizational perspective in *Türkiye Solu (1960–1980)*, published in 2007. According to Aydınoğlu, the party/group structure of, say, the TKP was very strong. But Dev-Yol, the biggest group in Istanbul, was different: it was a more fluid organization, and given Mahir Çayan (THKP-C) was killed in 1972 without writing much, it was unable to base its work or lineage on a "charismatic" intellectual figure. For Aydınoğlu, charismatic figures represent some "historical gain," and give groups historical legitimacy, connecting them to a social movement. More generally, Aydınoğlu makes the point that an organizational "deficit" characterized the rapidly growing mass leftist movement after 1974, so that despite its much larger numbers of activists and sympathizers it was less effective in influencing politics than TİP in the 1960s. For him,

> Devrimci Yol, Halk Kurtuluş, Kurtuluş etc., who in these years expanded to become powerful movements, can best be described not as organizations in the true meaning of the term but as interesting compounds of social movement and political sect. . . . An important sector of leftist political activities in the 1960s took place within modern political parties (TİP). The actions of this party and their related division of labor, like every modern political organization, was made within the bounds of administrative law. These regulations addressed all party members as equal and responsible individuals and provided a foundation for the necessary division of labor for political action. By contrast, after 1974 the great majority of those involved in leftist political action were not organized as such; political work was characterized by spontaneity and an organizational culture in which equality between political actors was largely degraded. . . . In that situation, groups were ruled by an "authority" that had somehow seized power, and who controlled members irresponsibly and without adhering to the principle of accountability. (Aydınoğlu 2007: 410–11)

Two more accounts—there are many others—of revolutionary strategy and their articulation with fateful divisions among leftist groups should be mentioned. One is Hamit Bozarslan's brief comment on a similar bourgeoning of Kurdish leftist groups in southeast Turkey after 1974, including KUK (Kurdistan National Libera-tionists), Tekosin (Militancy), Beş Parçacılar (Liberators of the Five Parts of Kurd-istan), and the PKK (Kurdish Workers Party). For Bozarslan, this intra-Kurdish radicalization reflected both a broader "plebian dynamic" and a "generational shift" in the late 1970s (2012: 8). For various reasons, these revolutionary Kurdish organi-zations were not prominent in Istanbul, while in the Kurdish areas state apparatuses made them the target of assault.[17]

Last, in *Cereyanlar* (Currents), his extensive study of political ideologies in Tur-key, Tanıl Bora traces the origins of a what he describes as a disturbing intra-leftist "culture of hostility" (to other leftists) back to the late 1960s and early 1970s, both to Mihri Belli's polemical propagating of the MDD (National Democratic Revolu-tion) against TIP and to an emerging youth radicalism that rejected TIP's parlia-mentarianism and legalism. Bora describes how with the fading of TIP's appeal (in the late 1960s),

> the left's most lively new element, the rapidly growing Dev-Genç, adopted as their watchword "violence against opportunism." This fierce culture of hostility and enmity internal to the left no doubt also reflected its inheriting of the global socialist tradition's contemporary state of divisions. One aspect of this was a puritanism that conceived separation and "purification" as a legitimate theoretical-political measure. The hope caused by the extraordinarily rapid growth of the left and the impatience fostered by the feelings of urgency induced by "Turkish modernity"; combined with inculcated forms of nationalist thought concerning "traitors" and "liberation"; and of course the tensions caused by the rapid escalation of anti-communist violence: all of this added to a culture of hostility. (Bora 2017: 655)

CONCLUSION

In sum, in the 1970s' contrasting conceptions of the character and historical ori-gins of social relations, of the revolutionary subject, of the nature of imperialism and domination, and of the temporality of revolution led to the enacting of radi-cally different political strategies—to varieties of socialist, communist, focoist, nationalist, fascist, and Islamist projects. All of these, as we have explored in chap-ter 4, articulated with a rich repertoire of urban spatial practices.

Yet was it inevitable that these profound differences in social analysis and disa-greements over strategic political action would lead to *violent* conflict between their respective advocates? Why did these fostered ways of grasping the city, its history, its built environment, and its inhabitants result in such antagonistic relationships

17. See Jongerden (2017) for an account of the formation and early spatial politics (in Ankara) of the PKK from 1973 up until its founding in 1978, in particular through its organization of study groups in private apartments.

between protagonists? After all, contrasting pedagogies of different groups in other skilled endeavors such as music aesthetics, for example, or the development of opposed psychoanalytic traditions that disagree on the fundamentals of the psyche and its social constitution do not result in civil war, even as they educate therapists that understand the psyche in very different ways (such that they are unable or unwilling to work with each other).

One apparently naive explanation acknowledges that activism in Istanbul, unlike, say, music making there, was solely political. By this I mean that its major intention was to *transform* urban life and social relationships, through redressing (or conserving) people's collective economic and social position in relation to others. Moreover (and again unlike music making), in doing so, political activism always mobilized opposition. Cooperation and conflict are germane to its endeavor, in intra-class alliances and inter-class competition. Class conflict and class solidarity were means to change (or to defend) the *terms* of labor exchange and work. Organization of the working class was aided in this endeavor by political analyses (such as Marxism) that drew attention to the instruments and policies through which such unequal economic exchange functioned, even as such analysis threatened the self-regard of the dominant class regarding their own magnanimity. (The women's political movement does exactly the same in its seeking to change the unequal *terms* of exchange that pertains between men and women, aided by feminism's debunking of men's justificatory accounts for them.) Political struggle between classes, then, was fierce, even as it drew into that struggle leftist and rightist student groups as proxy actors in their class conflict.

Nevertheless, the politics oriented to the redress or conservation of class relations does not fully explain the extensive and murderous violence between leftists and rightists, or the intense hostility between leftist groups themselves in Istanbul, none of which would cooperate to create a common front against the fascist menace. Two other elements should be considered in accounting for this political intolerance. First, in both Turkish and leftist politics there existed a democratic deficit. In the (leftist) activist enterprise, rival groups were unable to manufacture any joint agreement among themselves to recognize the limits of self-assertion in relation to other organizations. That is, they failed to establish any self-binding or autonomous laws of ethical action that would regulate their interactions.[18]

Second, alongside the reflections on group rivalry offered above by ex-activists themselves, a distinction between *instrumental* and *ontological* violence might also illuminate such enmities. For certain elements of the nationalist right and, as we have seen, for some sections of the *focoist* left, as much as violence was a device to stabilize or to challenge exploitative social relations, it also promised to be a means of intersubjective self-transformation. Both Çağlar (1990) and Bora (2017) draw

18. "Autonomous" literally meaning "norms" given to one's self.

attention to the influential work of ideologue Nihal Atsız in propagating a racist or supremacist stream in Turkist thought. For Atsız, in a world of nations naturally hostile to each other, one achieves one's spiritual Turkishness by assertive acts of violence against non-Turks, and more particularly in the 1970s against communists who have lost their Turkish qualities. The Turkishness that resides in the blood must be proven in performative and sacrificial modes of action. Bora describes Atsız's discourse as "heroic-suicidal" (2017: 280), an interesting counterpoint to Samim's diagnosis of Mahir Çayan's actions as "suicidal adventurism" (1981: 76). For those leftist groups inspired by the Cuban revolution and *focoist* imaginaries, spectacular action in itself was believed to be productive, particularly in exemplary (violent) events that might bring into existence a happening ruptured from "objective" political conditions. Ideologically, then, in some sections of both the right and the left, violence was celebrated for its potential for initiating new forms of being and self-alteration.

In the context of the Turkish Armed Forces' own propensity for regenerating its sovereignty over society through military violence in a coup d'état, this was a dangerous practice for political activists to pursue.

7

Pacification, Resistance, Reconstruction

Coup d'État, City of the Fearful, 1980–1983

12 September 1980. 3:00 a.m.

Tanks maneuver their way down Istanbul's Menderes-built boulevards, noisily moving soldiers out of their barracks and into the darkened public squares of the city.

İstiklal Anthem. Harbiye March. Ottoman military music (*mehter*) broadcast on state radio. General Kenan Evren, head of the National Security Council and commander of the Turkish Armed Forces, addresses the nation.

Wake up! Get up! *İhtilal olmuş* (An insurrection has happened), the army has taken over!

Imposing martial law. Suspending the constitution. Abolishing Parliament. Lifting immunity from the People's Representatives (*Milletvekilli*). Dictatorship of the National Security Council.

Full curfew. Stay in your homes until further notice. Resistance will be severely punished.

Hasan Mutlucan's deep voice, singing *Kahramanlık Türküleri* (Songs of Valor), interspersed with repeat readings of Edict Number 1 and Edict Number 2.

After dawn soldiers distribute bread. Turn back men on their way to Friday *namaz*. Send home those who had got up early to join council coal queues.

Roads empty, glimmering and still. A submarine sidles up the Bosporus.

Pigeons, cats, and dogs, centering the streets.

Could anyone imagine what was about to happen in Istanbul?

7.1 JUNTA SPATIAL POLITICS:
PACIFICATION OF THE CITY

For the first few days the city is quiet. Foregrounded in perception by its sudden absence, the non-sounds of gunfire or bombs echo loud. Soldiers in its streets, patrolling roads, tanks parked on their corners; shops, schools, government offices, ferries, theaters, airports, workplaces closed. "I was in Vienna on a training course when it happened. Flights into (and out of) Turkey were suspended for two days. In the hotel they said, "Your uncle has made a coup. (We had the same surname, but were not related.)" (Ömer). In many suburbs people's first response is relief: "Thank God, the chaos is finished."[1] Radios stay turned on, transistors pressed to ears for the military proclamations. Hidden from street view, neighbors gather in secluded back gardens of apartments, visit up and down stairs—quiet supporters of the coup.

The inhabitants of more politicized suburbs notice military preparations uneasily; the construction of checkpoints on street corners, the long buzz of passing army jeeps. Families shrink into themselves. Visiting friends and relatives is impossible. People start to talk in whispers. Fear takes hold as news or rumors of arrests circulate. Not every home has a phone. There is only state TV or radio. Decree Number 2 declares that the country is divided into thirteen martial law regions, headed by thirteen martial law commanders. Activists make preparations for an uncertain future. People dispossess themselves of books. Bury them in the earth. Journals and newspapers are abandoned or destroyed, cassettes hidden. At night, under cover, militants leave homes and addresses, moving to houses of acquaintances.

The radio announces that the ovens will open. People go out to buy bread, pushed into lines by shouting soldiers, a silent queue. Just like that, everyday life changes.

Haluk comes home to find that his illiterate grandmother has burned his books in the *soba* (stove), identifying the "*anarşik*" ones that worried her by the moustaches or beards of authors in the photographs. Gorki, Marx, Lenin, and Çayan, remembered by their empty shelves. He is angry at first, but his grandmother calms him down: "Don't worry. Let these days pass; the books can be bought again. I'll place them on the bookshelf. I know all their photographs; I remember all their faces" (in Asan 2010: 152).

But the arrests have already begun. On 14 September 1980 Tuğba is sent to Çanakkale to start her working life at a school there. "On my first day, no teachers came. They had all been detained (rightists and leftists)." The coup is well planned, made in lists. Soldiers round up politicians, heads of unions, leaders of mass

---

1. In Ömer Asan's edited collection titled *12 Eylül sabahı* (The morning of 12 September) a common reflection among writers is that for reasons of safety they were glad the coup occurred and that they could not imagine what would befall them in the days thereafter.

associations, journalists, writers, intellectuals, teachers, lecturers, and militants, all quickly placed "under security." Mug shots of dead activists begin to appear in the censured newspapers, ugly photos captioned "*yakalandı, öldü*" (captured, dead), or "İstanbul'da bir terörist ölü olarak ele geçirildi" (In Istanbul a terrorist was seized dead). Rumors of systematic beatings and torture spread like wildfire. Nothing is written in the newspapers or said on radio. On television, carefully placed prohibited books—ones the police call *altı* (six), after VI (Vladimir Ilyich) Lenin—exhibited next to terrorists' guns. Istanbul is under occupation.

What characterizes the junta's immediate spatial activism, its emergent architecture of violence, its own sonic and visual politics, and its occupation/transformation of place?

Silence. Curfew. Martial music. Checkpoints. Military graffiti: "Wanted" posters in public thoroughfares. Civil police loiter. "It is hard to pass the posters. Should I look? What if I saw myself, or someone I knew?" (Banu, Dev-Yol).

Occupation of suburbs and assaults on houses: in a word, *siyasal gecekondulaşma* (political squatting). Despite the claims of the junta, not everything changes—"thugs" still control the streets, even if they are different people. Violence, too, continues across the city, in prisons, barracks, and police stations. Suppressing activist repertoires of urban engagement, movement, and relationships, the state of emergency powerfully induces in partisans' new perceptions of Istanbul, fabricating a foreboding sense of place, even as it produces different urban experiences across the city: "On the other side of the E5, in the *gecekondu* areas, there were lots of police checks and house searching. At every crossing of the E5 down to Kartal there were checkpoints. But in Göztepe where I lived [between Bağdat Caddesi and E5] there were no house searches or road barricades. It was quieter the nearer you went toward the sea" (Ömer Faruk, Biliş).

Despite these differences, even in more middle-class suburbs arrests are made, sometimes with a firefight. Houses are attacked, doors smashed in, people shot. Scores of people are killed, including police. In *direniş* (resistant) shantytown suburbs the searches go on for days, of every house. For Özlem (Kurtuluş), "the city was turned into an unknown place. There was constant fear: people looked out secretly from behind curtains at police entering someone's house, and we thought, when will they come to us?" Neighbors become afraid to visit the house where somebody has been arrested, in case police come again. The armed forces' spatial politics erode solidarity, and activists begin to feel alone. Meeting with more than three people in public is made illegal, and police disperse groups of four or more. "It was as if life had finished," said Ümit.

Ironically, for hundreds of thousands of people the coup reinforces the city's perceived lawlessness, providing no legal certainty. "Things could happen on the whim of the area commander. You could be searched whenever, on the ferry for example" (Akın, CHP). Sometimes you could be lucky. Adnan remembers carrying

copies of a forbidden journal in a big envelope for distribution, on the bus: "Someone suddenly shouted, 'my wallet is stolen.' The chauffer immediately said, 'OK,
we're going to the police station.' '*Aah I'm finished*,' I said, torture, arrest, I imagined
everything that would happen to me. By chance there was a civil policeman on the
bus. He stopped the bus before we got there and made us get off one by one so he
could search us. When it came to me, I handed him the envelope with my magazines in them, he rifled through it then handed it back to me!"

Roadblocks stop the traffic. Once the twenty-four-hour curfew ceases, resched-
uled to a midnight one, moving through the city, to study or to work, exposes
activists to great risk. People are halted any time on the street. "There was a terrify-
ing atmosphere in the city," said Hilmi. Activists' concern is not to be detained.
Arrests are made through cutting the road and then searching everyone, lying
people down on the ground, taking them away if they don't have an identity card,
especially in the gecekondu. Place and ethnicity are targeted: "If your identity card
said *Tunceli*, the officer would say, 'seize him'" (Filiz, Dev-Sol). Buses are suddenly
boarded for searching. Streets are patrolled. Public places like tea gardens or cafés
are surrounded, controlled. Police demand to see identity cards or passports. For
Özlem (TKP) Istanbul is a city living in terror: "Our house was known, we took
our books somewhere else. I became pregnant in 1982 and seriously thought of not
having the baby (many friends didn't have children then). If there wasn't such a
fear the army and police would never have been able to silence five hundred thousand people. But we didn't resist, or do politics because we knew it wouldn't be
successful. I was scared: what if I was tortured and gave names?"

Overnight, mobilization gives way to mobility. Activists abandon their homes
or places of residence to avoid arrest or capture. They go into hiding, leave one city
to go to another, flee to the mountains, or try to escape the country. Others change
their names. Dilek (Kurtuluş) recalls that between 1980 and 1983 she and her husband moved house twelve times because someone they knew was arrested:

> How did we know? We would make a rendezvous. If the person didn't come, we'd go
> back the next day. If they didn't come, then we would assume they were arrested and
> immediately pack up our stuff and move. We were arrested because we broke our
> own rules: we assumed the man who had stayed in this house with us had forgotten,
> he had forgotten before: "We said, nothing will happen." The police came at mid-
> night, with the man in the car who probably thought we had moved. We were tor-
> tured immediately with wires/electricity, while my husband watched. "Where's the
> rendezvous?" they said. "Who with?"

The parents of activists often move too, after visits by police inquiring into the
whereabouts of their children. The sudden shifting of activists from one place
to another fragments organizations and fractures friendships and relationships.
Meliha said, "For months, even for years, I heard no news from, and couldn't

see the faces of friends that I had met with right up until the evening of 11 September. It was not known where they were, or if it was known it was kept secret" (in Asan 2010: 221). *Ülkücü*, too, are unsure of the situation: Reha (MHP) told me he went to Germany in a car the day after the coup, because it wasn't clear what would happen. "While there, I wrote a letter to Kenan Evren saying: 'You did well to stop those communists cooperating with Russia. But what about those who had to fight them because you (army) weren't doing it enough? Why are they being arrested?"[2] Similarly, Mehmet Metiner notes the fleeing of a small number of Akıncılar overseas, including its general president who escaped to Pakistan (2008: 8).

What is it like for those who remain behind? The junta's violent "pacifying" of the whole country, and their occupying and remaking of Istanbul's spaces not only curtail militant practice but also transform activists' mood. More middle-class or professional partisans experience a severe *diminishing* of the scope of their lives and sociality, as the military reengineer the city's "affective atmosphere" (Anderson 2009). As Bülent (TKP) put it, "Before the coup Istanbul was a cosmopolitan, noisy, twenty-four-hour city, full of marches. After the coup there was a great silence, no meetings or marches; we were even too scared to sing." He fantasizes about going deep into the forest, shouting out marches. Theaters close and cultural activities are suspended. With the destroying of social and political life, militants feel alone. Alongside this shrinkage of political ambition and efficacy, life withdraws into homes. There is a need to feel secure, and for solidarity. Fear and persecution make activists stick together. Akın recalls how the effect of the coup resembles the years after the revolution in Iran: "We were stuck at home, but at home there was more freedom. For years the visiting of like-minded friends was our main social activity. Only once things normalize do we stop doing that." Filiz (TKP) remembers how in those years "We had one piece of fortune: for two weeks a year we went on holidays with the same group of people, in a convoy of cars, people who thought the same. We chose always to be together."

For local activists in the gecekondu known by neighbors and shopkeepers, social ties begin to unravel. Police pressure acquaintances to reveal where they had last seen them. Doors close. Refuge is refused. The numbers of faction houses shrink, even as activists try to rent new houses to protect themselves away from home. The junta encourages neighborhoods to inform police about the activities of communists and terrorists. Those who remain at home sit by their windows, anxiously scanning the street. Police barricade entrances to the suburb, continuously searching houses and businesses. Rendered anonymous by masks, informers

---

2. Alparslan Türkeş famously defended himself in a similar manner during his trial, declaring, "My opinions and beliefs are the same as the generals who organized the 1980 Turkish coup d'état, yet I am in prison." The claim gives an idea of the junta's post-coup policies.

are brought into the coffeehouse; look at the faces of people one by one; signal to accompanying police. There is nowhere safe to go. In Hürriyet Mahallesi, Can (Dev-Sol) remembers hiding away from home for two days after the coup, returning to find that the police had searched his house and detained his friends:

> All our relationships with organization members were broken. Clearly that was a bad thing, but we had no idea about what was going to happen. At that time a friend named Rıza was arrested. I was sitting in the shop of a tailor that I knew. Suddenly a police vehicle stopped in front of the shop and Rıza got out, surrounded by police. "Is there anyone you recognize?" the police asked him. He looked over to me and said, "no-one." He didn't inform on me. But then I thought being alone was worse. Everyone is being tortured in detention, surviving in terrible conditions, but you are outside going around on your own. Of course, and this might appear comic, to be arrested is bad but not to be arrested was bad too. (in Mavioğlu 2008: 85)

Even worse is 1981. Like the French paratroopers in Pontecorvo's film *The Battle of Algiers*, the police establish special "desks" for each organization, collect names, file addresses, search for THKP-C activists, or Dev-Yol people. Organizations are targeted in stages. Gün (TKP) thought that the military hit organizations like Dev Sol, TIKKO, the ülkücüler first: groups that had been involved in organized violence or armed struggle. "But we were waiting for our turn. The first operation against TKP began in September 1981." (Mesut thought it was later, in 1982.) Under systematic torture activists divulge comrades' whereabouts, leading to a vicious circle: arrests; torture; more arrests; torture. "They had agents in every *örgüt*," said Ergun; "the state knew everything; the coup happened very easily." He felt that in his organization (HK) everyone was rounded up and put in prison. A whole legal system is set up, military tribunals in different cities. Eighteen leftists are officially executed, and only eight rightists (despite their high rates of murder). Activists try not to wear normal prisoners' clothes when appearing in court, sometimes appearing in underpants or wearing singlets.

Factual reports—carefully neutral—of events, arrests, charges, and punishments begin to appear in the newspapers:

Cumhuriyet 3 October 1980:
A DİSK lawyer for the Bursa district committed suicide yesterday by throwing himself off the fifth floor of the security building.[3]

---

3. Reported suicides were often executions or the result of people being beaten to death. "We didn't do a thing, Your Honor. Nobody did a thing. They kicked themselves. They twisted their own balls. We know nothing about it, sir. We have no information, nobody has." From Adalet Ağaoğlu's novel *Curfew* ([1984] 1997: 27). Before the coup, there was already a midnight curfew in Istanbul that had been declared in March 1980.

Cumhuriyet 5 October 1980:
The four Martial Law districts covering Malatya, Elazığ, Tunceli, Bingöl, Muş, and Bitlis have arrested 2,379 people since 12 Eylül.

Cumhuriyet 10 October 1980:
15 years' prison and a ban from working in government employ was given to an ülkücü who murdered two students in Adana.

Cumhuriyet 14 October 1980:
The Third Military Court gave death sentences to two people from THKP-C and MLSPB, for killing two people.

Tercüman 16 November 1980:
21 leftists tried in Adana for murder, assault, and robbery.

Tercüman 19 November 1980:
Izmir Dev-Yol lawsuit begins. According to the bill of indictment prepared by the Military Court of the Aegean Army and Martial Law Command, "they [Dev-Yol] attempted to alter, deform and extinguish by force part or all of the Republic's constitution, and forming a gang executed the following activities: six murders, shooting of many houses, throwing of explosive materials, setting fire to work places and associations, armed threats at various times, hanging posters with bombs, stealing dynamite, hijacking a policeman's personal car, burning a house, collecting money, distributing a manifesto, putting up placards, holding illegal meetings [*korsan gösteri*], and committing robbery in order to supply weapons for the organization." The court wants 5 to 25 years for defendants, and 32 death penalties.

Tercüman 22 December 1980:
460 militants captured in Istanbul.
The Ankara Emergency Rule Command dismisses 169 civil servants.

Cumhuriyet 1 September 1981:
Since the coup 33 Turks have sought political asylum from Greek authorities.

Cumhuriyet 2 September 1981:
In Istanbul 34 people, members of the illegal TKP were captured. The professions of those arrested included one doctor of economics, one doctor in agriculture, four architects and engineers, one lawyer, six businessmen, one teacher, one civil servant, eleven workers, and three housewives.

Cumhuriyet 10 September 1981:
Business Vocation high school student tried for showing disrespect to the İstiklal March.

Confessions extracted under torture condemn militants to years of imprisonment. Newspapers and television fail to report that activists of different factions are prohibited from reading their carefully prepared rebuttals in court. Indictments are publicized and sentences reported but newspapers are unable or unwilling to publish defendants' statements explaining their actions, motivations, and perceptions. One exception is the military case against the TİKP, in which Doğu Perinçek's defense is published in full. Not all political groups are equally persecuted. Hüseyin reported that although after the coup some people were arrested from Aydınlık (Doğu Perinçek is imprisoned for five years), "we were not declared to be enemies, because we half-supported the coup. On the whole, we stayed free, as we weren't perceived to be very dangerous." Some leftists feel that the ülkücü and MHP guerillas are charged with different crimes, so that they will be able to enter parliament and the public service later. Muhsin Yazıcıoğlu is a case in point.[4]

Muting/Amplifying: The Junta's Acoustic Activism

Political news is carefully disseminated, both through censorship of unauthorized views and reportage in the media and by distribution of approved material. Certain words are prohibited in publications because of the potency of their hidden meanings: *devrim* (revolution) for example or *nur* (light) (see Asan 2010: 197). Newspapers are forbidden from describing 12 Eylül as "*ihtilal*" (mutiny or insurrection). In its place, "*Ordu idareye el koydu*" (the military has taken possession of administration) is to be used. Despite their self-censorship, *Cumhuriyet* newspaper is closed down four times between 12 Eylül and 12 March 1984, for a total of forty-one days (Topuz 2003: 259). *Yeni Aysa* (newspaper) is shut on 4 October 1980, and its replacement paper *Yeni Nesil* on 4 November 1982 (in Asan 2010: 197–98). *Tercüman*, *Milliyet*, and the journal *Nokta* are closed on 29 August 1983 (333). According to Ümit (Aydınlık), the first "leftist" journal to appear after the coup is theirs, titled *Ufaklar*. "We published fourteen editions before being closed down, after a friendly warning from a MIT [Turkish intelligence service] agent. We were very careful in our words of criticism."

Alongside this diminuendo of leftist language and restricting of information, official accounts flourish and swell. Kenan Evren speaks, and the population is forced to listen. Activists remember TRT's televising "all day" details in black and white about the anarchists' "killings and terrorism." Although Mamak military prison is overburdened with three thousand political prisoners who are subject to torture and the notorious brutality of its guards, *Milliyet* newspaper publishes a series describing how the food given to prisoners is of better quality and cheaper than at the market, and it is distributed only after being tasted for quality control by the prison commander himself. The report goes on to say that leftists and rightists are remorseful about their acts and are reconciled with each other under the inspiration and influence of Atatürk's speeches (broadcast into every ward through

---

4. Muhsin Yazıcıoğlu, chairman of the Greywolves and of the Ülkücü Youth Association in the years before 12 Eylül, was charged with part-organizing the massacre of Alevis in Kahramanmaraş but was found not guilty. Arrested after the coup, he was declared innocent in 1987 and released from prison. He later became a member of parliament.

every keyhole) and that life in the isolation cells in which prisoners sentenced to execution are held (including Erdal Eren's) is much more pleasant than in the wards.[5] Prisoners could also avail themselves of supplies from the canteen, and read newspapers.

Control over what one sees, reads, and hears continues in others ways and in other fields. Gündüz Vassaf remembers that although no prohibition has been declared, the head of Boğaziçi University Library puts away books that would displease the military junta, among them Şerif Mardin's *Din ve İdeoloji* (Religion and ideology). "Just to be on the safe side, ya, because the book has *ideology* in its title."[6] The prints of the television series *Yorgun Savaşçı* (The weary warrior), adapted from the Kemal Tahir novel on the period of the Independence War and commissioned by the TRT, are burned in front of the military commission that condemned it, without it ever being broadcast, for containing scenes that were "anti-Atatürk." Hundreds of films and books are banned. The Kurdish language is silenced, films prohibited for sounding out a single sentence. The graphic humor journal *Gırgır* is suspended for printing on its cover a sartorial/satirical drawing of the singer Müşerref Tezcan.[7] Adorned in dresses designed from the Turkish flag, junta favorite Tezcan appears constantly on TRT-TV (and in film) singing her song "Türkiyem" (My Turkey, my Turkey). The charge against *Gırgır* includes "drawing a monstrous woman in the dress of the Turkish flag" (Ucube bir kadının üzerine Türk bayrağı elbise çizmek).[8]

Acoustic activism—the muting of certain music and sounds and the amplification of others—is central to the junta's spatial politics in Istanbul, as the post-coup ringing out of the song "Türkiyem" demonstrates. Because political worlds are also "sonically apprehended" (Feld 1996: 93) and because, as we have seen, activist

5. See Yıldıray Oğur, "12 Eylül'ün en güzel idam hücreleri," *Taraf* 24 July 2010. Erdal Eren was executed for the shooting of a soldier in Ankara, despite being under the age of eighteen and there being serious doubts about his role in the killing. The first ülkücü executed was Mustafa Pehlivanoğlu.

6. *T24*, http://t24.com.tr/yazarlar/gunduz-vassaf/turkiyede-universite-var-mi,16578, published 13 February 2017.

7. Satirizing daily political events, including through iconic caricatures of politicians (Demirel, Ecevit, Erbakan, etc.), the enormous popularity of *Gırgır* made it the third-best-selling comic journal in the world in the late 1970s, selling over three hundred thousand copies weekly. Indeed, so widespread was its influence that Ali (İGD) told me that the student experience of everyday life in Istanbul before 12 Eylül could be summed up as "laughing, crying, and fighting." He remembered that students would wait for *Gırgır* to come out, buying it on the first morning. It also reserved a "corner" for publishing caricatures sent in by prisoners.

8. I have taken this information from the Facebook page, Avanak Avni Hayranları (Fans of Avanak Avni). Avanak Avni was a popular cartoon character in *Gırgır*, drawn as a typical boy from the gecekondu. See https://www.facebook.com/115272118494062/posts/girgir-dergisio%C4%9Fuz-aral-y%C3%B6netiminde-1972den-1989a-kadar-t%C3%BCrkiyenin-en-%C3%A7ok-satan-/483715408316396/ (accessed 9 October 2018).

groups are "sound communities" who listen to certain makers and styles of music, the junta seeks to change activists' experience of place by reforming the city's aural ecology. What is heard changes. Nuriye (from Dev-Sol) remembers how "before 12 Eylül, the wooden carts sold cassettes. They often played the marches of the different leftist groups through little speakers. After the coup there was a silence, then they began to play *arabesk* music."

At the same time, leftist singers are prosecuted and possession of their albums is prohibited or criminalized: Ümit (HK) mentions that his possession of illegal Livaneli cassettes is used as evidence in the court case against him. The arrangements, words, and pieces of composer Sanar Yurdatapan, in exile after the coup, are all banned, as is the voice and appearance of his wife Melike Demirağ.[9] Popular protest singer Selda Bağcan is imprisoned three times between 1981 and 1983; other leftist artists flee the country or have their citizenship revoked. TRT's board of directors redetermines what will be broadcast on TV and on radio stations: according to Stokes (1992) they begin to reschedule and replace Turkish folk music with Turkish art music. Songs that combine Western instruments with the oud or the kanun are banned, as is the bouzouki. On New Year's Eve 1980, singer Orhan Gencebay appears on TRT singing "Yarabbim," his first appearance on television and a sign that certain types of *arabesk* music are to be rehabilitated.

The junta propagates its own urban soundscape, publicly silencing music and sound that was significant in the shaping of leftist political sentiments and loyalty. Anthropological questions about music recording and "how best to present and represent the sonorous enculturated worlds inhabited by people" (Samuels, Meintjes, Ochoa, and Porcello 2010: 329) suddenly appear naive. Post-12 Eylül, the very sonority of the city—what we might call its *akumena*, or acoustic phenomena (Smith 1967)—is partly produced by the junta. They compose a soundscape intended to pacify activism and to dull its "acoustemology"—activists' ways of sensing and knowing the city through sound (see Feld 1996). The junta's acoustic activism also involves censorship of selected, disliked sounds and practices (languages, concerts, music recordings). The junta claims such sounds and experiences revive or even create undesirable moods, feelings, and intentions in/for listeners. The engineering of affect and soundscape rings purest in the most regulated spaces—prisons and barracks.

In Istanbul's Metris prison—and doubtless in others around the country—three tones in particular structure its soundscape. The first is a recording of a statement by the martial law commander of Istanbul, General Haydar Saltık: "For the attention of prisoners" (Tutuklu personelin dikkatine), relayed through loudspeakers five times a day and beginning with the staccato words, "Hiçbir taviz verilmeyecektir" (No

9. See S. Yurdatapan, "Déjà-vu: Bu Filmi Daha Kaç Kere Göreceğiz?" *Biamag*, 3 March 2018, https://m.bianet.org/biamag/siyaset/194821-deja-vu-bu-filmi-daha-kac-kere-gorecegiz.

concessions will be granted). Prisoners make fun of the words. Ataturk's speeches and sayings are broadcast from the speakers as well. For prisoners, the soundscape's third sonic feature is even worse: the playing of Müşerref Akay's "Türkiyem" song hundreds of times a day at full volume, accompanying the sessions of torture, and intended as torture in itself.[10]

Not that the junta itself listens to "Türkiyem." That sonic environment is designed primarily for others, for the non-leftist public watching television, as well as for militants in prison. For itself, the junta creates a different acoustic space. A week after the coup, *neyzen* (*ney* player) Süleyman Erguner tells of being taken by army jeep to the Officers' Club in Harbiye, where the five members of the National Security Council are eating dinner. With three other musicians who also work for TRT, and accompanied by the singer Recep Birlik, the newly formed quintet give a one-off performance. Starting the program with a ney solo to "sit" the mode in the generals' ears, the musicians continue with a cycle of Rumeli folk songs, with which Kenan Evren, whose family is from Üsküp, is thought to be familiar. At the conclusion of the thirty-minute concert, "the Council members applaud ... shake our hands while congratulating us ... before we depart the salon to be taken in army vehicles through the silent and empty streets back to our homes" (in Asan 2010: 283–84).

Six hundred fifty thousand people are arrested.[11] Furthermore, the city—the country—is turned into an open prison. In prisons themselves the armed forces mobilize the violence of architecture, transforming them into disorienting sites of spatialized and acoustic brutality to destroy activists' emotional and bodily integrity. Torture is widespread, used on nearly everybody detained by police or the military, a systematic state policy and practice: punishment by the state for offending the state. For Fırat (Dev-Yol), torture occurred not because the torturers were sadists per se. "It was a systematic policy designed to break spirits, and feelings of resistance. People could be tortured for up to ninety days before being brought before the *savcı* [then you had to be officially charged]: this was in case people died under torture, so there would be no record." Ertuğrul Mavioğlu 2008) cites a psychiatrist (Mehmet Bekaroğlu) working in Metris prison after the coup saying, "They wanted me to treat the disease of communism." Treatment included the

---

10. The song's words read:

Treason infiltrated my hero nation / Pain and hatred in all hearts / My enemies aren't brave, all are despicable / There in no ally to Turks other than Turks / Let us be enlivened by the principles of Ata[türk] / Let us run toward the targets that he set / My Turkey, my Turkey, my heaven / My peerless nation / My Ata, the leader of Turkishness, of youth / This sacred homeland is your deed / As a nation we are in your footsteps fired by love / Long live the Republic, the beloved Fatherland.

11. That figure, probably conservative, is given in a report on the coup prepared by the Turkish Parliament in 2010.

forced cantillation of Atatürk speeches or of verses from the Koran, alongside constant brutality and torture.

And there is an ethnic dimension to the unequal distribution of torture, too. Özlem (ex-TKP) tells me of her recent visit to Diyarbakır as a lawyer to take down transcriptions of torture at Diyarbakır Prison after 12 Eylül. "It was beyond belief, the violence. Some of them didn't even know why they were arrested, and didn't know it was for being Kurdish. They learned in prison, as the coup targeted Kurdish identity for suppression." Fırat, himself, tortured in Istanbul, notes that there are some places—Tunceli, Diyarbakır, Artvin, Fatsa—where nearly everyone is tortured. In the newly constructed Diyarbakır Military Prison, torture takes on "ethnic characteristics" (Zeydanoğlu 2009: 10), an assault not just on leftist subjectivity but on Kurdish being as well. Kurdish speech is banned. Along with the constant military songs and speeches and the extreme violence, prisoners are forced to learn and sing Turkish nationalist songs, to recite the national anthem, to repeat nationalist slogans: in brief, to Turkify themselves through the shouted mechanism of their own voices.

Electric shocks; severe beatings; whipping of the soles of feet; hanging by arms and legs; blindfolding; stripping naked; high-pressure hosing; solitary confinement; attacks by dogs; burning by cigarettes; extraction of nails and teeth; sexual assault . . .[12]

In Istanbul interviewees remember being tortured in Metris Military Prison, in Davutpaşa Barracks, in Gayrettepe Police Station, and in Bayrampaşa Prison. Both Bülent (Partizan Yolu) and Ferhat (Kurtuluş) were already in prison when the coup happened. "We barricaded the doors so the soldiers couldn't enter. They came in by firing smoke bombs and guns. They beat us for a day." Similarly, Ferhat remembers that they (leftists) were in control of the prison until the coup: "Then the guards got their revenge on us." Levent recalls that his eighteen-year-old brother was arrested in 1981, after being denounced for writing a poster, "Down with the Military Junta," in English and sticking it up on a wall at Boğaziçi University. "For proof, they checked his handwriting. He was sentenced to two years prison, stayed in for a year and was tortured."

How long did this state of terror continue?[13] Bülent notices a feeling of general fear when he is released from prison in August 1983. For Adnan, who arrives in Istanbul in 1983 to study, the city feels like the film Missing. Although he isn't involved in politics, soldiers are everywhere and there are constant identity checks. "At university gates there are police. Everywhere in the city there are 'Aranıyor'

12. For two horrifying accounts of torture in Diyarbakır Military Prison after 1980, done to thousands of Kurdish men, see Zeydanlıoğlu (2009), and the film Prison No. 5: 1980–1984, by Çayan Demirel (2009).

13. The state of emergency, or martial law (sıkıyönetim) was not officially lifted in Istanbul until 19 November 1985.

[Searching for] posters, with photos taken from police files." Even in 1985, Filiz remembered being with a friend in a tea garden, and the man's arrest by "civil" police. "When I asked why at the station, they said because he was wearing blue jeans and sports shoes."

Finally, this urban pacification—particularly through arrests, imprisonment, and torture—has a transforming effect on activists' families, who are shocked by the fate of their children or relatives. According to Özlem, many of those families later become founding figures of human rights associations, which didn't exist in the 1970s. Cem remembers his transfer from Sultanahmet Prison to Metris: "The prison director instructed the soldiers to forcibly cut our hair, and then to beat us for more than an hour in the corridors. Our heads were torn apart, our faces were covered in blood. I'll never forget our families waiting outside the prison, among them my father, witnessing the smiles and the air of victory of the soldiers as well as our battered state" (in Mavioğlu 2009). Bade asks herself how she was to know that, a month after she married the man she loved, "our home would be raided by panzers, that the soldiers who had been given orders to kill if we didn't surrender would drag us out of our bed, that we would be taken to the barracks. I stayed in prison for five months, and for eleven years would go from prison to prison as the wife of the man I loved, spending my life's most productive years at their doors" (in Asan 2010: 67–68). Faruk tells me that sometime after the coup, four of his friends were taken from Sümer Bank lodgments for being members of illegal organizations. One, Nurettin Yedigöl, was tortured to death. Police deny that he was ever arrested. His body was never returned to his family. Thirty-two years later, in 2013, his family march down the street holding up posters with his photo in a sad but all too common urban ritual, declaring that he is missing still and that they are searching for him always. "Nurettin Yedigöl, 1954– . . . Arıyoruz. Unutulmadı; unutulmayacak!" (We are looking for him. He is not forgotten; he will not be forgotten!)[14]

7.2 "TO LIVE ONE MORE DAY": MICRO MODES OF RESISTANCE

How did activists respond to the junta's pacification of Istanbul, to its muting of the sounds of their political life, to its control over the city, and to its brutal acts of imprisonment and torture? Did they—could they—continue the revolutionary struggle? Were they able to devise a new repertoire of post-coup spatial tactics? Or did life move into the passive voice, such that activists were forced to "experience" the actions of more powerful others as survival became their chief concern? What might resistance mean, if resisting hopelessness becomes a political act?

14. For a video showing a commemoration march in his name please see https://www.youtube.com /watch?v=YWWGDNa-vjk.

The question of "resistance" has become an important issue in anthropology, involving debates around its scale, intentionality, openness, and embodied-symbolic characteristics. Is wearing jeans and sports shoes an act of defiance against the junta's attempt to nationalize and regularize post-coup bodies? What about the buzz of families crowding the streets at 12:45 at night—the curfew is at 1:00 a.m.—who would never be out so late otherwise? Are they pushing back against the political temporality imposed upon the city by the junta? Is it resistance to refuse to forget the killing of your son, commemorating for decades the anniversary of his disappearance and murder, stubbornly demanding justice even when you have lost hope that it is ever to be done?

In *Weapons of the Weak*, published in 1985, coincidentally the very year that martial law officially ended in Istanbul, James Scott makes a critique of what he diagnoses as Leninist assumptions about "real" resistance. For Scott, Leninist revolutionary or intentionalist theories presume that ideal resistance entails the social lucidity of movements or parties that are aware of both the current hegemonic order and of dominant popular (mis)-conceptions of it, and who in their organized and oppositional action articulate a radical alternative to it. By contrast, against such a model, he proposes to include as equally valid resistance activities that are "(a) unorganized, unsystematic, and individual, (b) opportunistic and self-indulgent, (c) have no revolutionary consequences, and/or (d) imply, in their intention or meaning, an accommodation with the system of domination" (1985: 292). Although Scott's concern is to comprehend the self-interested, unorganized, and diffuse "resistance" of a subordinated class of peasants against landowners in rural areas in Malaysia, his concept of the "weapons of the weak" illuminates the situation and some of the practices of activists in Istanbul post-12 Eylül, an irony given the Leninist political orientation of so many of their organizations.

What might resistance entail in the junta's terrible prisons? In his well-known poem "Some advice to those who will spend time in prison," Nazım Hikmet counsels socialists that in jail merely surviving, one day at a time, is a defeat of your enemies. Yet at the same time, he instructs them to cultivate, somehow, an intense orientation to the outside world:

> If instead of being hanged by the neck
>   you're thrown inside
> . . . you won't say,
> "Better I had swung from the end of a rope
>   like a flag"—
> you'll put your foot down and live.
> It may not be a pleasure exactly,
> but it's your solemn duty
>   to live one more day
>   to spite the enemy.

Part of you may live alone inside,
    like a stone at the bottom of a well.
But the other part
    Must be so caught up
    In the flurry of the world
    That you shiver there inside,
When outside, at forty days' distance, a leaf moves.[15]

    —Hikmet 1994

Hikmet reassures activists that in the face of grotesque violence in prison, it is enough simply to maintain life. There, bare survival is victory. Of course, in some places conditions are such that endurance is beyond most people. Suicide in protest or despair occurs. In 1982 in Diyarbakir Prison, "four young prisoners, Mahmut Zengin, Eşref Anyık, Ferhat Kurtay, and Necmi Öner, rolled up in newspapers and sprayed with paint and holding hands, burned themselves alive" (Zeydanlıoğlu 2009: 11). Other prisoners protest in different ways, imperiling their own lives through hunger strike, a method of self-annihilation that negates the consciousness engineering (and embodied-punishment) purpose of torture and that is understood by the state to constitute the ultimate act of defiance. In it, activists reassert control over the breaking of their bodies. Both Ertuğrul and Cem recall how in response to the hunger strike at Metris guards wheeled trolleys of *köfte* and coffee up and down corridors, which "made our stomach juices react and was designed to turn our action into torture" (Mavioğlu 2009). After twenty-eight days, the hunger strike was successful, and the regular torture sessions ceased. Cem remembered an air of victory in the shared cells, as well as the slogan: "If there is the oppression of the oppressors, there is our resistance."[16] Prisoners in Diyarbakır were not so fortunate. In 1982 four prisoners starved to death, and many others were crippled.

In such extreme conditions, interviewees perceived that refusing to "crack" is also an act of solidarity with fellow revolutionaries, even if they have become less committed to the politics and practices of their factions. Fehmi (Kurtuluş) told me that it was in prison that he decided to change his worldview, partly because of the Solidarity movement in Poland and its working-class resistance to the socialist state. "But I didn't tell anyone in my ward and continued to play a role. If I did, it would have been a victory to the fascists and it would have destroyed the morale of friends. It was important to be loyal to friends. I was contacted after getting out, but didn't go to the meeting. They must have been disappointed, as I was a pillar of strength, and never surrendered in prison."

15. See also Maureen Freely (2009), "The Prison Imaginary in Turkish Literature."
16. See also Kukul (1989) for prisoner narratives about the prison in the years after the coup.

Finally, in other prisons, once the first months of torture passed, interviewees remembered discreetly resuscitating certain revolutionary practices and values. Some quietly celebrated May 1. In the women's wards, Banu recalled, there was a strong ethos of sharing among political prisoners. "We distributed cigarettes, but according to their quality: twenty per person if filterless, ten or less if filtered. Families would bring them, or would send money."

Imprisoned City

Outside of prison, what forms of practice does resistance take? Under martial law the distinction between being inside and outside prison becomes less clear. Outside, hundreds of thousands of people are blacklisted; tens of thousands of people lose their jobs; tens of thousands of people are forced underground. Thousands flee the country, to face unemployment and incomprehension in places—Europe, Australia—that have no idea about their experiences or history. While torture is an existential issue for those in prison, their families outside dwell in fear for the welfare of relatives inside, reorienting their lives toward them, their own daily reality confined to worrying, writing letters, visiting, organizing legal support.

In such circumstances, maintaining a life in Istanbul also becomes an act of endurance and thus an act of resistance by activists and their families. "Imprisoned" in the city, some enact (whether they know the poem or not) Nazım Hikmet's phenomenological advice that a part of you must nevertheless "shiver" at the flicker of a leaf elsewhere. In response to the junta's radical spatial pacification of Istanbul, Özlem (TKP) describes how she rescaled and miniaturized her life, modifying the significance of the new city surrounding her through attentiveness to small things: "Some things carried much more weight than before, symbols became very important, and we gave small events a great importance. For example, if someone whistled a song that I knew, it had a huge effect on me. It was like a secret signal or sign, just as when you saw someone wearing a parka: it carried a greater meaning than its appearance. For us it meant, 'I'm not hiding: I'm making a challenge.'"

Expanding on the mood of those years, Özlem remembered that the first concert she attended after 12 Eylül was a performance by Zülfü Livaneli when he returned from exile in 1984. "Everyone was crying listening to those songs." The song she picked out was "Karlı kayın ormanı"(Snowy beech forest), Livaneli's setting of a Nazım Hikmet poem that ends with the beautiful lines, "Ne ölümden korkmak ayıp, ne de düşünmek ölümü" (There is no shame in being scared of death, nor in thinking of dying). In a moving comment that speaks to the relevance of core perceptual processes identified by phenomenology—consciousness's constitution of the meaning of the world; intersubjectivity and the centrality of our knowing and perceiving in relation to others; the temporality of our making sense of the world in the course of experience; and the role of perceptual horizons that enter into present perception as the history of one's body and as recollections, habits, and moods—she described how that concert evening "the meaning we weighed it [the music] with was entirely different." Here in response to the deadly transformation of the city by the junta we see Özlem's bestowing of fresh meanings on its now fugitive sounds; this is her act, not that of the junta.

Thus, even in undergoing an experience that is not of their own making—"to undergo means that we endure it, suffer it, receive it as it strikes us, and submit to it" (Heidegger 1959: 59)—activists still seek to claw back some sense of action for themselves. The poet and writer Muzaffer Erdost changed his name forever to Muzaffer İlhan Erdost, to preserve the memory and being of his brother İlhan, beaten to death after arrest by soldiers on his way to Mamak Prison in Ankara.

What happens to activists' political groups after the coup: Can they resist the junta, maintaining their own revolutionary values? Or with the arrests of so many of their militants, do political factions dissolve? According to Hamit Bozarslan, by the return of civilian rule in late 1983, the powerful fractions of the 1970s had been eliminated:

> The shock created by the military coup of 1980 was huge. While you were expecting a civil war, you face a military coup and within days you don't have any kind of space for maneuver. So what to do? Everything you have done in the past has stopped, become to some extent meaningless, and you ask "what happened to us?" and "how can we resist and survive?" The first issue is a concern with survival: "we should continue to exist" as an organization, as a political circle, as a political project.
>
> Herein lies the key. Not one party, illegal or legal, can rise up to its feet again after 1983. Everything is destroyed. The cadres of the parties are gone. . . . This is the case for all the parties. If you look at the radical Right party, the MHP, there is nothing left of them in 1983. Many of their members reconvert to Islamism, or withdraw into private, in some cases mafia business. . . . No one is occupying the same place as he was before. (Bozarslan 2012)

Precisely because of the rapid collapse of political organizations, interviewees remember vividly their own novel spatial tactics, confirming the necessity of provisional, individualistic, opportunistic, and pragmatic minor acts of resistance in certain contexts, just as Scott discovered for Malaysia. These range from hard-won practices of self-protection, including new urban movement protocols and domestic arrangements, to innovative modes of communication. For example, to move around the city, activists began to look more middle class, with a suit and tie or dressed up in one's "finest bourgeois woman's clothes." For security, they always met in a different spot. When meeting someone they went early to check out the place. If anyone was a few minutes late, they assumed they were arrested, and left straight away. Bülent explained how he did it: "To follow through with a rendezvous, I would get a friend to watch me pass, to see whether anyone was following me. He would follow me to the rendezvous point and watch from afar. After hand-ing over whatever documents we carried, I would leave and the same friend would wait to see it anyone was following the other person when they left."

According to Haydar, Kurtuluş decided after 12 Eylül that women had to finan-cially support their activist husbands, as the organization was incapable of doing so. But men were also to prepare their wives to be their substitutes, training them to do the professional organizing work.

Similarly, by necessity, the TKP took a decision that the period after the coup would be a time of retreat. While waiting for the operation to begin against them, the party informed members that their political duty was to pull back and protect themselves, to take precautions, find a new residence, change their identity, or leave their work:

> For example, a young man came from Izmir and lived with us. I moved to the Bakırköy office, and moved other staff around to other offices, but before I left, I destroyed my files with all the names of unionists, party affiliations, etcetera, because we had organized the management and workers. No one was arrested from Tekel. I resigned from the party in 1981, and was told to go "illegal." We moved house, broke off relations with relatives, tried to continue seeing people, to collect information about what was happening, collect money for new houses for rent. It was easier to be protected in Istanbul, so people moved here, working in new jobs. (My wife became an accountant after starting work for protection's sake in an accounting office!) It was also better to move to *siteler*, or middle-class suburbs, where there was less neigh-borly interest, unlike in the gecekondu.
>
> The party could help with a new identity: it tried to protect five hundred people, as well as others close to it. There were two methods of getting a new identity. One was just to make up a new card, with no historical validity. The better one was to take the identity of someone with no record (a "clean" person). You had to memorize everything about them, their parents' names, their place of residence, their high school: you became two people, with one identity. The party sometimes gave two new identities to people and said, "we married you," and left it up to the people them-selves as to whether they would enter into sexual relations: you could, or you couldn't. Or they advised people to marry. It was easier for a married couple to rent a new house. (Haydar, TKP)

Activists felt that communicating that one is still there, undaunted in the face of the junta's spatial politics, was important. To do so, a common strategy was the fleeting misuse of the affordances of Istanbul's public spaces and of its public objects/things. Activists gave false information to the contact telephone numbers written on the "Wanted" posters. But they devised more positive ways to commu-nicate their existence to residents in the city. Ömer explained how he and his friends would write slogans on a number of small bits of paper, jamming them somehow near the skylight in a bus, then get off. The paper would go blowing off across the streets. "Why? It was a sign that we were not defeated. When I saw oth-ers do it, I thought, 'there are maniacs out there still continuing.'" Activists secretly put leaflets in the letterboxes of apartment houses, or even under their doors. Others left them in the toilets of factories or (in pre-coup strongly-unionized state factories) on the seats of the service buses before work. Mehmet (TKP) told me how they filled a bag with pamphlets then sealed it with string, went up to the top floor of a building on İstiklal Avenue, hung the bag out the window, then put acid on the cotton seal and went running downstairs. When the acid reached the bag, it fell open and the leaflets went fluttering down onto İstiklal. "Aah, ne güzel [how beautiful]!" he grinned. "We learned this from the Portuguese communists, who used a candle." In all of these examples we see how activists performed a brief subversion of junta rule though the activation of space and objects, creating from them a fleeting alternative urban place.

The fact that the pro-Soviet TKP had international links, unlike more indigenous mass movements such as Dev-Yol or Kurtuluş and so on, as well as its being a middle-class and professional organization with better resources, meant that it had some advantages in protecting its members and in signaling its continuing existence. In a long interview with Mustafa (TKP), he explained his complex process of recording and distributing the "Voice of the TKP," which after the coup was broadcast in Turkish from East Berlin:

> We began to record, print, and reproduce the broadcasts. At first this was slow work: I had a typewriter, and not to make a sound I would put a pillow under it, on its sides, at its back, so the sound didn't reverberate. These were precautions: we had moved, we didn't know who the neighbors were; you couldn't trust anyone. We would put the carbon paper in the typewriter and could make three or five copies of the broadcasts/ announcement. This was very thin paper [pelur kağıt].
>
> We began to distribute to friends: we would roll the paper up with a cigarette, the first paper would be the typed one. You gave to friends: "al cigara kardeşim." We would make an inside compartment in the cover of a book and carry papers in there. We also put pages in a çay [tea] packet, as if we had been shopping. Some of these strategies we learned from other communist parties: it was international knowledge.
>
> Our problem, though, was how to produce more. I got a teksir [a primitive printing press], but found that it was impossible to find pelican ink in the city. The junta had banned it. Finally, I tracked some down through my wife's father's contacts, my wife found it in Sirkeci. I found that I could smear the ink on a leather briefcase, then through the machine, wearing gloves so as not to get ink on me. I could do forty or fifty before needing new ink, make hundreds in a night. This was a miracle! Now I could take a hundred pages to friends. On 4 April 1981 we printed "No to NATO" and distributed it. We pasted them on walls. We posted copies to the state institutions from different post office boxes: to Kenan Evren, who complained on TV that this propaganda was even coming to him, from outside Turkey. But my typewriter had a broken e key, and the pages had an e that was lower than the rest of the line.
>
> After 1982, I reconnected with someone from the party and gave them a report of activities, about which they were surprised.

Why was the party surprised? As we read above, operations against the out-lawed TKP that began in 1981 decimated the party. Indeed, the special police report made by the Istanbul Martial Law Command and repeated in *Cumhuriyet* newspaper makes more sense now: "In searching the residences, offices and work-places of the captured members of the organization, the following items were dis-covered: fake passports and identity cards, microfilms sent by the central party offices abroad containing their instructions, . . . the illegal printing material of the party, photographs and electronic materials used in the production of microfilms, . . . one car, several offices and hand-written documents belonging to the party" (*Cumhuriyet*, 2 September 1981).

7.3 POLITICAL RECONSTRUCTION OF WORK
AND URBAN ENVIRONMENTS

Through this harsh program of arrest, torture, sentencing (in military tribunals), and imprisonment the Turkish armed forces targeted for suppression the most dynamic actors of sociopolitical life in Istanbul in the latter half of the 1970s, as well as the places transformed by their spatial practices. At the same time, the junta authorized a huge number of revised laws and rules, establishing new politi-cal institutions intended to regulate Turkish society and to produce different ways of being students, activists, professionals, workers, consumers, and so on. To make this suppression permanent, the junta abolished the existing constitution and pre-pared a new one for ratification by referendum. According to interviewees, one succinct result of all this new legislation was a sharp increase in the power of the state vis-à-vis citizens, and of the Turkish bourgeoisie vis-à-vis Turkish workers. Legislating to enact "generational change," the junta promulgated (as we see below) new laws in the arenas of civil society (including for organizations, associations, and political parties); urban planning/housing; education, language, and ethnicity (universities and schools); and in labor relations.

A few days after the coup, in a speech given to the press on 16 September, Kenan Evren spelled out more clearly which groups of actors, along with the political par-ties, the military held responsible for the crisis, indicating which fields of social practice would be targeted with special laws. Educational institutions were identi-fied first:

> Unfortunately, the Turkish democratic regime based upon Atatürk's reforms was unable to defend itself by equipping the new generations with the Atatürkist perspective. . . . From the universities to the primary schools, where Atatürkism or, to put it differently, where a Kemalist education and production of ideas should have been pursued, the opposite happened with left, right, and reactionary ideas produced. Unfortunately, a number of those generating these ideas were teachers and professors taking a salary from the state treasury, creating a situation where first teachers and then professors

divided, and then our most treasured thing, our innocent children were fractured among opposing ideas. (2000: 20)

Civil society organizations were next: "The right to freely establish an association existing in democratic regimes was abused. Thousands of associations departed from the principal purpose for which they were founded and developed into organizations pronouncing opinions about the regime, openly or secretly beginning a war to demolish democracy" (21).

Thirdly, the activities of unions or associations devoted to the organization and education of workers were singled out for special opprobrium: "Hardworking, innocent Turkish workers, who have no thought other than ensuring security for tomorrow, who labored day and night sweating from their brow both to develop their country and to make ends meet for their families, were traitorously used by people with illicit authority [in Turkish, *birtakım ağalar*[17]] who wanted both another regime and to destroy democracy, placing a red flag and pictures of foreigners [presumably Lenin] in their hands" (Evren 2000: 21). One primary solution, proposed in each of Evren's speeches, was to reeducate the country in the principles and practices of Atatürk, as demonstrated in the broadcast addressed to the nation on the day of the coup:

In training and education and in the shortest possible time, measures will be taken to spread Atatürk nationalism once again to the farthest corners of the country. Precautions will be taken to prevent our children, who are the guarantors of the future, from becoming anarchists one by one after being educated in foreign ideologies instead of in the principles of Atatürk. Accordingly, there will be no permission given to our teachers, whom we all respect, to be separated by being members of associations or federations. At every level, a student's aim will be to attain productive knowledge and skill that conforms to Atatürk principles and nationalism. (2000: 16)

In sum, as Evren said in a speech delivered in Ankara for Republic Day (29 October, 1980), "Throughout their life, every Turk will hold to Atatürkist ideology like a flag high in the sky to ensure that the country and the nation will reach the aims identified by it."

In Decree No. 7, the junta prohibited the activities of all political parties, including their organization of youth or women's sections, one of their major links to broader society. The prohibition brought to an end the democratic experiments of the New Municipal movement. Imprisoning Istanbul's elected mayors and relieving from duty elected officials of local institutions, they appointed in their place the first of three soldier-mayors to control the city over the next four years. (The

---

17. The term is difficult to translate: in Turkish *ağa* literally means landlord, but here its meaning is made to resonate with connotations of exploitative, oppressive, and illegitimate authority over innocent but gullible followers.

first act of one of them, General Abdullah Tırtıl, was to announce that Istanbul's street *simit* [bagel] sellers would wear uniforms as part of their work). Replacing the new municipalism's innovative forms of cross-council union and engagement with urban dwellers, Istanbul councils were forcibly combined into one single, giant, centralized, and security-minded city municipality, resulting, as Yıldırım notes, "not only in inhabitants' political distancing from local administration but also in their physical-geographic distancing too" (1990: 34). The junta's constituting of a single Istanbul government authority, its return to a "bureaucratic and hierarchical administrative structure" (33), and its increasing of resources to municipalities paved the way for three major legislations in 1984 and 1985, the Metropolitan Local Government Reform Law, Urban Planning Law, and the Mass Housing Law. Through each of them, what Kayasu and Yetişkula (2014) call a neo-liberal transformation of the gecekondu is begun.

Exempting only the Turkish Aviation Association, the Society for the Protection of Children, and the Red Crescent, the same decree announced the closure of all foundations, democratic mass societies, cultural clubs, cooperatives, and professional associations, leading to the evaporation of civil society and to the termination of social movements. Two months after the coup TOB-DER (Society of All Teachers' Union and Solidarity), Turkey's largest teachers' association, was targeted, its staff all over Turkey arrested, in Ankara its chairman and sixty-three others taken before the military prosecutor of the Martial Law Command and accused of "dividing the Turkish nation into ethnic groups by advocating for the rights of everyone in Turkey to receive education in their own native language and for the abolition of chauvinist and assimilationist pressures on education related to language and culture, for seeking to destroy nationalist sentiments by defending teaching and education in languages other than the official language agreed to in Article 3 of the constitution, and for organizing the community so that one economic and social class can establish its dominance over other social classes" (*Tercüman*, 19 November 1980).

In response to TOB-DER's and to other organizations' and parties' (TİP and Dev-Yol, for example) acknowledgment of the "national subordination" of Kurds in Turkey, the junta re-banned the public speaking—and thus the urban hearing— of Kurdish. At the same time, they republished and disseminated the core assimilationist claims of the Republic concerning "those who think themselves Kurdish."[18] This included the notorious book by Committee of Union and Progress intellectual Habil Adem (published under the pseudonym Dr. Fritz), who proposed that Kurds, parasitic upon the genius of Turks, Arabs, and Persians, have no separate

---

18. The words are from a 1961 report on the "Eastern problem" commissioned by the Turkish military after the coup in 1960, which refused to use the word *Kurds*.

language, history, political autonomy, or culture/art of their own.[19] The "Armenian question" also received a new official "denialist" narrative, coordinated in 1981 by the creation of the Directorate General of Intelligence and Research, whose primary task was to "conduct research into and produce scholarship on the Armenian question" (Gürpınar 2016: 225), including the translation of its works into foreign languages. With the destruction of TOB-DER, the junta found no obstruction to its militarization of school curricula either. In what Kaplan calls their systematic intervention into children's subjectivities through the production of military ideals taught at school, the junta propagated "through reworked textbooks and pedagogical directives . . . earlier myths and images to emphasize a particularly visceral collective representation—'the Turkish soldier, defender of the Muslim faith'" (2002: 114).

The junta reorganized the universities in November 1981, establishing the Council of Higher Education (YÖK) to centralize control and to curtail university autonomy and student organizations. YÖK immediately expelled seventy academics thought to have leftist leanings. Hundreds more resigned so as not to be charged under Martial Law Act No. 1402, which stated that those found guilty were "never again allowed employment in public services," making reinstatement to their university positions legally difficult even once the "interim regime" of the junta handed back legal administration to civilian courts.[20] University students attended compulsory history lessons taught by army officers, complementing the compulsory religious lessons in nationalist Islam introduced into primary and secondary schools. Military personnel headed every university lodgment, with identity checks at doors and strict evening deadlines (9:00 p.m. for girls). University staff feared for their jobs and livelihood, sometimes betraying students as a consequence. Gündüz Vassaf remembers an event at Boğaziçi University, when small, handwritten placards reading "Long Live May 1st" were discovered placed on class blackboards:

> Scared, the first teacher to see the slogans told the dean. The dean told the president. The president told the police. The police reported it to the military command of Istanbul. On the same day, special teams dispatched to the university seized the posters. . . . The police then requested from university administration the enrolment application forms filled out by students. In the police laboratory, handwriting experts went over four thousand forms, shrinking down the names. Lecturers shared with

19. Entitled *Kürtlerin Tarihi* (Istanbul: Hasat Press), the book was first published in 1918 and has been periodically republished by the Turkish state ever since. See Dündar (2001) as well as Houston (2009).

20. See Baskın Oran's account of the legal processes that those dismissed from university under Clause 1402 went through to have their university termination reversed, which finally occurred in 1990, in "Rezil darbenin yıl dönümünde karşılaştırmalı bir muhasebe," *T24*, 21 July 2017, http://t24.com.tr/yazarlar/baskin-oran/rezil-darbenin-yil-donumunde-karsilastirmali-bir-muhasebe,17737.

police the exam papers of students left on the list. In three weeks, the students were identified.[21]

The military tribunal opened up a case against DİSK on 19 December 1980, arresting thousands of its members and torturing the confederation's leaders. DİSK-affiliated unions and their activists were charged under Article 141, accused of "forming an organization to establish a hegemony of one social class over other social classes." The prosecutor sought both DİSK's closure and, under Article 146, the death sentence for its leadership for "attempting to overthrow the existing constitutional institutions and social order by force," an ironic charge in light of the huge numbers of junta decrees and laws enacted in contravention of the 1961 constitution and of parliamentary legislation thereafter.[22] The right to strike was outlawed, and the collective bargaining process suspended, taken under control of the junta through their institution of the Supreme Arbitration Council. Gendarmes were placed at factory doors, detaining unionists and members of organizations. According to Bülent (Biliş), to make local collective agreements impossible, "the State declared that 10 percent of the workforce over the whole of Turkey have to agree to the negotiation. That is, if there are one million workers in metal factories over Turkey, one hundred thousand have to be included in any bargaining. This stopped the right to agitate collectively for better conditions for six or seven years, which allowed for a huge concentration of wealth in business owners' hands." Among other things, a wage freeze changed the fate of workers in Turkey, contributing to their relative impoverishment, increasing income inequality, and "establishing [again ironically] the hegemony of one class over others." Spitefully, the junta cancelled the May Day public holiday.

Most efficaciously, the junta consolidated all of these laws and institutions and their restructuring of social relations by abrogating the existing constitution and instituting a new one, prepared by a special commission appointed by the National Security Council, and ratified in a general referendum held under martial law on 7 November 1982. The armed forces' restitution of 1930s Kemalism, "Atatürkçülük" (Atatürkism) was declared the defining feature of the Third Republic. Political parties were required to show allegiance to the "nationalism, principles, reforms and modernism of Atatürk."[23] Otherwise they would face closure by the constitutional court (as has occurred numerous times since). To prevent minority representation (political or ethnic) in Parliament, the new constitution instituted a 10 percent vote threshold. In enshrining Atatürkism at the center of repressive power, the

21. See Gündüz Vassaf, "Türkiye'de Üniversite Var mı?," *T24*, 13 February, 2017, http://t24.com.tr /yazarlar/gunduz-vassaf/turkiyede-universite-var-mi,16578.

22. Sentences against DİSK leaders were only overturned on appeal in 1991. DİSK remained closed for twelve years.

23. Preamble to the Constitution of the Turkish Republic (1982).

1982 constitution ensured that propagating it became the primary ends of policy, governance, and even civil society itself, so that Kemalism ceased to be a means to something else—in its own terms to civilization, modernity, secularism, and so on. Indeed, the constitution's explicit circumscribing of the bounds of legal politics meant social and political dissent thereafter, of necessity, minimally had to reference itself in relation to Kemalism and maximally to mobilize against it. As we saw in chapter 2, one unintended result of the constitution has been a strong need felt by many intellectuals and ex-activists since the 1980s to critically reexamine the original years of Kemalism in search of clues to its present oppressive form, leading to a widespread crisis of belief in it.

Furthermore, given that a state of emergency existed during the period of its drafting and electoral ratification, the constitution was not an act of political autonomy—literally the giving of the law to oneself—by the people of Turkey. In the lead-up to the plebiscite, criticism of the proposed constitution was illegal, as was the organization of any political campaign to advocate against it. In the ballot room itself, electors had to choose between two colors: white paper for those voting Yes; blue for those choosing No. In public speeches Kenan Evren and other junta leaders told people not to vote blue. Some interviewees remembered that where they voted the color of the ballot paper could be publicly seen, discouraging the giving of a blue vote in front of soldiers and police. Through Provisional Clause 15, voter approval of the new constitution simultaneously ensured for the five members of the National Security Council a lifelong immunity from prosecution for overthrowing the government and making a military coup.

Post-coup City

Alongside this reconstruction of Turkish society through law and censure, what changes did interviewees themselves perceive in their suburbs, in their social relationships, and in the city's spatial forms? A number of activists lived in *mahalle* (neighborhoods) in the historic peninsula, and each mentioned significant changes in their areas in the 1980s. Any remaining houses with gardens were quickly torn down and replaced by apartments. In various suburbs e.g., Fatih, the student lodgments closed. Mesut remembers that after getting out of prison in 1984 he tried to revive the organization (Dev-Sol). "I still felt strongly about social justice. But by then things had changed a lot. Many of the neighbors had left; there were now factories where some apartments used to be. People had become more concerned for themselves; more individual, and neighborly relations/feelings had weakened." Adding insult to injury, the summer cinema had closed down. Bülent commented that whereas in the 1970s house doors were all made from wood, during the 1980s they came to be made of steel, so "people were like turtles with their protective shells."

Istanbul's gecekondu suburbs changed even more rapidly. One important cause was dual "amnesty" laws passed in 1983 and 1984 (Laws 2805 and 2981), which set in train a process for the retroactive legalization of residents' earlier occupation of state land, as well as for legal recognition of house ownership. To put it another way, the amnesties ensured the privatization of formally government-owned land—not of public space—through the transfer of land titles. At the same time, as gecekondu residents moved through the legal processes of land survey and documentation that confirmed property rights, the council also conducted its own cadastral and land registration surveys, increasing the legibility of the urban environment to the state. Thus, the amnesty laws also provided the central government with a greater semblance of state control over the informal suburbs of Istanbul.

More important for the spatial transformation of the gecekondus' built environment was a second aspect of the amnesty laws, the bestowal of construction rights on the newly authorized owners of legalized urban land in order to "improve" the building(s) on that land (see Uzun, Çete, and Palançıoğlu 2010). Development rights on legalized plots included permission to demolish existing dwellings and replace them with apartments up to four stories high. In partnership with small-scale builders or developers, former squatters were able to move into their newly-built apartment as well as rent out other floors of the block as flats or shop fronts, completing the commodification or commercialization of land in Istanbul. Over time, housing rent became for many gecekondu residents a significant source of income. Spatially, in less than a decade gecekondu suburbs were transformed from habitats characterized by independent small houses with gardens into suburbs of cheap apartments. As has been the case since the expansion of Istanbul northward in the early 1900s, many people interpreted living in an apartment as a mode of being modern, even as the possibility of extracting rent enabled former gecekondu residents "to obtain permanent location in political space as well" (Şenyapalı 2004: 15). And of course, because both heavy migration to Istanbul and the state's war upon the Kurdish areas of Turkey have never ceased, Istanbul's sprawling post-gecekondu suburbs have become increasingly internally fragmented, as more recent migrants and internally displaced populations seek to find precarious work and cheap housing as renters in the *apartkondu* city. Işık and Pınarcıoğlu (2001) call this "destitution by turn" (*nöbetleşe yoksulluk*), although the term deflects attention from the permanent existence and poverty of an underclass itself.

Lastly, what did all these changes entail for the reproduction of activist groups in the gecekondu? Can's memories of Hürriyet Mahallesi in the 1980s reflect his perceptions of the ending of an era. He recalls the destruction of the organization, and the rapid building of apartments on the main streets by house owners, as well as the showy buying of cars. The community's practical insistence in the 1970s on housing for need, not for profit, dissipated with the faction's disappearance. New markets, furniture stores, and white goods (appliances) stores opened up, as did many garment workshops with their new workers. Equally noticeable for him was the effect of the new environment on [ex-] militants, on their feelings of aloneness, and on its changing of their perception/constitution of objects as they came out of prison:

> In the 1970s no one thought about money. Whereas now that's all anyone ever talks about. This has such a powerful effect that within a few days the main purpose of even those who come out of prison is to make as much money as they can.... They set up work and refuse to recognize us, or their old friends. And virtually selling their memories for money is not the only damage they do. They both set a bad example, and in talking to people spread the belief that, "Look, we tried, nothing happened, in this country a revolution won't happen, it's just a pipe dream." On top of that, for a period certain flamboyant revolutionaries who couldn't withstand police torture appeared on television, saying, "This work is finished; we were defeated by the state."
>
> As these examples proliferated, the insecurity and fear felt by remaining revolutionaries built up. Apart from trying to help the families of those in prison, the activities of myself and the handful of friends left petered out. (Mavioğlu 2008: 88–89)

For Can, as for other interviewees, each day under martial law was experienced as a shrinking world until he, too, in the end, "was finished."

CONCLUSION

This chapter has concentrated on three temporally experienced and interrelated themes. The first describes the junta's immediate spatial and activist politics of 12 Eylül, embarked upon to punish activists and to intimidate and pacify the city. The second involves investigation of activists' and their families' responses and resistance to this assault on Istanbul's urban bodies and places, expressed sometimes in their care for each other while surviving one more day, sometimes in minor acts of dissent. The third section presents the junta's legal and institutional reconstruction of Turkish society, intended to drastically and permanently reorganize its political practices. Taken together, the themes chronicle Istanbul's shock entry into a reign of fascism and its slow exit over three years into a new authoritarian political and (*alla Turca*) neoliberal economic order.

The junta's defanging of the labor movement and its suppression of citizens' rights, alongside the civilian government's expansion of the rights to property engineered by the amnesty laws and a range of other new economic policies (lowering of trade barriers, liberalizing of capital flows, privatizing of government assets) led to a form of coerced consent to the new order by many activists, as we see in Can's experience above. Consent to political order, like resistance to it, is no straightforward matter. Consensualist theories of political legitimacy presume that ideal consent entails the social lucidity of movements or people who are aware of oppositional alternatives to the current order and yet who support it. By contrast, as with resistance, consent may be individual, opportunistic, pragmatic, or cynical. It may entail no assent to a system's ideological claims nor possess any system-reproducing consequences. It may take place imperceptibly, over longer or shorter periods of time. It may also be studied diagnostically, as revealing the operations of political power, as Abu-Lughod (1990) argues for the case of resistance.

Existentially, in instituting the new regime, the Turkish armed forces, custodians of the Atatürk Cumhuriyeti (Atatürk Republic), declared, "I exist." Or perhaps more accurately, on 12 Eylül the junta asserted, on behalf of the military and of core segments of the state, "We exist—against you."

Thus, in the coup d'état the armed forces announced to socialist, labor, municipal, Kurdish, Islamist, and Turkist movements and to their [un]civil societies that "you have had your day; it is our turn now." The junta proclaimed that they could wait no longer: that their well-intentioned warnings to politicians to restrict their programs to an Atatürkist perspective had been unheeded; that they had been "compelled" to act, forced to move from passivity to agency, from inertia to action. In doing so, the coup sought the restitution of state dominance over both the political system and society through a politics of punishment and revenge. It entailed the exercise of "infrastructural power," defined by Eugene Rogan as "the capacity of the state to actually penetrate civil society, and to implement logistically political decisions throughout the realm" (Rogan 1999: 3).

"We exist against you." According to the junta, in certain crucial fields of social and spatial relations, implementation of the will of the Ataturk Republic had been obstructed. As Kenan Evren broadcast on the morning of the coup, "the armed forces are forced to take possession of administration in order to reestablish the lost authority of the state" (2000: 16). Embarking upon a martial remaking of the city, the military short-circuited Istanbul's emergent social relations, ensuring the autonomy of the state from the people. Five weeks later in a speech in the Anatolian/Black Sea town of Çorum, Evren explained further why the coup was necessary. According to him, in certain other [unnamed] places in Anatolia,

> They established a separate authority. It was as if there was no Turkish Republic. There was a local committee, and people's courts. Citizens could not go to the state courts; the people's court decided their applications. The decisions given by it were the decisions implemented. Council services, even if illegal, even if forced, were done on the directives of the municipal chief. There, among these anarchists, several people from every profession took a state salary. . . .
>
> And there in the government offices they hung calendars, and on the pages of the calendar, on the large monthly pages of the calendar, there are pictures of the anarchists killed in that region. Underneath the photos there are poems dedicated to them. And on the pages' right-hand side there are Nazım Hikmet poems. All of this, in government offices, hung on the walls of that town's government offices. (Evren 2000: 39)

In the eyes of the Junta, what were the core offences of such legitimately elected political actors? Was it not their emergence as political movements that sought to generate autonomous local institutions and alternative political practices, and/or more socialist forms of social relationships and self-governance? The gecekondu themselves were a case in point: in the absence of state construction, transport, and distribution of consumer goods, or even of the infrastructure required for water or electricity, residents were forced to organize their own networks. Building upon that self-organization, leftist groups in Istanbul sought to politicize it, to revolutionize society so as to revolutionize an unjust order and state. One consequence was socialization in alternative political perceptions and attachment to non-state-authorized political values. "Did you know," writes Ali Yıldız (Dev-Sol), "that in the games of children in Nurtepe there were revolutionaries, fascists and police? Did you know that when asked, children in Nurtepe would say, 'when I grow up I want to be a revolutionary'? They took their first education by writing on walls."[24] Similarly, Can recalls that in 1979, "when we heard that a police inspector had bad mouthed Mahir Çayan, five hundred people gathered and we walked to Harbiye. They were forced to move that inspector from Çağlayan" (Mavioğlu 2008: 86).

From the junta's perspective both events (and others like it) were anathema, an existential threat to a certain type of historical state and to propagation of a desired national (*milli*) consciousness. Should not the people march, on the contrary, in protest to insults against Ataturk, as they were organized to do in 1955? Should it not be his photo on government walls or in calendars? Should not children thrill to imagine their soldierly participation in the independence war? Should it not be the *şehit* (martyrs) of the Turkish nation and of the Republic that are commemorated and remembered? The armed forces brooked no rival authority, no political mobilization of alternative aims and motivations. In the coup event, militant citizens were made subservient to the nation and its state, transformed from activists to survivors and then, as the decade unfolded, into passive citizens, forced to dwell within and engage with the "New Order."

Let me conclude chapter 7 by simply listing the raw dimensions of the coup. The figures are given in an unprecedented and extraordinary report prepared by a parliamentary commission established in 2012 on behalf of the Turkish Grand National Assembly, to investigate all aspects of military coups in Turkey:[25]

- 650,000 people were arrested.
- 1,683,000 people were blacklisted.

24. See Sosyalist Forum, file:///Users/mq20057577/Desktop/CityoFearless/MU%CC%88CADEL EYLE%20DOG%CC%86AN%20BI%CC%87R%20SEMT_%20C%CC%A7AYAN%20MAHALL ESI%CC%87%20NURTEPE%20-%20Sosyalist%20Forum%20-%20Sosyalizm%20Okulu.htm (accessed 9 October 2018.

25. Source: The Grand National Assembly of Turkey, Parliamentary Investigative Commission into "Coups and Memorandums in Turkey" (published November 2012). Summarized in *Wikipedia* https://en.wikipedia.org/wiki/1980_Turkish_coup_d%27%C3%A9tat, accessed 3 March 2017.

- 230,000 people were tried in 210,000 lawsuits.
- 7,000 people were recommended for the death penalty.
- 517 people were sentenced to death.
- 50 of those given the death penalty were executed (26 political prisoners, 23 criminal offenders and one ASALA militant).
- The files of 259 people, which had been recommended for the death penalty, were sent to the National Assembly.
- 71,000 people were tried by articles 141, 142, and 163 of Turkish Penal Code.
- 98,404 people were tried on charges of being members of a leftist, a rightist, a nationalist, a conservative, or other organization.
- 388,000 people were denied a passport.
- 30,000 people were dismissed from their firms because they were suspects.
- 14,000 people had their citizenship revoked.
- 30,000 people went abroad as political refugees.
- 300 people died in a suspicious manner.
- 171 people died by reason of torture.
- 937 films were banned because they were found objectionable.
- 23,677 associations had their activities stopped.
- 3,854 teachers, 120 lecturers, and 47 judges were dismissed.
- 400 journalists were recommended a total of 4,000 years' imprisonment.
- Journalists were sentenced to a total of 3,315 years and 6 months' imprisonment.
- 31 journalists went to jail.
- 300 journalists were attacked.
- 3 journalists were shot dead.
- 300 days in which newspapers were not published.
- 303 cases were opened against 13 major newspapers.
- 39 tons of newspapers and magazines were destroyed.
- 299 people lost their lives in prison.
- 144 people died in a suspicious manner in prison.
- 14 people died in hunger strikes in prison.
- 16 people were shot while fleeing.
- 95 people were killed in combat.
- A "natural death report" was given for 73 persons.
- The cause of death of 43 people was announced as "suicide."

8

Phenomenology, Event, Commemoration

Conclusion

8.1 PHENOMENOLOGY OF ACTIVISM

In *Istanbul, City of the Fearless*, I have explored the political perceptions, relationships, moods, memories, and practices of militants in Istanbul during the years before and after the military coup of 12 September 1980. Thinking from a phenomenological perspective, I described in both their and my words activists' ordinary and extraordinary experiences of urban places, political factions, ideologies, violence, sounds, objects, events (i.e., the coup d'état), and people. By phenomenological, I simply mean an approach that identifies and analyzes certain elementary processes through which people—here activists—apprehend and engage with the meaningful environment in which they dwell. In writing about activists' perceptions, I hope to have productively reversed a more typical relationship between subject and object found in many social science accounts of those years that presuppose the prior objective existence and abstract definition of entities—class structure, ideology, culture, the state, the city, and so on—and use such views about what something must be like to causally explain people's experiences of them. Phenomenology criticizes such an approach for its naivety in assuming "entities" self-evidently exist regardless of the subject's—in this case the scientist's or the analyst's—apprehension of, and mode of attentiveness toward, them. By contrast, in *Istanbul, City of the Fearless*, we have attended to how activism, the practical pursuit of urban transformation and of social justice, produces an attunement or orientation toward places, ideas, people, and objects that simultaneously confers significance upon them, constituting their meaning or *sensefulness*. To put it bluntly, if you were an activist in the 1970s and early 1980s, you "had" a different Istanbul.

In concluding, perhaps the benefit of beginning with militants' lived experiences rather than with social scientific theories or deductive inferences is better demonstrated than merely asserted. Two misleading features recur in many academic accounts of the late 1970s and of the 1980 coup d'état and its aftermath, especially in works whose primary focus is some other more contemporary sociological event and that narrate (constitute) the significant dimensions of those years literally in passing. These features are especially clear and especially problematic when put alongside—when putting aside—the perceptions and the *memories* of perceptions expressed by activists themselves. The first is a standard summary that concentrates on the violence of the period and of its anarchistic militants, their conflicts often "explained" through vulgar sociological, economistic, and/or psychological schemas. The second is the commencement of the present "neoliberal" time of Istanbul in 1980 or in 1983, without seeking to present anything of the fertile connections between the policies of the post-junta era begun under Turgut Özal and the (apparently unimportant) years before the coup.

To give just one example, in a new book on contemporary political developments in Turkey, the authors write,

> This urban unrest, that plagued Turkish cities for over a decade, dates back to 1968. Turkish university students, many of whom were originally from rural areas, were experiencing anxieties over their cultural displacement and alienation in the cities. They, like their fellow students across Europe, took to the streets in protest over their future prospects and job opportunities.
>
> These tensions came to the fore when economic conditions deteriorated after the petrol crisis in 1973. . . . This was particularly devastating to *gecekondu* residents who were already the hardest hit by the economic meltdown. . . .
>
> It is in this context that Turkey's cities began to experience gang warfare, political insurgency and brutal government crackdowns. An estimated 4500 lives were lost in urban political conflict, in addition to the thousands wounded between 1976 and 1980, before the military finally intervened to restore order.[1]

Finally? Do they mean if only they had done it earlier? Condensing the 1970s and the coup to three paragraphs, the authors attribute violence to civil society (not the military), even as they present it as symptomatic of other explanatory

---

1. In Waldman and Calışkan (2017, 148). That this has become the shorthand version of the period is shown in another newly published and generally excellent book on the reception and interpretation of Kemalism in the Soviet Union, which similarly proffers: "In the 1970s, Turkey offered a prime example of a cleavage between center and periphery, new and old, modernity and tradition. Students and youth, in particular, formed large, marauding gangs that roamed the streets and entered universities, beating up those who did not immediately identify themselves as sympathizers. Killings gradually spread, from targeted assassinations to widespread, indiscriminate raids on coffeehouses, public meetings, market squares, and shops" (Ter-Matevosyan 2019, 147).

theories—activists' cultural alienation, economic meltdown and/or self-interest, "gang" warfare, the crisis of tradition.

In contrast, by studying the meanings and descriptions of violence as given by political actors themselves, we can identify the intentionalities that constitute its meaning for them in order to disclose its features in a radically different way. Indeed, in the chapters above we have already encountered numerous adumbrations of violence generated by political actors themselves.[2] Thus the violence of the police, gendarmerie, and armed forces may be understood as punishment of those challenging the sovereignty of the state, for their exceeding the bounds of their allotted spheres of action. In the killing of police, who were also murderers (by Dev-Sol for example), we have been confronted with the meaning of violence as revolutionary justice. In certain acts of armed revolt by groups inspired by the life and deeds of Mahir Çayan and comrades, or in the work of *ülkücü* ideologist Nihat Atsız, we have seen how violence is understood as potentially self-altering, both individually and collectively. In Diyarbakir prison, extreme violence was designed not to form but to deform selves, an identity-negating program to erase from prisoners the strain/stain of Kurdishness that Turkism posits as the basis for never-ending civil war. This ego-enacted torture was accompanied by the apparently anonymous violence of architecture, in its structuring of physical forms that dictated interactions between prisoners and between prisoners and place, and in its vengeful use of sound. For torturers themselves, violence may have been pleasurable. However, in the court case opened up by Doğan Eşlik against the junta in 2012 for his being forced into the role of a torturer in Mamak Prison, his legal proxies contended that he was "compelled [to do so] by threats of being beaten," and that in inflicting torture on activists "his emotional well-being has been permanently destroyed, he has received psychiatric treatment, and . . . he was so traumatized that he has never been able to marry." Here the very act of afflicting torture upon others was experienced as self-dissolution. "They broke our mind, our will and made us beat inmates like animals," Eşlik said (in Cockburn 2012). Self-violence in the form of a hunger strike was conceived as changing one's body into a weapon, "threatening to die rather than submit oneself to the state" (Bargu 2014: 3). In the struggle in the gecekondu we have seen violence conducted as resistance to oppression and as self-defense, what Yonucu (2018) defines as "urban vigilantism" for the physical and ethical protection of residents. For members of many groups, violence was also connected to male heroism. For post-1983 Turkish feminism, the gendered distribution of violence in all of its expressions is understood as an aspect of a fostered masculinity that manifested itself in both rightist and leftist movements.

2. See Smith (2016: 51–59) for a clear description of Husserl's notion of *adumbrations* and its claims concerning the core perspectival features of experience.

In brief, phenomenological research allows us to see that violence is not one thing, but "is given each time with a different meaning" (Crowell 2006: 21). In ignoring these different meanings of violence, as well as the variety of ways that intentional consciousness constitutes its content, the received wisdom concerning the era radically simplifies—and delegitimizes—the rich diversity of political practices pursued by different activist groups, including their political acts of pacifism.[3] It also presents the Atatürkism of the junta as politically neutral or even as nonideological, disguising both its profound influence over leftist and rightist ideologies as well as its own violent nationalism. Further, the standard account retells—knowingly or unknowingly—the narrative of the junta. As we have seen, according to them intervention was forced upon the armed forces by the anarchy of the city. But given the extent to which elements of the broader state—the police, gendarmerie, secret service, legal system, and the military—were implicated in much of that "anarchy," as well as the systematic violence perpetrated in post-coup prisons, the junta's justification for intervention rings false. Not narrating the violence of the suppressing of violence similarly obfuscates, too, how 12 Eylül destroyed all types of democratic movements and rights, in the name of restoring democracy and order.

A second feature prominent in much social science research on Istanbul in the years after the coup is its dating of the empirical starting point of the event under investigation—commoditization of housing, gated towns, new models of public housing, the rise of political Islamism, and so on—to reforms made in the early 1980s without backgrounding the 1970s as the relevant pre-given horizon. The literature on neoliberalism is a case in point, given that nearly all analyses of it trace its origins to the post-junta era of civilian rule. To use just one example, Kayasu and Yetişkul (2014) distinguish between two phases of neoliberal urban policies in Turkey, "roll-back" and "roll-out," and date the first period to the "economic restructuring" policies of the 1980s. Yet strangely they do not discuss what it was that was rolled-back or re-structured! Equally typically, although the era of 1970s activism and the coup are not mentioned (let alone investigated), the article attributes meaning to them as a spectral past whence these changes somehow emerge. In sum, in many standard social science accounts of present-day Istanbul these two ways of talking about the years 1974–1983 appear. The first presents a junta-inspired shorthand summary that is a travesty of the lives and activities of activists before passing onto other concerns; the second dates (as if created from nothing) many contemporary social processes to the post-junta era without considering the relevant "prehistory" of those occurrences.

---

3. To give just one example, in doing this research for this project I was impressed by the journal *Mimarlık* and its articles' concerns for equality, spatial justice, and rights to the city, all rendered mute for post-coup generations by repetition of the junta's story.

8.2 THE URBAN EVENT AND ITS FUTURES

Yet these two features are the least of their "sins." What appears most strange in many such accounts of Istanbul is their implying that the consequences of the spatial activism of the revolutionary movements in the 1970s and of the 1980 coup d'état are now insignificant, because they are "completed" historical happenings whose influences over people's subjective perceptions have passed. Yet, on the contrary, in virtually every chapter in this book we have heard how each were convulsive events that majorly transformed the city, establishing new tutelary state institutions while permanently modifying inhabitants' perceptions of its places and their urban knowledge and agency.[4] To conclude this study, therefore, let me describe in two final short sections some of the ways in which in the last decade ex-activists and others continue to reckon with the events of 1970s activism and the coup. This contending is pursued not only to redefine their meaning but also, given they were political events, to pragmatically make—as phenomenology appreciates—something from them, using them to do further politics with.

Elsewhere I have sketched out a model of the "urban event" that conceives it as possessing generative efficacy—a source of novel spatial arrangements, urban moods, built environments, and new forms of social division that exert their force and influence into the future. The urban event begins in a moment of time but is not necessarily ever concluded: its congeries of political practices may continue over years, conjoining new urban developments and subjects, none of which could unfold or exist in the way they do without this prior primary event (Houston 2019).

Understood, then, as urban events, the spatial politics of activists and the repression of the junta live on in the lives and perceptions of millions of people who experienced them—roughly, anyone over the age of fifty in Turkey. If the political events of the years 1974–1983 are treated as simplistic, resolved, or as irrelevant (as in the examples cited above), it is impossible to hear, let alone to do justice to, the diverse ways that huge numbers of Turkish citizens react to the forceful influence—embodied, affective—that these critical events continue to exercise over (and in) their own being. Filiz told me that at a special screening of the film *Eve Dönüş*[5] for ex-militants of Dev-Yol in 2006, when the lists of people arrested,

---

4. To give just one brief example: activism in Istanbul changed the basic experience of walking in the city. Prost's building of a modernist Gezi Park in the 1940s as a place for an emerging Turkish middle class to promenade contrasts with the experience of activists in the 1970s, for whom moving through the city required a different attuning to space, involving constant visual and sonic attention to which group controlled the space.

5. The 2006 film *Returning Home* (director Ömer Uğur) begins its narrative on the day of the coup, to which the apolitical working-class couple at the center of the drama is oblivious. Denounced by his landlord as a communist (for not paying the rent) the man is arrested, accused of being a member of an illegal organization, tortured, dismissed from work, and expelled from home, while witnessing in prison the murder of other victims.

tortured, and killed came up alongside Kenan Evren's picture, people screamed in tears at his image, "You destroyed a generation!" (Bir nesil mahvettin!) To some sure extent, the consequences of powerful, intersubjective political relations of the past continue in the present, despite their completion as discrete events, so that new incidents are perceived in the light of such previous relations and happenings.[6] In brief, what phenomenology describes as horizons (of the past and of the future) are activated in every present act of perception and experience.

Nevertheless, if certain components of urban events are irreversible—say the "death of an anarchist"—this does not mean that the significance of such acts cannot be further determined and their sensefulness changed. Thus ex-activists do more than merely *cope* with past horizons. Many seek to perpend on their experiences in a more activist way, even intervening in the very configuration of the past in an attempt to control its unfolding meaning and agency into the future. The fate of the song "Türkiyem" (My Turkey) is a case in point. In 2009, decades after its sonic employment in prison, an ex-Metris prisoner took his revenge on it, buying the copyright of the "torture song" to silence it forever, "so that it can never be used again as *meze* [entree] for torture. Hey torturers, *geçmiş olsun*; because you'll have to find another song with which to demoralize people," exalted Ertuğrul Mavioğlu.[7] Here the past is haunted by the present.

Indeed, as phenomenology also attests, the new status of "Türkiyem" indicates how the sense and force of things reside less in themselves intrinsically and more in their exposure to the future, where their affect for individuals is always liable to revision by new constituting acts of meaning. Furthermore, this alteration and control over the unfolding signification and reception of past urban events is contested, related in part to changes in balances of political power. Most critically, because laws and jurisprudence judgments possess the capacity to acknowledge and address historical injustices, struggles over them have been paramount in the endeavors of varied segments of Turkish society to challenge dominant representations of the event and their related legal privileges, most clearly demonstrated in the self-granted immunity of the junta. Those groups' decades-long concern to bring the junta to justice, both for the intervention itself and for its brutal abuses, is evidence of the importance victims give to legal action as providing some (temporary) closure in the present as well as new expectations of the future.

People too, as much as songs, remain vulnerable to what befalls them, as seen in the fate of Kenan Evren himself. Despite ten years' rule as the most powerful man in Turkey, a constitutional package put to the people by the AKP in a referendum—held symbolically on 12 September 2010, the thirtieth anniversary of the coup

6. "Not the intense moment isolated, with no before and after, but a lifetime burning in every moment," writes T. S. Eliot in *Four Quartets*.

7. "Darbenin şarkısına en ağır darbe," *Radikal*, 12 August 2009.

d'état—proposed twenty-six amendments to the 1982 constitution, one of which allowed civilian courts to try military personnel while banning military courts from trying civilians except in times of war. Another annulled Provisional Article 15, which exempted the coup leaders from prosecution. The reforms were passed with 58 percent of voters in favor.

The very next day (13 September 2010), Turkish human rights groups filed petitions in Istanbul, Ankara, and Izmir courts to have the leaders of the coup tried for crimes against humanity.[8] A year later the Izmir Bar Association opened a court case to have the honorary doctorate awarded to Kenan Evren in 1982 by the Faculty of Law at Istanbul University cancelled.[9] In early 2012 the Ankara court accepted indictments against Kenan Evren (aged ninety-four) and Tahsin Şahinkaya (eighty-six), the last two surviving members of the junta, with the prosecutor seeking life imprisonment. Two years later, in June 2014, both were found guilty of "crimes against the authority of the state," stripped of their officers' commission, demoted to private, and given life sentences.[10] Being sick, neither went to prison.

Thirty years after 12 Eylül, then, and despite the junta's attempt to mandate immunity and devise a statute of limitations for their acts, the slip-knot of history reopened, enabling political actors to bestow (for now) a new legal and ethical signification on the urban event of the coup d'état, as a criminal act. Alongside this "correction," municipal parliaments pursued a related spatial politics, erasing anything associated with the coup from the names of streets, schools, parks, fountains, and so on. Thus, in Urfa in late 2009, the municipality renamed 12 Eylül Caddesi as Demokrasi Street.[11] Similarly, in Muğla, the major thoroughfare Kenan Evren Bulvarı was changed to Cumhuriyet Boulevard, while a park named after Kenan Evren's wife Sekine Evren in one of the town's suburbs was changed to Türkan Saylan Parkı after Istanbul's famous leprosy doctor. With the decision to change Evren Paşa (General Evren) primary school and Kenan Evren Middle School to Armutalan primary and secondary schools respectively, "the [council] commission completely erased Kenan Evren's name, leader of the 12th September coup, from every school in the district."[12]

Emboldened by both the referendum and the legal possibilities it facilitated, the Parliament also sought to deconstruct the military's justifications and to deny the legitimacy of the military coups and memorandums of the Turkish armed forces, producing in 2012 a report endorsed by members of all four of its major political parties. In it they state:

8. "Call to Try Turkish Coup Leaders," *Al Jazeera*, 14 September 2010.
9. "Evren'den o cüppeyi geri alın," *Radikal*, 6 October 2011.
10. "Kenan Evren'e müebbet hapis cezası," in *Milliyet*, 18 June 2014.
11. "Şanlıurfa'da Kenan Evren'e 12 Eylül darbesi!," *CNN Turk* (accessed 1 December 2018).https://www.cnnturk.com/2009/turkiye/12/07/sanliurfada.kenan.evrene.12.eylul.darbesi/554511.0/index.html.
12. "Kenan Evren'in adı okullardan da kaldırıldı," in *Posta*, 30 April 2014.

By grounding themselves and their coups in the founding will and founding ideology of the Republic, the doers of coup d'états justify their dominion over the state by proclaiming their strong love for the homeland and nation.

They performed their coups always declaring that they loved their homeland more than its citizens did. They endeavored to establish their monopoly over the legitimate sphere by discrediting lawful politics and its representatives.

No coup d'état is national [Hiçbir darbe milli değildir] even if all military interventions were executed by the means of those institutions named "national." Because the coup-makers justified their coups as being "for the nation despite the nation," and "for the people despite the people," they created institutions of guardianship like the "National Unity Committee," the "National Security Council," and the "National Security Commission." . . .

In forbidding the airing of even a single oppositional statement against the constitution that they devised, they forced the approval of the constitution upon a society whose leaders, legitimate representatives and spokespeople were either imprisoned or exiled. If people did not oppose it, that is because they did not wish to encounter a catastrophe greater than the coup itself.[13].

8.3 COMMEMORATING ACTIVISM, COMMEMORATING 12 EYLÜL

Amending the military's constitution. Annulling constitutional impunity. Prosecuting the junta. Expunging references to the coup in the names of places. Reasserting the inalienable right of the parliament to govern. Each act conferred negative new meanings on 12 Eylül.

Did these developments rehabilitate the ethical significance of the deeds of activists that the discredited and now criminal junta had once targeted for extreme punishment? Or are events and laws somehow out of sync with each other, so that even as the military intervention is condemned, the contested politics of the contemporary public sphere generate suspicion and hostility toward the activism of militants in the 1970s? The latter situation appears more the case. To give just one example: in a critical speech act inaugurating the state of emergency five days after the failed coup in July 2016, President Tayyip Erdoğan addressed the public who confronted the soldiers on the streets of Istanbul and Ankara on the night of the coup attempt, declaring that "Our nation has lived for years with its regrets that it was unable to protect Menderes and his friends. The nation's grief is still fresh from its inability to stand up for our young people against the ideologies of the left and

---

13. The Grand National Assembly of Turkey, Parliamentary Investigative Commission into "Coups and Memorandums in Turkey," 2012: 16, https://www.tbmm.gov.tr/sirasayi/donem24/yil01/ss376_Cilt1 .pdf.

the right at the 1980 coup. This [action] has become a turning point that has brought that terrible course of events to an end."[14]

Here the president attributed to the nation long-held regrets concerning its inability to resist the interventions of the Turkish military, regrets that included its failure to protect (sahip çıkmak) young people in the 1970s from radical political ideologies that are posited in the very same utterance to be un-national and illegitimate. Yet because both left- and right-wing ideas and endeavors continue, his mention of Adnan Menderes and his barb at 1970s ideologies is not "merely" historical but seeks to unlock particular political sentiments (horizons) in AKP supporters in the present.

In the final few pages of this study, I will offer five brief illustrations of how in the face of continuing hostile interpretation of 1970s activism, leftist political parties, unions, and civil society groups memorialize it and the coup to counter such politics in the present. The touring of the mobile *Museum of Shame* is a case in point, showing how important it is for ex-activists to cooperatively communicate to younger generations both the aims of their struggle and the losses—death, torture, prison, unemployment, family problems, injury, loneliness—accruing to its participants, especially given the audibility of decades of militaristic education and official history-telling since 1980. There is no mention of coups or torture in the Military Museum (Askeri Müze) in Istanbul, packed full of school children each day.[15] Because people's lives are embroiled in urban events in different ways there is always *poly-verity* in history. Commemorative acts in the *Museum of Shame* testify to experiences younger people could not know.

Commemorations also take place in places. More accurately, places themselves are commemorated in commemorations, given their unavoidable role in inhabitants' experiences of urban events. Remembering the thirtieth anniversary of 12 Eylül in 2010, DİSK members held a press conference and ceremony outside Istanbul's Davutpaşa Barracks, where the confederation's administrators and worker-representatives were tried in 1980. The barracks are now part of the campus of Yıldız Technical University. Participants then marched, despite police obstruction, to nearby Otağ-ı Hümayun Köşkü, the Ottoman Imperial Pavilion in which the DİSK executive and many others were tortured after the coup. Speaking in front of the building and calling for its reconstruction into a human rights museum, DİSK Chairman Süleyman Çelebi declared:

> Without a doubt 12 Eylül directed its greatest attack and lawlessness against DİSK and its member unions. Thousands of DİSK members were arrested, filling the military prisons. 27 unions and 600,00 members became the primary target of the junta. This building bears witness to all that happened. Like Mamak, Metris, and Diyarbakır

14. See *T24*, 21 July 2016.
15. Thanks to Max Harwood for this information.

this building was turned into a torture workshop. . . . As a member of DİSK's steering committee, I was tortured in this building, eyes blindfolded. . . . Those days are not forgotten nor will they be forgiven. Leaving its deep traces in the memory of DİSK members, *Otağ-ı Hümayun* too cannot be forgotten.[16]

Istanbul's places, then, hold and exude multiple moods and feelings, all dependent upon people's "social history, personal and interpersonal experiences, and selective memory" (Kahn 1996: 167). Yet more than this, the reservoir of meanings and even trauma deposited in Otağ-ı Hümayun Köşkü by its co-option for torture also bears witness to the violence of "architects": to the way their uses of buildings as prime sites of spatial intervention may reorchestrate earlier design and over-determine people's experiential realities of place. Far from any agency of inanimate things, places subsist under the reign of their controllers.

On the same day four years later, once again in front of Otağ-ı Hümayun Köşkü, DİSK's current general secretary narrated a similar history of the building. But post-conviction of the junta, he declared the legal process "a show-piece of political propaganda by the government . . . in which no one guilty of crimes has gone to prison. More, the aims of those who praise the symbolic trial of the junta have been shown again and again to be no different from the makers of the coup. Today the ideas of the 12 Eylül fascist junta are in power. Above all else, the military coup of 12 Eylül was an assault of capital on the working class."[17] Commemorating 12 Eylül may now also evince other purposes, to protest a perceived continuity between the practices of the junta and the contemporary politics of the ruling AKP government. As the banner carried by DİSK protesters read, "12 Eylül is continued by the AKP!"

Two closing examples illustrate how in commemoration activists create alternative and fleeting public spaces in Istanbul by theatrically exhibiting histories and projecting political identities, as well as by claiming ownership of the dead. Amid a heavy police presence, at a Remembrance Day ceremony I attended in 2013 in Topkapı cemetery for well-known Turkish communist Dr. Hikmet Kıvılcımlı (founder of the Fatherland Party), three different socialist groups visit his grave in turn to make speeches, singing songs and standing for a minute of silence in memory of socialist martyrs. Like airplanes maneuvering on a runway, groups shout their slogans to each other as they progress around the cemetery's paths. "Kıvılcımlı öncümüz yaşatıyor gücümüz' (Our leader Kıvılcımlı makes our strength live). As

16. "DISK Üyelerine 'Otağ-ı Hümayun Müdahalesi,'" in *DISK* Newspaper, 27 November 2010 (accessed 6 December 2018), https://disk.org.tr/2010/12/disk-uyelerine-otag-i-humayun-mudahalesi/.

17. "12 Eylül; Susmayacağız, unutmayacağız, affetmeyeceğiz," *Tekstil İşçileri Sendikası* newspaper, 15 September 2014 (accessed 20 November 2018), https://disktekstil.org/12-eylul-susmayacagiz-unut mayacagiz-affetmeyecegiz.html.

much as it fabricates unity, commemoration may thus also contribute to factional fractures by engaging in a struggle for political patrimony.

Even earlier, in September 2009 I encountered the weekly protest of the mostly Kurdish "Saturday Mothers," a group of some one hundred people sitting motionlessly on Istanbul's busy İstiklal Caddesi. Holding A4-size photos of sons or daughters, the placards simply stated "Yakalandı Kaybedilmiş" (Arrested Lost) or "Kayıp" (Missing). On each, the name of the person and the date when the event happened were also written. Most portraits were dated between 1993 and1996. But on some 1981 was writ large, twenty-eight years ago to the day. Employing the crowds and noise as affordances, the group powerfully marked the commemoration with silence, stillness, and quiet. The AKP prohibited the gatherings in August 2018.[18]

In sum, in an era that repudiates the 1980 coup d'état (and coup d'états in general), commemorative acts revealing its particular human damage are one core practice whereby different groups seek to inflame in participants (and in the "public") certain affective feelings about that event. Symbolic remembering of harm, suffering, and terror, whose possibilities of urban memorialization open and close with political developments, is vital for activists in intervening in the crowded spatial politics of Istanbul. For "historically stigmatized populations" (Yonucu 2018) such as Kurds, Alevis, non-Muslims, and LGBTs, intervention in the city is a fragile spatial practice. The same pertains to socialists, for whom commemorating activism and its losses or gains always runs the risk of becoming an illegal act. And yet . . .

18. "Soylu'nun emriyle: 'Cumartesi Anneleri'nin eylemine ters kelepçeli gözaltı,'" *DİKEN*, 25 August 2018 (accessed 7 December 2018), http://www.diken.com.tr/soylunun-emriyle-cumartesi-annelerinin -eylemine-ters-kelepceli-gozalti/.

EPILOGUE

2010. The first official May Day meeting for thirty-three years. Thirty-three years since the 1977 Labor Day massacre.

Songs, slogans, music, speeches, banners, union symbols, faction colors, placards, photographers, cameras. A hundred thousand people and more march triumphantly into Taksim Square.

Türk-İş and the CHP stride up from Unkapanı.

DİSK and the TKP from Nişantaşı and Mecidiyeköy.

Dev-Yol partisans and comrades from Gümüşsuyu, arms interlocked, protest songs hurled into the air.

A flood of Maoists chanting along Tarlabaşı Bulvarı.

The tide of history ebbs and flows.[1]

1. For now (2018), the AKP government has again prohibited May Day celebrations.

BIBLIOGRAPHY

Abu-Lughod, L. 1990. "The Romance of Resistance: Tracing Transformations of Power through Bedouin Women." *American Ethnologist* 17(1): 41–55.

Ağaoğlu, A. (1984) 1997. *Curfew.* Austin: University of Texas Press.

Ahmad, F. 1993. *The Making of Modern Turkey.* New York: Routledge.

———. 2003. *Turkey: The Quest for Identity.* Oxford, UK: Oneworld.

Akbulut, M., and S. Başlık. 2011. "Transformation of Perception of the Gecekondu Phenomenon." *METU: Journal of the Faculty of Architecture* 28(2): 1–44.

Akçam, Taner. 2013. "Namus bekçileri," *Taraf*, 21 November.

Akpınar, İ. 2010. "İstanbul'da modern bir pay-i taht: Prost planı çerevesinde Menderes'in icraatı." In *İmparatorluk başkentinden cumhuriyet'in modern kentine: Henri Prost'un İstanbul planlaması (1936–1951)*, ed. F. Bilsel and P. Pinon. Istanbul: Istanbul Araştırmaları Enstitüsü.

———. 2015. "Menderes imar hareketleri Türkleştirme politikalarının bir parçası mıydı?" *Arrademento Mimarlik Dergisi*, May, 85–90.

Aksakal, P. 2007. *Fatsa gerçeği.* Istanbul: Penta.

Akşin, S. 2007. *Turkey from Empire to Revolutionary Republic.* London: Hurst & Company.

Aktar, A. 2000. *Varlık vergisi ve Türkleştirme politikaları.* Istanbul: İletişim.

———. 2006. *Türk milliyetçiliği, gayrimüslimler ve ekonomik dönüşüm.* Istanbul: İletişim.

Alexandris, A. 1983. *The Greek Minority of Istanbul and Greek-Turkish Relations 1918–1974.* Athens: Centre for Asia Minor Studies.

Anderson, B. 2009. "Affective Atmospheres." *Emotion, Space and Society* 2(2): 77–81.

Asan, Ö. 2010. *12 Eylül sabahı.* Istanbul: Heyamola Yayınları.

Aslan, Ş. 2004. *1 Mayıs Mahallesi: 1980 öncesi toplumsal mücadeleler ve kent.* Istanbul: İletişim.

Aydınoğlu, E. 2007. *Türkiye solu (1960–1980).* Istanbul: Versus.

Bachelard, G. 1994. *The Poetics of Space*. Boston: Beacon Press.

Bali, R. 2008. *1934 Trakya olayları*. Istanbul: Kitabevi.

Bargu, B. 2014. *Starve and Immolate: The Politics of Human Weapons*. New York: Columbia University Press.

Basso, K. 1996. "Wisdom Sits in Places: Notes on a Western Apache Landscape." In *Senses of Place*, ed. S. Feld and K. Basso, 53–90. Santa Fe, NM: School of American Research Press.

Batuman, B. 2006. "Turkish Urban Professionals and the Politics of Housing, 1960–1980." *METU: Journal of the Faculty of Architecture* 23(1): 59–81.

Baturayoğlu-Yöney, N., and Y. Salman. 2010. "Mass Housing Development by a Government Agency and the Politics of Urbanization." Unpublished paper from 14th International Planning History Conference, Istanbul, 12–15 July 2010. Accessed 8 October 2016. http://www.iphs2010.com/abs/ID204.pdf.

Bektaş, C. 1996. *Hoşgörünün öteki adı: Kuzguncuk*. Istanbul: Tasarım Yayın Grubu.

Belge, M. 1979. "Sosyalist bir topluma geçişte örgütlenme nüvesi olarak belediyelerin önemi." *Mimarlık* 2: 16–18.

Benjamin, W. 1940. *Theses on the Philosophy of History*. Marxists. org. Accessed 8 April 2016. https://www.marxists.org/reference/archive/benjamin/1940/history.htm.

Berik, G., and C. Bilginsoy. 1996. "The Labor Movement in Turkey: Labor Pains, Maturity, Metamorphosis?" In *The Social History of Labor in the Middle East*, ed. E. J. Goldberg, 37–64. Boulder, CO: Westview Press.

Berkes, H. 1964. *The Development of Secularism in Turkey*. Montreal: McGill University Press.

Bertram, C. 2008. *Imagining the Turkish House*. Austin: University of Texas Press.

Bilsel, F. 2010. "Henri Prost'un Istanbul planlaması (1936–1951): Nazım planlar ve kentsel operasyonlarla kentin yapısal dönüşümü." In *İmparatorluk başkentinden cumhuriyet'in modern kentine: Henri Prost'un Istanbul planlaması (1936–1951)*, ed. F. Bilsel and P. Pinon. Istanbul: Istanbul Araştırmaları Enstitüsü.

Bora, T. 2015. "Şehitler ve Şahitler," *Birikim*, 16 September. Accessed April 25, 2018. http://www.birikimdergisi.com/haftalik/1567/sehitler-ve-sahitler#.Wt_hvdNuYUQ.

———. 2017. *Cereyanlar: Türkiye'de siyasi ideolojiler*. Istanbul: İletişim.

Bourdieu, P. 1977. *Outline of a Theory of Practice*. Cambridge: Cambridge University Press.

———. 2001. *Masculine Domination*. Stanford, CA: Stanford University Press.

Bozarslan, H. 2012. "Between Integration, Autonomization and Radicalization: Hamit Bozarslan on the Kurdish Movement and the Turkish Left." *European Journal of Turkish Studies* 14. http://journals.openedition.org/ejts/4663.

Bozdoğan, S. 1994. "Architecture, Modernism and Nation-Building in Turkey." *New Perspectives on Turkey* 10 (Spring): 37–55.

———. 2001. *Modernism and Nation Building: Turkish Architectural Culture in the Early Republic*. Seattle: University of Washington Press.

Can, K. 2011. *12 Eylül 1980: Akıl tutulması*. Istanbul: Boyut.

Carpenter, E. 1960. "Acoustic Space." In *Explorations in Communications*, ed. E. Carpenter and M. McLuhan, 65–70. Boston: Beacon Press.

Casey, E. 1987. *Remembering: A Phenomenological Study*. Bloomington: Indiana University Press.

————. 1996. "How to Get from Space to Place in a Fairly Short Stretch of Time: Phenomenological Prolegomena." In *Senses of Place*, ed. S. Feld and K. Basso, 13–52. Santa Fe,
NM: School of American Research Press.

————. 2001. "Between Geography and Philosophy: What Does It Mean to Be in the Place-
World?" *Annals of the Association of American Geographers* 91(4): 683–93.

Castoriadis, C. 1987. *The Imaginary Institution of Society.* Cambridge, UK: Polity Press.

————. 1997. "The Imaginary: Creation in the Social-Historical Domain." In *World in Fragments: Writings on Politics, Society, Pyschoanalysis, and the Imagination*, ed. C. Castoriadis, transl. D. A. Curtis. Stanford, CA: Stanford University Press.

Cengizkan, A. 2009. *Fabrika'da barınmak: Erken cumhuriyet döneminde Türkiye'de işçi
konutları: Yaşam, mekan and kent.* Ankara: Arkadaş Yayınevi.

Clark, K. 2013. "European and Russian Cultural Interactions with Turkey: 1910s–1930s."
Comparative Studies of South Asia, Africa and the Middle East 33(2): 201–13.

Cockburn, Patrick. "Working as a Jail Torturer Ruined My Life," *The Independent*, Wednes-
day, 15 February 2012. https://www.independent.co.uk/news/world/europe/working-as
-a-jail-torturer-ruined-my-life-6917392.html.

Connerton, P. 2008. "Seven Types of Forgetting." *Memory Studies* 1(1): 59–71.

Constitution of the Republic of Turkey. 1982. UNHCR. Accessed 10 February 2013. http://
www.unhcr.org/refworld/docid/3ae6b5beo.html.

Copeaux, E. 1996. "Hizmet: A Keyword in Turkish Historical Narrative." *New Perspectives
on Turkey* 14: 91–114.

Crowell, Steven. 2006. "Husserlian Phenomenology." In *A Companion to Phenomenology
and Existentialism*, ed. H. Dreyfus and M. Wrathall, 9–30. Oxford: Blackwell Publishing.

Çağaptay, S. 2006. *Islam, Secularism, and Nationalism in Modern Turkey: Who Is a Turk?*
Oxon, UK: Routledge.

Çağlar, A. 1990. "The Greywolves as Metaphor." In *Turkish State, Turkish Society*, ed.
A. Finkel and N. Sirman, 79–101. London: Routledge.

Çavdar, T. 1978. "Toplum bilinçlenmesinde araç olarak katılımsal tasarım: İzmit yenilikçi
yerleşmeler projesi." *Mimarlık* 154(16): 55–60.

Çelik, Z. 1986. *The Remaking of Istanbul.* Washington: University of Washington Press.

————. 2007. "İstanbul, bir tema parkı olarak kentsel koruma—Soğukçeşme Sokağı." In
Şehirler ve Sokaklar, ed. Z. Çelik, D. Favro, and R. Ongersoll, 97–112. Istanbul: Kitap
Yayınevi.

Çoker, F. 2005. *6–7 Eylül olayları: Fahri Çoker Arşivi.* Istanbul: Tarih Vakfı.

Davis, D. E. 2005. "Cities in Global Context: A Brief Intellectual History." *International Journal of Urban and Regional Research* 29(1): 92–109.

Davison, R. 1998. *Turkey: A Short History.* London: Eothen Press.

Debray, R. 1967. *Revolution in the Revolution? Armed Struggle and Political Struggle in Latin
America.* London: Penguin Books.

De Cauter, L. 2011. "Towards a Phenomenology of Civil War: Hobbes Meets Benjamin in
Beirut." *International Journal of Urban and Regional Research* 35(2): 421–30.

de Certeau, M. 1984. *The Practice of Everyday Life.* Berkeley: University of California
Press.

Deringil, S. 1998. *The Well-Protected Domains: Ideology and the Legitimation of Power in the
Ottoman Empire,1876–1909.* London: I. B. Tauris.

————. 2003. "'They Live in a State of Nomadism and Savagery': The Late Ottoman Empire and the Post-Colonial Debate." *Comparative Studies in Society and History* 45(2): 311–42.

Der Matossian, B. 2014. *Shattered Dreams of Revolution: From Liberty to Violence in the Late Ottoman Empire.* Stanford, CA: Stanford University Press.

Desjarlais, R. 2003. *Sensory Biographies: Lives and Deaths among Nepal's Yolmo Buddhists.* Berkeley: University of California Press.

Desjarlais, R., and J. Throop. 2011. "Phenomenological Approaches in Anthropology." *Annual Review of Anthropology* 40: 87–102.

Dressler, M. 2013. *Writing Religion: The Making of Turkish Alevi Islam.* Oxford: Oxford University Press.

Dubetsky, A. 1976. "Kinship, Primordial Ties, and Factory Organization in Turkey: An Anthropological View." *International Journal of Middle East Studies* 7: 433–51.

Duranti, A. 2009. "The Relevance of Husserl's Theory to Language Socialization." *Journal of Linguistic Anthropology* 19(2): 205–26.

Dündar, F. 2001. "İttihat ve terakki'nin etnisite araştırmaları." *Toplumsal Tarih* 16: 43–50.

————. 2014. "Empire of Taxonomy: Ethnic and Religious Identities in the Ottoman Surveys and Censuses." *Middle Eastern Studies* 51(1): 136–58.

Eldem, E., D. Goffman, and B. Masters. 1999. *The Ottoman City Between East and West: Aleppo, Izmir and Istanbul.* Cambridge: Cambridge University Press.

Eliot, T. S. 1934. *The Wasteland and Other Poems.* New York: Harcourt Brace & Company.

Epstein, A. 1964. "Urban Communities in Africa." In *Closed Systems and Open Minds: The Limits of Naivety in Social Anthropology,* ed. M. Gluckman, 83–102. Edinburgh: Oliver & Boyd.

Erder, S. 1996 *İstanbul'a bir kent kondu: Ümraniye.* Istanbul: İletişim.

Ergün, N. 2004. "Gentrification in Istanbul." *Cities* 21(5): 391–405.

Erman, T. 2001. "The Politics of Squatter (Gecekondu) Studies in Turkey: The Changing Representations of Rural Migrants in the Academic Discourse." *Urban Studies* 38(7): 983–1002.

————. 2012. "Urbanization and Urbanism." In *The Routledge Handbook of Modern Turkey,* ed. M. Heper and S. Sayarı, 293–302. Abingdon: Routledge.

Evren, K. 2000. *Seçme konuşmalar (12 Eylül 1980–6 Kasım 1989).* Istanbul: Doğan Kitapcılık.

Faubion, J. 2010. "From the Ethical to the Themitical (and Back Again): Groundwork for an Anthropology of Ethics." In *Ordinary Ethics: Anthropology, Language, and Action,* ed. M. Lambek, 84–101. New York: Fordham University Press.

Feld, S. 1996. "Waterfalls of Sound: An Acoustemology of Place Resounding in Bosavi, Papua New Guinea." In *Senses of Place,* ed. S. Feld and K. Basso, 91–136. Santa Fe, NM: School of American Research Press.

Ferguson, J. 1999. *Expectations of Modernity: Myths and Meanings of Urban Life on the Zambian Copperbelt.* Berkeley: University of California Press.

Finkel, A. 1990. "Municipal Politics and the State in Contemporary Turkey." In *Turkish State, Turkish Society,* ed. A. Finkel and N. Sirman, 185–217. London: Routledge.

Freely, M. 2009. "The Prison Imaginary in Turkish Literature." *World Literature Today* 83(6): 46–50.

Geniş, S. 2007. "Producing Elite Localities: The Rise of Gated Communities in Istanbul." *Urban Studies* 44(4): 771–98.

Gibson, J. 1979. *The Ecological Approach to Visual Perception*. Boston: Houghton Mifflin.

Gökarıksel, B., and K. Mitchell. 2005. "Veiling, Secularism, and the Neoliberal Subject: National Narratives and Supranational Desires in Turkey and France." *Global Networks* 5(2): 147–65.

Göktürk, D., L. Soysal, and I. Türeli. 2010. "Introduction." In *Orienting Istanbul: Cultural Capital of Europe?*, ed. D. Göktürk, L. Soysal, and I. Türeli, 1–24. London: Routledge.

Guenther, L. 2017. "Epistemic Injustice and Phenomenology." In *The Routledge Handbook to Epistemic Injustice*, ed. I. Kidd, J. Medina, and G. Pohlhaus, 195–204. New York: Routledge.

Gül, M. 2009. *The Emergence of Modern Istanbul: Transformation and Modernization of a City*. London: I. B. Tauris.

Gül, M., and R. Lamb. 2004. "Urban Planning in Istanbul in the Early Republican Period." *Architectural Theory Review* 9(1): 59–81.

Gülalp, H. 1997. "Modernization Policies and Islamist Politics in Turkey." In *Rethinking Modernity and National Identity in Turkey*, ed. S. Bozdoğan and R. Kasaba, 52–63. Seattle: University of Washington Press.

Gunter, M. 1989. "Political Instability in Turkey during the 1970s." *Conflict Quarterly* Winter.

Gürpınar, D. 2016. "The Manufacturing of Denial: The Making of the Turkish 'Official Thesis' on the Armenian Genocide between 1974 and 1990." *Journal of Balkan and Near Eastern Studies* 18(3): 217–40.

Güven, D. 2005a. *6–7 Eylül olayları fotoğraflar-belgeler, Fahri Çoker Arşivi*. Istanbul: Tarih Vakfı.

———. 2005b. *Cumhuriyet dönemi azınlık politikaları bağlamında 6–7 Eylül olayları*. Istanbul: Tarih Vakfı.

Heidegger, M. 1959. "The Nature of Language." In *On the Way to Language*, ed. P. Hertz. New York: Harper & Row.

Hikmet, N. 1994. *Poems of Nazım Hikmet* (trans. by R. Blasing and M. Konuk). New York: Persea Books.

Hilgers, M. 2013. "Embodying Neoliberalism: Thoughts and Responses to Critics." *Social Anthropology* 21(1): 75–89.

Holod, R., and A. Evin. 1986. *Modern Turkish Architecture*. Philadelphia: University of Pennsylvania Press.

Holston, J. 1989. *The Modernist City: An Anthropological Critique of Brasilia*. Chicago: University of Chicago Press.

Hough, C. 2010. "Obscured Hybridity: The Kurdishness of Turkish Folk Music." *Pacific Review of Ethnomusicology* 15. https://ethnomusicologyreview.ucla.edu/journal/volume /15/piece/480

Houston, C. 2001. *Islam, Kurds and the Turkish Nation State*. Oxford: Berg.

———. 2008. *Kurdistan, Crafting of National Selves*. Oxford: Berg.

———. 2009. "An Anti-History of a Non-People: Kurds, Colonialism and Nationalism in the History of Anthropology." *Journal of the Royal Anthropological Institute* 15(1): 19–35.

———. 2015a. "Neither Things in Themselves nor Only for Someone: Anthropology, Poetry And Phenomenology." In *A Sense of Perspective: Phenomenology in Anthropology*, ed. K. Ram and C. Houston. Bloomington: Indiana University Press.

———. 2015b. "Politicizing Place Perception: A Phenomenology of Urban Activism in Istanbul." *Journal of the Royal Anthropological Institute* 21(4): 720–38.

———. 2015c. "Kemalism and Beyond." In *The Oxford Handbook of Contemporary Middle-Eastern and North African History*. Oxford: Oxford University Press.

———. 2019. "Event-stanbul? Contemporary Istanbul as Site of Intersecting Urban Events." *Ethnos* (February 13).

Houston, C., and B. Şenay. 2017. "Humour, Amnesia and Making Place: Constitutive Acts of the Subject in Gezi Park, Istanbul." *Social Analysis* 61(3): 19–40.

Howard, D. 2001. *The History of Turkey*. Westport, CT: Greenwood Press.

Humphrey, C. 2008. "Reassembling Individual Subjects: Events and Decisions in Troubled Times." *Anthropological Theory* 8(4): 357–80.

Humphreys, M. 2002. *The Politics of Atrocity and Reconciliation: From Terror to Trauma*. London: Routledge.

Husserl, E. 1962. *Ideas: General Introduction to a Pure Phenomenology*. New York: Collier Books.

Ingold, T. 2000. *The Perception of the Environment*. London: Routledge.

———. 2005. "Epilogue: Towards a Politics of Dwelling." *Conservation and Society* 3(2): 501–8.

———. 2011a. "Worlds of Sense and Sensing the World: A Response to Sarah Pink and David Howes." *Social Anthropology* 19(3): 313–17.

———. 2011b. *Being Alive: Essays on Movement, Knowledge and Description*. London: Routledge.

Ingold, T., and E. Hallam. 2007. "Creativity and Cultural Improvisation: An Introduction." In *Creativity and Cultural Improvisation*, ed. E. Hallam and T. Ingold, 1–24. Oxford: Berg.

Insel, A. 2001. "Giriş." In *Modern Türkiye'de siyasi düşünce: Kemalizm*, 17–28. Istanbul: İletişim.

Irzık, S. 2010. "The Constructions of Victimhood in Turkish *Coup d'État* Novels: Is Victimhood without Innocence Possible?" In *Betraying the Victims: Constructions of Victimhood in Contemporary Cultures*, ed. F. Festic. Newcastle upon Tyne: Cambridge Scholars Publishing.

Işık, O., and M. Pınarcıoğlu. 2001. *Nöbetleşe yoksulluk, Sultanbeyli örneği*. Istanbul: İletişim.

Jackson, M. 1998. *Minima Ethnographica: Intersubjectivity and the Anthropological Project*. Chicago: Chicago University Press.

Jongerden, J. 2017. "A Spatial Perspective on Political Group Formation in Turkey after the 1971 Coup: The Kurdistan Workers Party of Turkey (PKK)." *Kurdish Studies* 5(2): 134–56.

Jongerden, J., and H. Akkaya. 2018. "The Kurdistan Workers Party (PKK) and Kurdish Political Parties in the 1970s." In *Routledge Handbook on the Kurds*, ed. M. Gunter, London: Routledge.

Kahn, M. 1996. "Your Place and Mine: Sharing Emotional Landscapes in Wamira, Papua New Guinea." In *Senses of Place*, eds. S. Feld and K. Basso, 167–96. Santa Fe, NM: School of American Research Press.

Kalaycıoğlu, E. 2005. *Turkish Dynamics: Bridge across Troubled Lands*. New York: Palgrave.

———. 2012. "Political Culture." In *The Handbook of Modern Turkey*, ed. M. Heper and S. Sayarı. New York: Routledge.

Kandiyoti, D. 1977. "Some Implications of Social Change for Housing Design." *METU: Journal of the Faculty of Architecture* 3(1): 101–17.

———. 2002. "Introduction: Reading the Fragments." In *Fragments of Culture: The Everyday of Modern Turkey*, ed. D. Kandiyoti and A. Saktanber, 1–21. London: I. B. Tauris.

Kaplan, S. 2002. "*Dinu-Devlet* All Over Again? The Politics of Militarism in Turkey Following the 1980 Coup." *International Journal of Middle Eastern Studies* 34(1): 113–27.

Karpat, K. 1976. *Gecekondu: Rural Migration and Urbanization*. Cambridge: Cambridge University Press.

Kayasu, S., and E. Yetişkul. 2014. "Evolving Legal and Institutional Frameworks of Neoliberal Urban Policies in Turkey." *METU: Journal of the Faculty of Architecture* 31(2): 209–22.

Kemal, Y. 1964. *Aziz Istanbul*. Istanbul: Istanbul Fetih Cemiyeti.

Keyder, Ç. 1987. *State and Class in Turkey*. London: Verso.

———. 1993. *Ulusal kalkınmacılığın iflası*. Istanbul: Metis.

———. 1999a. "The Setting." In *Istanbul between the Global and the Local*, ed. Ç. Keyder. Lanham, MD: Rowman & Littlefield.

———. 1999b. "The Housing Market from Informal to Global." In *Istanbul between the Global and the Local*, ed. Ç. Keyder. Lanham, MD: Rowman & Littlefield.

———. 2003. "The Consequences of the Exchange of Populations for Turkey." In *Crossing the Agean: An Appraisal of the 1923 Compulsory Population Exchange between Greece and Turkey*, ed. R. Hirschon, 39–52. Oxford: Berghahn Books.

———. 2005. "Globalization and Social Exclusion in Istanbul." *International Journal of Urban and Regional Research* 29(1): 124–34.

———. 2010. "Istanbul into the Twenty-First Century." In *Orienting Istanbul: Cultural Capital of Europe?*, ed. D. Göktürk, L. Soysal, and I. Türeli. London: Routledge.

Knibbe, K., and P. Versteeg. 2008. "Assessing Phenomenology in Anthropology: Lessons from the Study of Religion and Experience." *Critique of Anthropology* 28(1): 47–62.

Kolluoğlu-Kırlı, B. 2002. "The Play of Memory, Counter-Memory: Building İzmir on Smyrna's Ashes." *New Perspectives on Turkey* 26: 1–28.

Küçükkaya, Y. 2011. *Darbe şakacıları sevmez*. Istanbul: Cumhuriyet Kitapları.

Kukul, S. 1989. *Bir direniş odağı metris: Metris tarihi*. Istanbul: Haziran Yayınevi.

Kutal, M. 2003. "Türkiye'de kamu görevlilerinin sendikal örgütlenme hakları." *Sosyal Siyaset Konferansları*, no: 45, 141–54.

Laidlaw, J. 2002. "For an Anthropology of Ethics and Freedom." *Journal of the Royal Anthropological Institute* 8(2): 311–32.

Lambek, M. 2010. "Introduction." In *Ordinary Ethics: Anthropology, Language and Action*, ed. M. Lambek, 1–38. New York: Fordham University Press.

Lefebvre, H. 1991. *The Production of Space*. Oxford: Blackwell.

Levinas, E. 1995. *The Theory of Intuition in Husserl's Phenomenology*. Evanston, IL: Northwestern University Press.

Lewis, G. 1999. *The Turkish Language Reform, A Catastrophic Success*. Oxford: Oxford University Press.

Lipovsky, I. 1992. *The Socialist Movement in Turkey 1960–1980*. Leiden, Netherlands: Brill.

Low, S. 1996. "Spatializing Culture: The Social Production and Social Construction of Public Space in Costa Rica." *American Ethnologist* 23(4): 861–79.

Luft, S. 1998. "Husserl's Phenomenological Discovery of the Natural Attitude." *Continental Philosophy Review* 31(2): 153–70.

Marchand, T. 2010. "Preface." In *Making Knowledge: Explorations of the Indissoluble Relation between Mind, Body and Environment*, ed. Trevor Marchand. West Sussex: Wiley-Blackwell.

Mardin, Ş. 1978. "Youth and Violence in Turkey." *Archives Europeenes de Sociologie* 19: 229–54.

———. 1997. "Projects as Methodology: Some Thoughts on Modern Turkish Social Science." In *Rethinking Modernity and National Identity in Turkey*, ed. S. Bozdoğan and R. Kasaba, Seattle: University of Washington Press.

Mauss, M. 1973. "Techniques of the Body." *Economy and Society* 2(1): 70–88.

Mavioğlu, E. 2008. *Bizim çocuklar yapamadı: Bir 12 Eylül hesaplaşması*. Istanbul: İthaki Yayınları.

Mazower, M. 2004. *Salonika, City of Ghosts: Christians, Muslims and Jews 1430–1950*. London: HarperCollins Publishers.

McCarthy, J. 1995. *Death and Exile: The Ethnic Cleansing of Ottoman Muslims, 1821–1922*. Princeton, NJ: The Darwin Press.

Mello, B. 2010. "Communists and Compromisers: Explaining Divergences within Turkish Labour Activism, 1960–1980." *European Journal of Turkish Studies* 11(1): 1–21.

Merleau-Ponty, M. (1945) 2002. *Phenomenology of Perception*. London: Routledge.

Metiner, M. 2008. *Yemyeşil şeriat, bembeyaz Demokrasi*. Istanbul: KaraKutu.

Mignon, L. 2014. "Minor Literatures and Their Challenge to 'National' Literature: The Turkish Case." In *Turkey and the Politics of National Identity: Social, Economic and Cultural Transformation*, ed. S. Brennan and M. Herzog, 194–214. London: I. B. Tauris.

Mills, A. 2010. *Streets of Memory: Landscape, Tolerance and National Identity in Istanbul*. Athens: University of Georgia Press.

Moran, D. 2000. *Introduction to Phenomenology*. London: Routledge.

Myers, F. 1991. *Pintupi Country, Pintupi Self: Sentiment, Place and Politics among Western Desert Aborigines*. Berkeley: University of California Press.

Navaro-Yashin, Y. 2009. "Affective Spaces, Melancholic Objects: Ruination and the Production of Anthropological Knowledge." *Journal of the Royal Anthropological Institute* 15(1): 1–18.

Nora, P. 1989. "Between Memory and History: Les lieux de memoire." *Representations* 26: 7–25.

Odabaşı, Y. 1991. *Bir Kürdün Eylül defterleri (1975–1985)*. Istanbul: Broy Yayınları.

Oran, B. 2003. "The Story of Those Who Stayed: Lessons from Articles 1 and 2 of the 1923 Convention." In *Crossing the Agean: An Appraisal of the 1923 Compulsory Population Exchange between Greece and Turkey*, ed. R. Hirschon, 97–115. Oxford: Berghahn Books.

Öz, O., and M. Eder. 2012. Rendering Istanbul's Periodic Bazaars Invisible: Reflections on Urban Transformations and Contested Space. *International Journal of Urban and Regional Research* 36(2): 297–314.

Özbek, M. 1991. *Popüler kültür ve Orhan Gencebay Arabeski*. Istanbul: İletişim.

Pamak, M. 1992. *Kürt sorunu ve Müslümanlar*. Istanbul: Selam Yayınları.

Pamuk, Ş. 2014. *Türkiye'nin 200 yıllık iktisadi tarihi*. Istanbul: İş Bankası Yayınları.

Parla, T., and A. Davison. 2004. *Corporatist Ideology in Kemalist Turkey.* Syracuse, NY: Syracuse University Press.

Perouse, J. 2004. "Deconstructing the Gecekondu." *European Journal of Turkish Studies* 1: 1–8.

Pilsel, F., and Pinon, P. eds. 2010. *İmparatorluk başkentinden cumhuriyet'in modern kentine: Henri Prost'un Istanbul planması (1936–1951).* Istanbul: Istanbul Araştırmaları Enstitüsü.

Pinon, P. 2010. "Henri Prost'un şehirciliği ve İstanbul'un dönüşümleri." In *İmparatorluk başkentinden cumhuriyet'in modern kentine: Henri Prost'un Istanbul planması (1936–1951),* ed. F. Pilsel and P. Pinon. Istanbul: Istanbul Araştırmaları Enstitüsü.

Pope, N., and H. Pope. 1997. *Turkey Unveiled: Atatürk and After.* London: John Murray.

Preziosi D. 1991. "Introduction: The Mechanisms of Urban Meaning." In *The Ottoman City and Its Parts: Urban Structure and Social Order,* ed. I. A. Bierman, R. Abou-El-Haj and D. Preziosi, 3–11. New Rochelle, NY: Aristide D. Caratzas.

Rabinow, P. 1989. *French Modern: Norms and Forms of the Social Environment.* Chicago: University of Chicago Press.

———. 1996. *Essays on the Anthropology of Reason.* Princeton, NJ: Princeton University Press.

Ram, K., and C. Houston. 2015. "Introduction: Phenomenology's Methodological Invitation." In *Phenomenology in Anthropology: A Sense of Perspective,* ed. K. Ram and C. Houston. Bloomington: Indiana University Press.

Rogan, E. 1999. *Frontiers of the State in the Late Ottoman Empire: Transjordan, 1850–1921.* Cambridge: Cambridge University Press.

Rubin, B. 2005. "Foreword." In *Turkish Dynamics: Bridge across Troubled Lands,* ed. E. Kalaycıoğlu, New York: Palgrave.

Salah, M. 1984. "The Turkish Working Class and Socialist Movement in Perspective." *Khamsin* 11: 86–116.

Samim, A. 1981. "The Tragedy of the Turkish Left." *New Left Review* 1(126): 60–85.

Samuels, D., L. Meintjes, A. M. Ochoa, and T. Porcello. 2010. "Soundscapes: Towards a Sounded Anthropology." *Annual Review of Anthropology* 39: 329–45.

Sartre, J. P. 1976. *The Emotions.* New York: Philosophical Library.

Sasanlar, B. 2006. "A Historical Panorama of an Istanbul Neighbourhood: Cihangir from the Late Nineteenth Century to the 2000s." Unpublished Master's Thesis, Boğaziççi University, Istanbul.

Sassen, S. 2009. "The Immutable Intersection of Vast Mobilities." *Urban Age.* Accessed 10 February 2014. http://lsecities.net/media/objects/articles/the-immutable-intersection-ofvast-mobilities/en-gb/.

Saunders, R., and K. Aghaie. 2005. "Introduction: Mourning and Memory." *Comparative Studies of South Asia, Africa and the Middle East* 25(1): 16–29.

Sayyid B. 1997. *A Fundamental Fear: Eurocentrism and the Emergence of Islamism.* London: Zed Books.

Scott, J. 1985. *Weapons of the Weak: Everyday Forms of Peasant Resistance.* New Haven, CT: Yale University Press.

Secor, A. 2004. "'There Is an Istanbul That Belongs to Me': Citizenship, Space and Identity in the City." *Annals of the Association of American Geographers* 94(2): 352–68.

Seddon, D., and R. Marguilies. 1983. "The Politics of the Agrarian Question in Turkey: Review of a Debate." *Journal of Social Studies* (19): 1–44.

Sen, B. 2013. "The Production of Autonomous Settlements for the Working Class by the Turkish Socialist Movements." Draft paper for Resourceful Cities Conference, Berlin, 2013.

Şen, I., and Ş. Şoher. 2015. "Becoming a Permanent Construction Site: Istanbul after 1923." In *Under Construction: Building the Material and the Imagined World*, ed. E. C. Heine. Berlin: Lit Verlag.

Şenay, B. 2015. "Masterful Words: Musicianship and Ethics in Learning the Ney." *Journal of the Royal Anthropological Institute* 21(3): 524–41.

Şenyapılı, T. 2004. "Charting the 'Voyage' of Squatter Housing in Urban Spatial 'Quadruped.'" *European Journal of Turkish Studies* 1: 1–19.

Shull, N. 2012. *Addiction by Design: Machine Gambling in Las Vegas*. Princeton, NJ: Princeton University Press.

Silverstein, B. 2008. "Disciplines of Presence in Modern Turkey: Discourse, Companionship and the Mass Mediation of Islamic Practice." *Cultural Anthropology* 23(1): 118–53.

Sinclair-Webb, E. 2003. "Sectarian Violence, the Alevi Minority and the Left: Kahramanmaraş 1978." In *Turkey's Alevi Enigma: A Comprehensive Overview*, ed. P. J. White and J. Jongerden, 215–36. Leiden, Netherlands: Brill.

Smith, J. 2016. *Experiencing Phenomenology: An Introduction*. London: Routledge.

Smith, Joseph. 1967. "Insights Leading to a Phenomenology of Sound." *Southern Journal of Philosophy* 5(3): 187–99.

Stevens, W. 1990. *The Collected Poems of Wallace Stevens*. New York: Vintage Books.

Stokes, M. 1992. *The Arabesk Debate: Music and Musicians in Modern Turkey*. Oxford: Clarendon.

———. 1999. "Sounding Out: The Culture Industries and the Globalization of Istanbul." In *Istanbul Between the Global and the Local*, ed. Ç. Keyder, 121–40, Lanham, MD: Rowman & Littlefield.

Tanpınar, A. 1949 (2011). *Huzur*. Istanbul: Dergah Yayınları.

Taylor, C. 2007. *A Secular Age*. Cambridge, MA: Harvard University Press.

———. (1988) 2009a. "Yakın geçmişten bugüne belediye programlarının oluşumu: Sosyal Demokrat belediyecilik–ANAP belediyeciliği." In *Cumhuriyetin Belediyecilik Öyküsü (1923–1990)*. Istanbul: Tarih Vakfı Yurt Yayınları.

———. (1998) 2009b. "Türkiye'de cumhuriyet döneminde kentsel gelişme ve kent planlaması." In *Modernizm, modernite ve Türkiye'nin kent planlama tarihi*. Istanbul: Tarih Vakfı Yurt Yayınları.

Tekeli, İ, 2009c. "Cities in Modern Turkey." *Urban Age*. Accessed 2 July 2017. http://www.urbanage.net/publications/newspapers/istanbul/articles/07_IlhanTekeli/en_GB/.

Ter-Matevosyan, V. 2019. *Turkey, Kemalism and the Soviet Union: Problems of Modernization, Ideology and Interpretation*. London: Palgrave.

Throop, J. 2015. "Sacred Suffering: A Phenomenological Anthropological Perspective." In *A Sense of Perspective: Phenomenology in Anthropology*, ed. K. Ram and C. Houston, 68–89. Bloomington: Indiana University Press.

Toprak, Z. 2012. *Darwin'den dersime: Cumhuriyet ve antropoloji*. Istanbul: Doğan Kitap.

Topuz, H. 2003. *II. Mahmut'tan Holdinglere Türk basın tarihi*. Istanbul: Remzi Yayınevi.

Torre, S. 1996. "Claiming the Public Space: The Mothers of the Plaza de Mayo." In *The Sex of Architecture*, D. Agrest, P. Conway, and L. Weisman, 241–50. New York: Harry N. Abrams.

Touraj, A., and E. Zürcher. 2004. *Men of Order: Authoritarian Modernization under Atatürk and Reza Shah*. London: I. B. Tauris.

Tschumi, B. 1994. *Architecture and Disjunction*. Cambridge, MA: MIT Press.

Tunc, A. 2001. *Bir maniniz yoksa annemler size gelecek: 70'li yıllarda hayatımız*. Istanbul: YKY.

Üngör, Ü. 2011. *The Making of Modern Turkey: Nation and State in Eastern Anatolia, 1913–1950*. Oxford: Oxford University Press.

———. 2012. "Creative Destruction: Shaping of a High Modernist City in Inter-War Turkey." *Journal of Urban History* 39(2): 297–314.

Uzun, B., M. Çete, and M. Palancıoğlu. 2010. "Legalizing and Upgrading Illegal Settlements in Turkey." *Habitat International* 34: 204–9.

Vassaf, G. 2011. *Prisoners of Ourselves: Totalitarianism in Everyday Life*. Istanbul: İletişim.

Waldman, S., and E. Calışkan. 2017. *The "New Turkey" and Its Discontents*. Oxford: Oxford University Press.

Weiss-Wendt, A., and Ü. Üngör. 2011. "Collaboration in Genocide: The Ottoman Empire 1915–1916, the German-Occupied Baltic 1941–1944, and Rwanda 1994, *Holocaust and Genocide Studies* 25(3): 404–37.

White, J. 2002. *Islamist Mobilization in Turkey: A Study in Vernacular Politics*. Seattle: University of Washington Press.

———. 2013. *Muslim Nationalism and the New Turks*. Princeton, NJ: Princeton University Press.

Whitman, W. (1855) 1986. *Leaves of Grass*. New York: Penguin Books.

Wroe, N. 2004. "Occidental Hero." *The Guardian*, 8 May. Accessed 10 February 2014. http://www.theguardian.com/books/2004/may/08/fiction.orhanpamuk.

Yeşilkaya, N. 1999. *Halkevleri: İdeoloji ve mimarlık*. Istanbul: İletişim.

Yıldırım, S. 1990. "Yerel yönetim ve demokrasi." Paper given at Turkish Foundation for Social, Economic and Political Research, February 1990.

Yıldız, A. 2011. "Mücadeleyle doğan bir semt: Çayan mahallesi." *Sosyalist Forum*. Accessed 9 August 2018. https://www.sosyalistforum3.net/showthread.php?t=49236.

Yonucu, Deniz. 2018. "Urban Vigilantism: A Study of Anti-Terror Law, Politics and Policing in Istanbul." *International Journal of Urban and Regional Research* 43(4): 408–22.

Yücel, C. 2005. *Gökyokuş/Kuzgunun yavrusu*. Istanbul: Doğan Kitap.

Yumul, A. 2009. "A Prostitute Lodging in the Bosom of Turkishness: Istanbul's Pera and Its Representation." *Journal of Intercultural Studies* 30(1): 57–72.

Zeydanlıoğlu, W. 2009. "Torture and Turkification in the Diyarbakır Military Prison." In *Rights, Citizenship and Torture: Perspectives on Evil, Law and the State*, ed. W. Zeydanlıoğlu and J. Parry, 73–92. Oxford: Inter-Disciplinary Press.

Zigon, J. 2007. "Moral Breakdown and the Ethical Demand: A Theoretical Framework for an Anthropology of Moralities." *Anthropological Theory* 7(2): 131–50.

———. 2009. "Phenomenological Anthropology and Morality: A Reply to Robbins." *Ethnos* 74(2) 286–88.

Zileli, G. 2002. *Havariler*. Istanbul: İletişim.

Zürcher, E. 1984. *The Unionist Factor*. Leiden, Netherlands: Brill.

———. 1995. *Modernleşen Türkiye'nin tarihi*. Istanbul: İletişim.

INDEX

Founded in 1893,
UNIVERSITY OF CALIFORNIA PRESS
publishes bold, progressive books and journals
on topics in the arts, humanities, social sciences,
and natural sciences—with a focus on social
justice issues—that inspire thought and action
among readers worldwide.

The UC PRESS FOUNDATION
raises funds to uphold the press's vital role
as an independent, nonprofit publisher, and
receives philanthropic support from a wide
range of individuals and institutions—and from
committed readers like you. To learn more, visit
ucpress.edu/supportus.